The Salmon of Knowledge

The Salmon of Knowledge

Stories for Work, Life, the Dark Shadow, and OneSelf

Nick Owen

Crown House Publishing Limited
www.crownhouse.co.uk
www.crownhousepublishing.com

First published by

Crown House Publishing Ltd
Crown Buildings, Bancyfelin, Carmarthen, Wales, SA33 5ND, UK
www.crownhouse.co.uk

and

Crown House Publishing Company LLC
6 Trowbridge Drive, Suite 5, Bethel, CT 06801-2858, USA
www.crownhousepublishing.com

British Library Cataloguing-in-Publication Data
A catalogue entry for this book is available
from the British Library.

ISBN 978-184590127-1

LCCN 2008936748

Printed and bound in the UK by
Cromwell Press Group

Softness triumphs over hardness, gentleness over strength. The flexible is superior to the immovable. This is the principle of influencing things by going along with them, of mastery through adaptation.
Lao Tzu

I do not know what I may appear to the world, but to myself I seem to have been only like a boy playing on the sea-shore, and diverting myself in now and then finding a smoother pebble or a prettier shell than ordinary, whilst the great ocean of truth lay all undiscovered before me.
Isaac Newton

Man did not weave the web of life. He is merely a strand in it. Whatever he does to the web, he does to himself.
Chief Seattle

Our scientific power has outrun our spiritual power. We have guided missiles and misguided men.
Martin Luther King, Jr.

Contents

Foreword

Zen Master Dennis Genpo Merzel

All of us are on a journey, a journey that could be called returning home, to what we say in Zen is our original nature or our original heart-mind. We're all engaged, whether we realise it or not, in an evolutionary process of waking up to who we really are and what we're here to do. It's a process we experience as individuals, but it has universal meanings and milestones.

On a universal level, for all of us, it's about becoming more conscious, more realised, and finding out how to live this life in a more compassionate, more heartfelt, loving way towards our fellow beings—our families, our friends, the people we work with, the ones we work for or that work for us—trying, as Aldous Huxley once said, to be a little kinder to our neighbours.

On the individual level, it's about finding our passion in this life, what it is that we love to do, and how to use this passion to serve others, how to be there for others, how to put our own self-interest off to the side, but not neglect it, to contribute and make a difference in the lives of others.

Discovering that there's something greater than our ego-centred self—something that goes by many names including God, Reality, Truth—and that it is within each of us, gives us the key to finding and taking responsibility in our lives rather than being victims of circumstances. This process awakens what I call Big Heart, which is unconditional love and compassion for all beings and the ability to embrace all beings including the great earth, without being overwhelmed by this love and compassion towards others. Integration of the self with that which is greater than self is an important milestone on our journey.

If we look at our self, this body, mind, and spirit, and imagine that we're sitting cross-legged on the floor, we look something like a triangle with our left and right knees forming the base, and our head at the top, the apex. Imagine that this triangle embraces our whole self. On one side, say the left knee, we have the human elements, the human components of our human beingness. So all those qualities of being human, the emotions, feelings, thoughts, ideas, concepts, behaviours, the five senses—all of these together are the human side. Here we have preferences, likes and dislikes, we want this, we don't want that. On the other side of this triangle, let's say the right knee, we have our beingness. This is the part that most of us are not so familiar with, if we're familiar with it at all. It's the part that is at peace, at home, tranquil in a state of presence, awareness, awakeness, where everything in this present moment, here now, is seen as perfect, complete and whole. This is what we refer to in Zen as our True Nature, what I call Big Mind. This is the place where we lack nothing. We do not feel inadequate or insufficient at all. In fact, we are empowered; we are empowered in our beingness, where we don't need to be doing anything to feel good about ourself. We don't need to become anything to improve ourself, we are absolutely perfect as we are.

The third point of the triangle I call the apex, but really it includes the entire triangle; it bridges and integrates the seemingly fundamental differences between the other two points, the human and beingness. Here we see that we are all human beings, and from this place we consciously choose to be a human being and embody this transcendent place that includes all of our faults, all of our shortcomings, our ups and downs, our emotional upheavals and see all of these human qualities as perfect and complete and whole. This allows us to live our life as fully integrated human beings, the masters of our own lives who take full responsibility for action and reaction, for cause and effect.

In the Zen tradition we have always used stories to help us transcend our self, which means to go beyond, but not neglect, the self. We include and embrace our self, but go beyond it, to a level of awareness or awakening that allows us to cope with our lives in a much wiser and more compassionate way, to let go of our emotions more quickly, particularly anger, rage, hatred, defensiveness, and to feel empowered, or to be empowered to live as a fully integrated and free-functioning human being.

These stories, often in the form of dialogues between teacher and student, are what we call koans in Zen. They cannot be understood or grasped by our discursive and intellectual mind but move us beyond our dualistic way of thinking to a non-dual reality, allowing us to see the other as oneself and oneself as the other. They enable us to recognise our equality and sameness, and yet appreciate our uniqueness and differences. Much like if you build a bunch of snow people, and some of them are milkmen or milkpersons, mailpersons, whatever persons, and yet it's all the same snow. These stories break down the barriers and the separations that divide each of us from one another, and enable us to come from a place where you are me and I am you, and yet you are you and I am I.

In this volume, Nick Owen, who is a student of mine, has gathered a wonderful treasury of stories, metaphors, koans, and anecdotes from spiritual and secular wisdom traditions spanning many eras and cultures to draw us directly into our human beingness, regardless of our background. The stories, engagingly told and wisely chosen, speak directly to our intuitive minds to show us what we do and what is important to us on a universal scale, helping us to reintegrate and make whole what has become separated.

Zen Master Dennis Genpo Merzel

Preface

A man fell into a deep hole in the middle of the road and a crowd quickly gathered. It was obvious that with a little help the man could be pulled out. 'Give me your hand,' onlookers cried as they reached down towards the man. He stood at the bottom of the hole with his arms tightly folded, shook his head and refused.

A storyteller came upon the scene and moving to the front of the crowd he looked at the man at the bottom of the hole. 'Take my hand,' he said. The man immediately reached up and grabbed the storyteller's hand and was pulled to safety.

The crowd was perplexed. 'Why did he accept your help and refuse ours?' they asked. 'Look at him,' the storyteller replied. 'He couldn't give to save his life, but he can easily take.'

Nick Owen is like that storyteller. He has a discerning eye and able to read the character of those whom he meets. Like all great storytellers, he is able to communicate to each and every one of us in language appropriate to who we are and what we need.

The Salmon of Knowledge, Nick's third book on metaphors, is deeper and darker than his earlier work. It explores the great themes: Work, Life, the Dark Shadow and the OneSelf.

Nick, the storyteller, weaves through these stories, laughing at his own foibles, embracing his own shadow, as the princess in the fairy story embraces the wet frog: loving it as it is.

Whatever its source, each story in this book has been touched and reworked by Nick. And in the touching, each story has reshaped Nick.

This collection has found you. The stories will change you and you will change them. They have a life of their own; they seek listeners, readers, recorders and retellers.

It doesn't matter how you read this book, sequentially or pages opened randomly. Somewhere your story is waiting for you.

As Nick the storyteller reminds us, 'It is written.'

Pete Lawry
Leadership Mentor

Prologue

Beneath the Surface of Things

The land is parched and a man digs a well to find water for his gardens. After working for several hours in a place recommended by the water diviner he finds nothing and gives up in disgust. He has dug about four metres.

As he sits dejectedly on the great mound of soil he has dug, a traveller passes by. The traveller laughs at him for digging there, and indicates a much more likely spot. So the man starts a new well, but after digging for five or so metres, he has still found no sign of water.

Getting tired and despondent, he finally accepts some different advice from his old neighbour who assures him that he'll find water in yet another place. After he's given up on that one too, his wife comes out of the house and says, 'Where are you, man? Have you lost your brains? This is no way to sink a well. Stay in one spot and go deeper and deeper there!'

The next day, having slept well and recovered his strength, the man returns to the first hole and spends all his time and concentration in that one place, and finds abundant water deep below the surface.

The more disarmingly simple a story, the more abundant and rich are the possible interpretations that lie beneath the surface. A brief inventory here might suggest the following incomplete list:

- Follow your outcomes through to the end.
- Don't give up too easily.
- Don't get distracted.
- Don't get dejected if things don't work out at first.
- Don't dissipate your energy on too many projects.
- Advice is cheap and often unreliable.

- Some people know what they're talking about; find out who they are.
- Practical people make good partners.
- Pay attention to quality feedback.
- Trust your own judgement and stick to your guns.
- Take responsibility for your own actions.
- Meditation isn't about losing yourself; it's about focusing on and attending to one thing at a time in great depth.
- The richest jewels lie in the deepest seams.
- Wisdom is attained through struggle with yourself and the world you inhabit.

The stories in this book, collected from storytelling and wisdom traditions around the world, offer deep wells of insight into ways in which we might consider how to live our lives with greater wisdom, understanding, intelligence, serenity, and success.

It is the central tenet of just about every major wisdom tradition in the world—whether spiritual, secular, pagan, or humanist—that if you wish to know God, The Buddha, True Nature, or the Truth then first you must study yourself. And that is what this book is about: studying ourselves and our human condition, on a planet inhabited by myriad other living systems, through the medium of story.

Between these covers are stories that embrace time and space. They are ancient and modern, spiritual and secular, short and long, spoken and written, and originate from all points of the compass. Some are based on lived experience; some are deeply metaphorical. All of them offer ways of looking at our 'reality' from different, unusual, or humorous perspectives and which may, if we are open to the possibilities of change and redirection, allow us to become more awake, more energised, and more connected to ourselves, other people, our work, and our planet.

I particularly resonate with stories that stretch the bounds of imagination, that offer challenging and provocative perspectives, that enquire into the conventional order of things, so that having read or heard such a story, I might feel a great desire to laugh out loud, or change something within, or see the world in a refreshingly new light, or be opened to something previously hidden within myself.

In particular I'm attracted to stories that are irreverent, insightful, and which offer the hidden promise of wisdom to be uncovered at the bottom of the well.

Such stories are found everywhere, in all societies, within all cultures, among all traditions, across all time. Great stories have no boundaries, and in a sense belong to no one for it is the nature of stories to be told and shared. And in each new telling they assume a new shape, a new identity, a new meaning until in the end no one can tell whether it is the teller shaping the story or the story shaping the teller, or the context in which the story is given and received that shapes story, teller, and receiver too.

And that is exactly as it should be because each one of us has our truth to discover, our story to tell, and our pathway to tread.

Tir na n'Og

There is an old Celtic legend about a man who chooses eternal youth, the fullness of his heart's desire, the love of a beautiful woman ... and then lives to regret it. But the story also speaks of loyalty, comradeship, service and—the sting in the tale—the courage to defy convention by staying utterly true to what lies in the innermost depths of one's heart and spirit.

The story tells of Oisin[1], son of Fionn Mac Cumhail, leader of a band of the Fianna, warriors who roamed the length and breadth of ancient Ireland, doing good deeds for the common people, and doing whatever it was that warriors loved to do. He's happy and he's content and his fame is spreading far and wide ...

> But it's one thing to be content, another to resist magic. For as he was sitting on the seashore one bright summer's day minding his own business, Niamh of the Golden Hair saw him from far across the seas where she lived in Tir na n'Og, the land of Eternal Youth. And she made a resolve there and then that she would have him for her lover.
>
> And so on her magical white mare she crossed the wide sea to Oisin in less time than it takes to blink an eye and made her proposal.

3

She offered him not just herself, but all the things a warrior could desire: fighting a-plenty, gold and silver, feasting and drinking, music and good company, and—just as a clincher—eternal youth.

Yet still it was a difficult choice for Oisin to give up the companionship of his band of warriors, to let go of his deep attachment to his native land even for a beautiful woman and the gift of eternal youth. He agonised the whole night before making up his mind. And then he went with Niamh who whisked him up on her horse and off they went to Tir na n'Og in a blink of the other eye.

And it was all that he had been promised and more. He fought all day, feasted and danced each evening, and coupled all night with the resourceful Niamh. But after a few months Oisin began to grow distracted and more than anything he missed his friends and the great forests of ancient Eire.

'Let me go back just for a day, just to see how they're all getting on,' he pleaded. At first Niamh refused, knowing that he hadn't yet understood that time passes differently in Tir na n'Og than in the marketplace world that you and I inhabit. In fact the three months that had passed for Oisin in Tir na n'Og were exactly three hundred years here in the world of impermanence.

'Oisin,' said Niamh, 'your friends are long dead, everything has changed. It can never be the same.' But Oisin, not entirely believing her, pressed until Niamh relented. She gave him her white mare warning him in no uncertain terms that he should not dismount.

***

Oisin arrives in Ireland to find everything has changed. The forests have been replaced by pastures, and the people who live there are surprisingly small, scarce half the size of the men of his day. Searching for traces of his old life, he finds a group of men trying to move a huge stone. 'Do you know where I can find Fionn Mac Cumhail and the Fianna?' he asks. The men laugh, 'He's just a legend that our grandmothers used to tell us. It's all ballox.'

Oisin is hurt but he still knows his duty. 'Can I help you with that stone?' 'Sure,' they scoff, 'if you can.' Oisin bends over, picks it up with one hand, and raises it high. And just at that moment with a loud snap, the girth of the saddle breaks and off he falls. No sooner does he touch the ground than his years in Tir na n'Og overcome him. His skin cracks, his hair greys, his teeth fall out. As for the mare, it skips back across the sea to the land of eternity.

'What have I done?' cries Oisin. 'I had it all and gave it up just to see my homeland once again.'

Now news travels faster than the speed of lips in Ireland. Within a day or so St Patrick arrives to find out more about this triple centenarian with a magic horse. He orders his monks to write down Oisin's story, and all the tales that Oisin can remember about Fionn Mac Cumhail and the Fianna. And a good thing too for in so doing the monks immortalised Fionn and the Fianna, keeping them in our memory eternally young.

But above all the good Saint Padraig's going to save Oisin's soul and convert him to Christianity before imminent death inevitably takes him. 'I'm going to baptise you in the name of Christ,' says the Patriarch, 'so you can be saved and go to Heaven with all the Blessed Saints.'

Oisin thinks about this for a moment and then asks, 'What happened to Fionn and all the warriors? Were they baptised in the name of Christ?' 'Indeed not,' replies St Patrick loftily, 'they were sinners all; they died unrepentant and went to Hell.'

'Well in that case,' retorts Oisin, 'If Heaven's not good enough for Fionn and the Fianna, then I'm damn sure it's not good enough for me either.' And with these words he died and went to join Fionn and the band of brothers. And whether he joined them in Hell or in Tir na n'Og no one can tell. At least not in this life.

Stories as Connectors

One of the attributes of good stories is that they are great connectors. They remind us that whoever we are, in whatever context we live, we're not really so very different from people living in other cultures and even in eras other than our own. The issues that are addressed in the story of Oisin and Niamh, issues that were presumably hot in third century Ireland, are universal themes that each of us has probably considered and faced up to in some way or another at different stages of our own twenty-first century lives.

In fact, this story is particularly rich in archetypal themes, and demonstrates just how effective story can be in expressing complexity in simple and elegant ways. The story takes the heroic dream of Youth—that Death can be fought and overcome—and counterpoints it with the inevitability of Death that we must all accept in later years. It compares different ideas of Eternal Life from both pagan and religious perspectives. It warns us against the danger of wanting everything and not being content with the gifts we are given. And it also celebrates the quality of the person who can recognise and own what is *really* important in life and death, and stay true to those values whatever the consequences.

Like all great wisdom stories—whether from pagan, secular, or spiritual traditions—the story of Oisin and Niamh expresses deeply complex universal ideas with simplicity and elegance. It also includes some of the key themes that are explored in this book: Work, Life, the Dark Shadow, and OneSelf.

Four Key Themes

1. Work

For Oisin, at least before he meets Niamh, work is a deeply satisfying expression of what he loves to do, what he does well, and what gives him sufficient challenge to learn and grow. At the same time, his work allows him to make a significant and valuable contribution to the band of warriors he leads, and the community he serves. As a result he feels happy and fulfilled within himself, while others praise his actions and build his reputation.

People of our own time may spend upwards of forty years in work and many get nowhere near the satisfaction that Oisin enjoys during his time with the Fianna. The stories in this book do not offer answers, but they do put forward various perspectives for looking at the nature of work and the contribution it enables us to make to ourselves, others, and our world in a variety of different ways.

The stories explore possibilities for deepening the personal and professional satisfaction we can derive from our work, enhancing the level of contribution we can make at many different levels, and recognising that the more we notice the systemic and interconnected nature of the world we inhabit, the more we can make wiser and more mature decisions and choices.

Above all, the stories suggest that the more of ourselves, particularly our core values and beliefs, that we bring into the workplace the more we and our work are likely to thrive and flourish.

2. Life

It is sometimes said that there are two great adversaries golfers must face when playing: the course and ourself. That strikes me, a non-golfer, as a particularly good metaphor for life. Another way of saying it is that life is a dance between what happens to us, over which we have no control, and how we respond to what happens to us, over which we appear to at least have some control.

As with Oisin, life offers us a constant series of opportunities and challenges that we have to navigate as best we can. We make choices, some easy, some difficult, and then have to live with them. And even if we recognise that everything we do will have consequences, it's very hard to see far enough ahead to predict what some of those consequences might be. This is Oisin's reality and our own.

The great test for Oisin, which is primarily a test of his personal integrity, comes at the end of his life when he is required to choose between one set of values—salvation in Christ—and another set of values—salvation in kin, clan, and community. It is not important which he chooses for anyone else but himself; what is important is that he knows what his own values are and remains steadfastly true to them. This is an act of supreme courage and integrity.

The stories in this book on the theme of life raise important existential questions like: Who am I? Why am I here? What's my purpose? What and whom do I serve? They also encourage us to laugh at ourselves, to treat ourselves and others with greater compassion, and to explore some of the great paradoxes of life—such as coming to terms with our twin and seemingly contradictory blessings of magnificence and insignificance, wisdom and foolishness, rationality and intuition, and many more besides. What wisdom might we gain, the stories enquire, through working to integrate these great opposing qualities that possess each one of us at different times in our lives?

3. The Dark Shadow

Symbolised by his escape to Tir na n'Og, the Land of Eternal Life, the great Dark Shadow for Oisin is Death. Oisin thinks he can cheat death and gain immortal life. He is even prepared to forsake what he holds most dear—kith, kin, clan, and community—to achieve his victory over death. But much as he feels at home in Tir na n'Og, the mortal world still calls to him; some deep part of Oisin feels incomplete, and he determines to return to the ordinary world 'just for a day'.

The story itself is unusual in that it combines an archetypal Youthful Hero story with elements of mid-life and late-life stories.[2] The first part of the tale is typical of a Youthful Hero story. In the first part of our lives we tend to be idealistic and think of ourselves as indestructible, even immortal. Death exists but as a distant figure, one that can be fought if necessary—especially in the service of a noble ideal—and conquered. I can think of several times in the earlier years of my own life when, having overcome serious illness or narrowly avoided a nasty accident, I arrogantly thought of myself as powerful and resourceful enough to cheat and overcome death. Why else would I have delayed paying into a pension fund till I was forty! Death was something that happened to others.

It was only in mid-life that I fully began to accept the truth of the graffiti I once saw painted on the side of an Austrian railway carriage: 'Life is a near-death experience.' Mid-life is the time when we stop counting the years since birth and begin wondering how much time remains till the exit strategy. Death is recognised at this point, indeed it is acknowledged as ever present, and can even seem attractive—a dancing partner that gives greater meaning and piquancy to life. And so at this stage in our personal development it is not uncommon to want to explore more deeply into ourselves; to start finally being more truthful with ourselves and about ourselves. It is time to face up to our own Dark Shadow.

The Swiss psychologist Carl Jung was the first to bring Western attention to the idea of our Shadow but its origins go way back. The story of Milarepa [Story 5.13], the Buddhist yogi, is one such example. Since Jung, the Shadow has been written about and explored extensively. It is central to archetype theory and psychotherapy, and it is essential in any approach to spiritual practice or in simply deepening awareness of oneself.

The 'shadow' consists of those parts of ourselves that we find hard to come to terms with, the bits we don't much like about ourselves, the parts we suppress or ignore. In extreme cases, we refuse to even see these qualities in ourselves, no matter how much our friends and our enemies can! We can live in complete denial of them: 'I'm not competitive.' 'I don't do anger.' 'I'm not narcissistic.'[3]

Unless we fully own these parts of ourselves, parts we spend a huge amount of energy suppressing, and hiding from the judgement of convention, we cannot begin truly to know ourselves or liberate ourselves from the 'stuckness' of our pretence. It is only, for example, when I truly own the narcissist that exists within me that I can truly begin to love and appreciate myself just as I am, which in its turn frees me to love others unconditionally too. When I fully own this or any other shadow voice, it no longer runs me, and it no longer emerges covertly. That, I find, is both liberating and empowering.

Sometimes we even deny our most positive and most nurturing qualities. Fearing to be the nail that stands proud of the floorboard, we disown our unique perspective, our personal wisdom, our insight, our deep sensitivity—anxious as we can sometimes be not to be seen as 'special' or 'clever' or 'powerful' by others.

The stories in this book on the theme of the Dark Shadow invite us to take a step back, to a safer more contemplative space, and look at ourselves with greater serenity and compassion, to laugh at our ridiculousness, and to open ourselves to new possibilities of self-honesty and truth.

***

When Oisin falls back to earth and becomes mortal once again, the storyteller is offering us a simple truth: that as a human being Oisin has access to two separate yet interconnected worlds, the finite and the infinite, the relative and the absolute. When the girth of his saddle breaks, Oisin returns from the eternal, absolute world represented by Tir na n'Og, to the relative, messy, finite world of struggle and death.

But even now, at over three hundred years old he still remains reluctant to move on. He becomes temporarily as stuck in the material world as before he was getting stuck in the eternal world. It takes St Patrick to offer him a choice, a choice that reconnects him with what he truly values—his old comrades and the warrior codes—that finally allows Oisin to own his shadow and embrace death as a welcome friend, a gateway to absolute reconnection to that which he holds eternally enduring and important.

In finally owning the shadow with style and humour, Oisin validates the integrity of his own unique, separate, and mortal self, and at the same time becomes one with everything he holds sacred and good: not a denial of his individuality but an empowerment of it.

4. OneSelf

The idea of the One and the Self—*OneSelf*—has fascinated humankind way back to the beginnings of time. It is the notion that perhaps other worlds, or parallel worlds, or interior worlds exist as well as the one we so materially inhabit. This is a notion that exists not only in the spiritual, contemplative, and wisdom traditions, but also in a great deal of modern scientific thought: particularly in quantum physics, relativity, systems theory, and chaos theory. These post-rational scientific theories perceive the universe in terms of indivisible integration and interconnection—'implicate order' to use the terminology of theoretical physicist, David Bohm.

These ideas have come to fascinate me more and more in recent years. I'm not a physicist, I'm not religious, I'm not a philosopher, and I'm not an academic. And although I have an interest in wisdom and spiritual pathways, I'm not particularly affiliated or attached to any one of them.[4] Rather, it is my own deepening and experiential awareness of a very tangible interior spaciousness opening up within me, which includes yet goes far beyond any sense of my individual self, that I want to explore through the stories that populate this book. This fascination started just a few years ago when I stopped being so busy being busy in my life; and what follows is my own personal take on it.

Drawing from a wide variety of traditions both spiritual and secular, the notion of OneSelf recognises the existence of two strands of human experience and awareness. The first is a *separate individual self*—an egoic, relative, rational, doing self—that feels alone and unique and which ends at the surface of our skin. It is the self we bring to our marketplace world. It is busy and practical and it gets things done. It is Oisin working hard to make third century Ireland a better place. The other is an *extended self* that has the effortless ability just to be, to flow and merge with—and into—all other things, material and non-material. This *OneSelf* has a sense of infinite connection. It is boundless, absolute, and at one with everything. In some traditions it is simply called No-Self, Beyond-Self, or the Absolute.

It is a space where the 'I' disappears; a space where there is no subject/object division.[5] I prefer to call it the Awakened Self because it is a state of absolute presence, of living in the moment, here and now, fully attentive to whatever is happening inside or out.

In fact, this *extended* or *awakened* self goes under many names depending on the tradition: Empty Mind, Beginner's Mind, Big Mind, Essence, Oneness, True Nature, the Source, the Non-Dual, and countless others. Whatever we call it, it's a space where we can find inner space and time to contemplate, reflect, and experience

11

a much vaster canvas of awareness than we are able to do when inhabiting the busy marketplace self of our everyday world. Whereas the *individual* self is brilliant at getting stressed and worrying about an infinite number of day-to-day considerations, No-Self, the awakened self is totally chilled. It just doesn't do stress. It's accepting, wise, deeply compassionate, and serene. Here, everything is OK just as it is.

Everyone, even the most rational among us, has glimpsed this space. Many people connect with it through meditation, and I have also found it when listening to great music, at extremes of physical exertion, when seriously ill, and when surrounded by great natural open spaces. Artists, warriors, and top sports stars often report that they perform at their peak when they simply empty their minds and respond to the immediate issues that arise in each moment. In modern parlance we call these states 'flow', 'the zone', and 'presence'. They are states—as everyone who has inhabited them knows—of heightened awareness.

There is a short story that I first heard from Zen Master Genpo Roshi at a Big Mind[6] seminar in London that draws attention to these two aspects of the human mind:

> A monk returned to the monastery after a long day working in the fields. The Abbot saw the monk, streaked with mud and perspiring heavily, as he made his way to the communal washroom.
>
> 'I see one who has been hard at it!' said the Abbot.
>
> 'Then, Master,' the monk retorted, 'you should also see the one who's not hard at it.'

The story is a koan, a puzzle that invites the merging of the different elements of a paradox, the merging of two opposites. The first element is the small, separate, egoic mind, the one that's *hard at it*. This one has to keep proving itself to the world and to the self. It is the mind that is always busy, always striving, always seeking, never fully satisfied. The second element is the non-seeking, non-doing, awakened mind; the mind of emptiness. This mind has nothing to prove; nothing to do. The monk challenges his Abbot to acknowledge both elements. The notion of OneSelf recognises these two aspects of the mind—the individual and the awakened—that are always available to each and every one of us.

The story of Oisin explores this notion of OneSelf in a number of ways. The first is when Oisin goes to Tir na n'Og. Here he shifts from the one who is hard at it to the one who has nothing to do. In this place everything is provided; there is nothing to be done. *Nothing needs to be done because that's how life is* in the absolute world. Oisin doesn't have to actively look for the fun of a good fight each day; the universe provides it. He doesn't have to find a wife; the universe has provided that too. In all the different wisdom traditions this sense of trusting the universe to provide whatever is needed is central to the teaching, whether it's a pre-Christian Fenian legend as in Oisin and Niamh, or in the spiritual teachings of the Kabbalah, the Tao, Sufism, Zen, or Christianity.[7]

> So why do you worry about clothing? Consider the lilies of the field, how they grow: they toil not neither do they spin; and yet I say to you that even Solomon in all his glory was not arrayed like one of these.
>
> Matthew 6: 27–29

Another way in which this theme is explored is through the concept of relativity: time in this case. Time in Tir na n'Og is different to time in the marketplace world. Oisin, when connected to the flow, totally present to whatever he is immersed in—be it fighting, feasting, or love making—simply doesn't notice the passing of time. And it's so easy to get here: you just jump onto a magic white mare: a simple metaphor for the speed and ease of the journey out of the marketplace self and into the awakened self each time we fully *connect* to the absolute energy that flows through and within us.

But Oisin begins to realise that something is missing in this rarefied world of the absolute where there is nothing to do and nothing to be done. He craves just one more connection with the fleshy, messy, mundane, experiential world of mortality and mates. In other words, he longs to embrace both parts of his True Self: the *individual* self as well as the *absolute* self.

A third way in which the idea of OneSelf is explored is at the story's end when Oisin recognises—with glorious and playful ease—how simple it is to surrender and sacrifice himself to a consciousness far greater and more enduring than his own limited self. When Oisin fully owns his lineage, the world to which he truly belongs, he instantly makes the leap from the small self to the One, the Absolute. He merges into eternal connection with his kin and clan, and the codes and standards by which he has lived.

Through consciously choosing his destiny in this way, Oisin recognises and integrates the two aspects of what it is to be a fully mature, freely functioning human being. He is *human* in that he inhabits and takes full responsibility for his small self with all its limitations and knowledge of deep separation. He is *being* in that he can fully connect with that deeper flow of energy that is always available to him and through which, like a wave in the ocean, he is simply part of the infinite source. And at the end of his life he embraces both aspects of who he is with complete mindfulness. He becomes both *human* and *being—human being*![8]

The many stories in this book on the theme of OneSelf explore what it means to inhabit the spaces of the Self and the One, sometimes separately, and sometimes together. They examine the idea that if we wish to operate in our marketplace world at deeper levels of insight, wisdom, and consciousness, then perhaps a readily available place to bring that mindfulness from is the absolute space of No-Self, Oneness, the Awakened Self.

The stories also describe from a variety of perspectives and traditions how life is ultimately unknowable, just as we ourselves are beyond full description, and that if we wish to fully engage with this life, we need to do so with faith, trust, and intuition just as much as with logic, analysis, and reason.

***

The symbols:

indicate which of the above four themes (Work, Life, the Dark Shadow, OneSelf) is present in each story. The symbols are displayed in a four quadrant box next to each title.

Stories and the Art of Making the Complex as Simple as Possible

Over the many years that I've been telling, collecting, and writing stories, those that have resonated with me the most have usually been from the wisdom traditions, whether pagan and secular like the story of *Tir na n'Og*, or spiritual. There is something deeply compelling about the way stories from these traditions are able to convey complex ideas that can be notoriously hard to write about—such as relationships, compassion, non-duality, mindfulness, awareness, intuition, life and death—with marvellous, insightful simplicity.

This has much to do with the skill of the ancient storytellers, and also because their job was to explore deeply into these issues. The storytellers of the wisdom traditions were griots—poets who preserved their community's history and culture—shamans, monks, priests, healers, seers, and spiritual masters. They were the psychologists and therapists of their day. The stories they used were a key instrument of their teaching, and one of the most effective methods of transmission through which their teaching would be remembered and handed down from generation to generation.

Of all the literary forms, the two that appear to be best equipped to translate complexity into tangible everyday ideas, which are memorable, applicable, and easy to grasp, are story and poetry. These two forms also happen to be the great carriers of image and metaphor. At their best they are experiential, contextual, and leave enough space between the lines to invite a mysterious dance of meaning between writer and reader, speaker and listener. It is surely no coincidence that these two literary forms are just as effective in spoken as in written form, sometimes more so.

Stories, in short, allow us to explore wisdom and truth from multiple perspectives, and in so doing they enable us to understand that there are both personal truths which differ, and universal truths that don't. They offer insights to resolve paradoxes and other seeming contradictions. They have the power to teach, inform, heal, and make aware. And in a world that can seem increasingly fractured and fragmented, stories offer well-trodden, well sign-posted pathways to healing, integration, and deep connection.

Science, Wisdom, Spirit, and the Role of Stories in the Twenty-First Century

There are many different perspectives from which we can usefully observe ourselves in order to study and understand ourselves bet-ter. This book focuses mainly on stories and the wisdom traditions to do so. But I'm also intrigued by the way a great deal of contemporary science seems to be pursuing a parallel pathway. Many of the great themes of contemporary science resonate strongly with many of the key themes of this book.

Einstein, for example, spent much of the later part of his life seeking to prove the existence of a 'universal field'. The general idea, developed from the theory of relativity, was that if you could get far enough away you would see the patterns, harmony, and order in the universe that are impossible to see close up. From sufficient distance, went the theory, you would see that ultimately everything connects to everything else.

This is very much what most well crafted wisdom stories do, at least in a metaphorical way. They offer us a remote vantage point from which to observe, evaluate, and engage with the world of human interaction: the stories hold up a mirror to human behaviours, values, and relationships. Universal and particular issues and challenges are acted out at a distance by characters struggling to make sense of the narratives they find themselves in, just as Oisin in the story of *Tir na n'Og*.

This distancing effect, often a distancing in time as well as in space and perspective, can be extremely liberating, enabling us to identify and recognise truths about ourselves and the human condition which pass us by in our busy, close-up, day-to-day lives.

Stories enable us to consider aspects of our own lives through the situations and experiences that others find themselves in. And since we cannot change what we do not acknowledge, one of the great gifts of stories is to point us towards a greater recognition and understanding of ourselves and to the possibility that we can—if we wish—find ways out of the ruts we have dug for ourselves.

The great spiritual pathways too offer similar distancing strategies for knowing and seeing ourselves more clearly, and for increasing our awareness of the deep patterning, harmony, and intricate order of the universe. These strategies are deep reflection, contemplation, and meditation. From these meditative spaces, sitting in a non-judging, non-attached flow of not-knowing, not-seeking, not-striving, not-doing we can pay attention to the life of our ordinary individual self, our busy marketplace self, and just notice how it's doing. So that when we return to the marketplace world, that small relative self might have access to some new insights about how it could improve the quality of its life, and operate in the world with a greater degree of conscious awareness.

Some spiritual pathways seek to diminish, overwhelm, or even destroy the egoic, relative self. But that makes no sense to me. This small individual self is what makes me human and gives me my individuality. It's strong and self-willed, and though frequently immature and misguided, it does its best to protect me, and it drives me to take whatever actions I need to survive in a challenging world. No, I reckon the best way to be able to connect deeply and whenever I want to my non-striving, non-thinking, non-attached, awakened mind is to have my small self actively engaged as a supportive ally and comrade.

It's also worth remembering that the story of Oisin pointed to the fact that it's just as possible to get stuck in the non-doing world of the absolute as it is in the limited perception of the relative mind. So the question becomes: How can I integrate and make the best of both minds? For this, it's useful to go to another place, even more remote—a higher level of consciousness if you like—from which to integrate the relative and the absolute and have them work together in harmony and greater awareness.

Although many traditions have ways of doing this, one of the most elegantly integral is that developed by Zen Master Dennis Genpo Merzel and embedded in his transformational Big Mind process.

He uses a simple yet dynamic visual metaphor that deeply supports and embodies the integration of the One and the Self. It's based on the spiritual geometry of one of the world's oldest and most mystical of symbols, the equilateral triangle. The relative and absolute elements form the bottom left and right corners of the triangle; True Self, which includes and transcends both, forms the apex.[9]

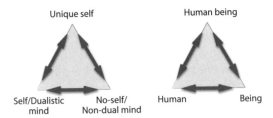

Unique self   Human being

Self/Dualistic   No-self/   Human   Being
mind   Non-dual mind

Wisdom stories, spiritual pathways, and contemporary science have more in common than may at first meet the eye. Scientists across a range of disciplines are increasingly engaging in the exploration of indivisibility, connection, and integration, placing notions such as paradox, stages of psychological development, levels of consciousness, and universality at the centre of their attention.[10]

There is still, it is true, plenty of resistance among some scientific communities to anything beyond the logical, rational, and material. Yet significant numbers of scientists, particularly those working in the realms of relativity and quantum physics, are looking at the world in ways that differ widely from the classical scientific approaches of the last three hundred years, the 'Age of Reason'.

Einstein often expressed his fascination for the relationship between two seemingly contradictory elements of human processing. He distinguished them as *reason* and *intuition*. Reason, as he variously described it, equates to the logical practices and intellectual processes that predominate in the marketplace world. Intuition, on the other hand, is a state of deeper awareness and connection—a flow state—that operates in the self-forgetting realms of the absolute.

Einstein labels intuition as 'divine', a quality he clearly and care-fully distinguishes from the 'servant' mind: 'The rational mind's a faithful servant; the intuitive mind a Divine gift. The tragedy of modern life is that we've begun to worship the servant while defil-ing the Divine.'[11]

Einstein certainly didn't dismiss the importance of logic and reason, recognising their enormous contribution to humankind's progress in understanding and manipulating material reality and natural laws. But he argued forcefully and frequently that rational-ity by itself was limited and insufficient. To truly understand the laws of the universe, and the human condition itself, something much more subtle was necessary. For Einstein, that was to be dis-covered in the absolute realms *beyond* rationality: 'There is no logi-cal way to the discovery of elemental laws. There is only the way of intuition, which is helped by a feeling for the order lying behind the appearance.'[12]

In the modern world it was the Swiss psychologist, Carl Jung, who first made discussion of the importance of intuition accept-able in scientific circles. Now, it is a key principle of cutting edge scientific investigation. Post-rationality, or that which includes and goes beyond reason, is central to many branches of scien-tific and philosophical enquiry. Ken Wilber talks of 'vision-logic' as an essential stage of development for exploring the non-dual. Malcolm Gladwell in his widely researched work, *Blink*, refers to the extraordinary 'power of thinking without thinking'. Theoretical physicists, such as David Bohm in his groundbreaking work *Wholeness and the Implicate Order*, have stressed the seriously limited reductionism of the purely rational: 'The primary physical laws cannot be discovered by a science that attempts to break the world into its parts.'

Bohm cites three particular aspects of quantum theory and quan-tum mechanics that have extraordinary parallels with many wisdom and spiritual traditions. Firstly, the notion of universal 'indivisibility', that there is nothing else but wholeness and inter-connectedness. Secondly, 'wave particle duality' which demon-strates that under certain conditions a wave can manifest as a particle and a particle can manifest as a wave whereas in classical physics these properties are intrinsic and non-interchangeable.

Thirdly, the concept of 'non-locality' in which particles in environments remote from each other can be shown to influence each other energetically.[13]

Bohm frequently pointed to the uni-perspectival stuckness of our Western thinking and how our ways of thinking are conditioned by our cultural perceptions. Classical science, the basis of modern educational systems, has taken 'parts' as the primary concept of study and research for the last three hundred years and 'wholeness' as a by-product of this. Classical science is a rational and logical analysis of the world *as we think we see it* broken down into its constituent parts. This has been very useful in many ways: in the engineering of machines and other mechanical processes, for example. And it is hardly surprising, as Bohm himself recognised, that we can be very unwilling to let go of this way of thinking which has brought such success and prosperity to much of the planet.

Classical science works … and yet it is only a partial truth. It is only one way of looking at things. The fact is that this purely rational, deconstructionist approach, with its focus on the parts rather than systemic interconnected wholes, has become deeply ingrained in our culture and ways of perceiving. And it is, perhaps, one of the key reasons why so much fragmentation exists in the world today, and why so many of the solutions aimed at 'fixing' current social, political, economic, and organisational issues are so deeply unsustainable. The fact is, our thinking is not very joined-up! Too many people still operate within a silo mentality. And today, in a world imminently in danger of collapse, we need more than ever to start thinking systemically, globally, and in *deeply* sustainable ways.

Quantum theory works too! And it can also embrace and include classical science without contradiction. It offers a bigger picture, a much broader canvas. According to the relativity theorists and the quantum theorists it is just as scientifically sound to take the *whole as primary* and its parts as secondary. And this way of perceiving—which is the basis of chaos, complexity, and systems theories—enables us to see much more patterning, harmony, order, structure, and deep systemic connection in the universe than the traditional approaches of classical science.

From the perspective of quantum mechanics everything exists together in a dynamic, flowing, unbroken universe. What was seen before as a small part is, when examined closely, a system in itself. And this system is connected to other systems—all the way up and all the way down—until everything can be shown to be connected to everything else. Introduce change to any small system in a small way, and it will very likely have consequences elsewhere in the wider systems; consequences that may be immediate, or may equally well be remote in time and space.

In our busy day-to-day marketplace lives it is easy to get disturbed by events going on around us. It is easy to take the setbacks and challenges life throws at us personally. Before we know it, we have got ourselves into negative spaces and negative emotions: frustration, irritation, resentment, lack of forgiveness, and so on, both with ourselves and with others. And because we're attached to our emotional point of view, we often give these negative states, and the behaviours that caused them, an importance they really don't deserve.

We need to get some distance away and see ourselves and the situations we find ourselves in from a different and more remote perspective, a perspective from which we can see ourselves in a more proportionate, more detached, and more awakened way. This helicopter view, or balcony position, gets us out of our narrow view and enables us to notice several things: that we are not one separate, distinct, discrete *part* of the universe but deeply enmeshed in myriad numbers of systemic interconnections; that from sufficient distance we notice our negative states drop away and we become less attached to our emotions, our values, and the need to be right about everything; that from this remote perspective we can generate new and creative choices and interventions that were not available to us before. From this more distant perspective we can think much more strategically and with much greater awareness and consciousness in relation to our situation as a *whole*.

Whether we make these shifts of perception based on the application of scientific principles, by moving to the apex of the triangle, or because of insights we take from a story, is immaterial. They are, in any case, aspects of the same indivisible, integrated, and interconnected process. The important thing is that we *do* shift, and in so doing become more aware, awake, and conscious of ourselves, others, and the world we inhabit.

From whichever remote perspective we take, we can choose to embrace the egocentric view of things that is natural to our individual self, the sense of connection to our culture and community which is a rather more mature stage of our development, or a much more systemic, world-centred awareness that points to the deep connection of all things. Any position which empowers us to include and transcend the totality of who we are is much more likely to enable wise, appropriate, and sustainable action and change in the world and in ourselves.

The Salmon of Knowledge

This ancient Celtic story, from the same Fenian cycle as *Tir na n'Og*, captures the whole essence of indivisibility, integration, and connection with which we've been playing. And it's important to remind ourselves that storytellers as far back as third century, pre-Christian Ireland were focused on exactly the same complex sets of relationships as Einstein and Bohm seventeen centuries later.

It is a sophisticated and elegantly simple story of connection and healing, of making whole, of recognition and integration, and it introduces just about all the key themes that are to be found and explored within these pages. Many versions of this story exist in books and widely on the internet. This is my version of it.

> Centuries ago, there lived a great fish in the upland reaches of the River Boyne, in the northern part of Ireland, that was known as the Salmon of Knowledge. Legend had it that anyone who ate of its flesh would become the wisest man in all Ireland, which at that time was as good as saying the whole wide world. All a person had to do was catch this fish and cook it to perfection. Oh, and the legend also said that the Salmon of Knowledge would be caught by a man named Fionn. Many Fionns (and plenty of non Fionns too if truth were told) had tried; all had failed.
>
> So it was that Fionngas, or Fionn the Seer, a Druid of great wisdom, had made the snaring and consuming of this great fish his

lifetime's work. With detailed research, consummate logic, ancient PowerPoints and spreadsheets, he had tracked it down to a particular deep pool where he finally managed, after great struggles and copious cursings, to net the magnificent beast.

Now all he had to do, after these many years of seeking and painstaking labour, was cook it. He cleaned and gutted the fish, skewered it on a long and green spear of alder wood, and set it to roast over glowing embers. Every five minutes he would turn the fish, for legend clearly had it that the fish must be perfectly cooked for the result to be optimal.

But then Fionn the Seer had a sudden and disturbing realisation: he hadn't collected sufficient firewood to complete the cooking to perfection. He was honest enough with himself to admit that it was his own impatience and over-eagerness that had caused this foolish miscalculation. And then looking deeper into his own Shadow he also acknowledged that somewhat more than a hint of greed and vanity were at work too.

Wondering what he could do, for the fish would need turning while he was collecting enough firewood, a young man appeared.

Not one to miss an opportunity the Druid roared, 'Come here, boy. Now while I'm away fetching firewood turn this fish just so every five minutes, and swear to me by all you hold dear in life that you'll not dare so much as taste a morsel of it. For by God if you do, I'll have your testicles on this spit faster than a pike can swim.'

Now while this young man had nothing more on his mind that morning than enjoying the great glory of the universe that he had been born into, he was very mindful and respectful of the great power of Druids. Especially so, as he'd been brought up in the Wild West of Ireland by a Druid or two himself. So he set to work with concentration and a determination to do what had been asked of him to the very best of his ability.

But it was indeed a lovely hot summer's day, and as he listened to the bees a-buzzing and the larks a-singing, and watched the butterflies a-fluttering and the fish in the river a-leaping, his whole spirit came alive to the beauty and magnificence of the day. And the next thing ... was that he could smell fish flesh a-burning. 'Oh my heart and balls,' he cursed to himself as he turned the fish over. And there on the hot side of the Salmon of Knowledge was a blister the size of a small acorn.

He blew on it. Nothing! He politely asked it to disappear. Nothing! He turned the fish faster on the spit. Nothing! Finally he looked around and, seeing no-one, he gently pushed the blister back into place.

And as he did so ... Psssshhhtt! Three golden drops of red-hot salmon oil spurted out, scalding the boy's finger. Would you have done any different nursing a scalded finger? Truth is, with a yelp of pain and anguish, he put it straight into his mouth to cool it ...

And at that very moment the Druid returned.

'Boy,' he said noticing a new fire in the young man's eyes and an added dash of presence and stature in his posture, 'Look me in the face and tell whether you have partaken of my salmon.'

And the boy not knowing how to tell a lie told him the whole unvarnished truth of what had happened. Told him with the voice and grounded authority of one who begins to see the complex relationships beyond the surface of all things.

It would not be truthful to say that Fionn the Seer was not a dash disappointed. But he took it in good grace. 'What's your name, son?' he asked finally with remarkable gentleness and compassion.

'Fionn, sir. Fionn Mac Cumhail, son of Uail Mac Baiscne.'

'So you are, indeed. So you are. So you are the Fionn who was destined from the oldest days of history to eat the great fish, and know all that is to be known, and gain the great wisdom as the prophesy foretold.'

And that is how Fionn Mac Cumhail became the wisest man in the land, leader of the Fianna, and Ireland's greatest warrior and poet too.

A Brief Interpretation

Storytellers, seers, shamans, and spiritual masters were the psychologists and psychotherapists of ancient times, and not so ancient times too. And story was, and remains still, one of their most potent and incisive instruments. The legend of the Salmon of Knowledge goes right to the heart of the human condition, pointing up themes of disconnection and connection, separation and integration.

Like yin and yang in classical Chinese thought,[14] or Apollo and Cassandra in the minds of ancient Greece,[15] Fionngas and Fionn represent different aspects of what it is to be fully human. They are the two opposing yet ever connected sides of the same human coin. The story expresses their coming together in integration to access the fullest potential of human existence represented as warrior and sage, healer and fool; and also as rational mind and awakened mind.

Fionngas, the seer, represents the rational mind. It takes hard work plus a calculating, tactical excellence nurtured by years of experience to locate, catch, and prepare the salmon. But so trapped is Fionngas in his obsession and desire to achieve the 'prize' that he is not sufficiently present or awake to what the critical moment requires.

Fionn, on the other hand, represents the intuitive awakened mind. He represents youthful innocence, healer, and fool—or to put it another way, spirit or soul. He has planned and prepared nothing at all. But he is present enough, awake enough, and intuitive enough to instinctively respond to what the critical moment calls for when he accidentally stumbles upon it.

Yet Fionn could never have tasted the fish without the years of painstaking work that Fionngas has put into his project. The salmon would not have been on the spit to be tasted. And fortunately perhaps for Fionn, the old seer is mature enough, and compassionate enough, to graciously accept the pre-eminence of the young man's gifts: the ability to show up at precisely the right moment, to instinctively do what has to be done, to straightforwardly own the truth, to be present to what is, and to see beyond the surface of things.

In the modern world of the creative arts this state of intuitive presence is often referred to as 'the flow'. In the world of sport it is known as 'the zone'. To get there requires intensive training and highly disciplined physical, mental, and emotional preparation. But there comes a point when something extra kicks in, a state of complete integration and flowing harmony between inner and outer worlds, a difference that absolutely makes the difference. The point being, of course, that we need to embrace both the rational *and* the intuitive parts of ourselves to get to it.

The story of *The Salmon of Knowledge* has complete resonance with the modern world.

In business the young protégé, who just happens to be in the right place at the right time, slips unnoticed into the position of status and power that the experienced tactical thinker has manoeuvred for, and coveted, for so long. In sports, the hugely successful US rowing team not only grinds out the hard miles in the gym and on the water, they also employ the services of Jon Kabat-Zin, internationally renowned mindfulness and meditation teacher, to add inspiration, spirit, and heightened awareness to the dynamic flow of their graceful and strenuous work.

The symbolism of *The Salmon of Knowledge* speaks to us across time and space. It urges us to pay attention to the personal disconnection that a focus on the solely rational can induce. And it also suggests there are limitations in the purely intuitive and spiritual too. Neither, by themselves, is enough to allow us to taste of the Salmon of Knowledge.

Stories as Tools for Healing

The Salmon of Knowledge is an 'apex' story.[16] Its core message is that we should know when to call upon our rational, calculating, marketplace self, and when to call on our intuitive, in-the-moment, awakened self. From the apex we can embrace both. From the apex we can transcend and include both. And as each element informs and deepens the other, it liberates, enriches, empowers, heals, and offers us more appropriate and more mature choices to act upon in our marketplace reality with greater wisdom, awareness, and compassion.

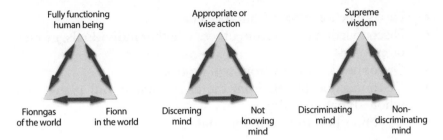

In more complex versions of the Salmon legend, Fionn does not wander into the Druid's kitchen simply by chance. He has a clear purpose in travelling the length and breadth of Ireland which is to attain as much wisdom as he can. It is for this reason that he is seeking out Fionngas in order to learn from him. Fionn has an instinctive recognition that the seer has a gift for him with which he needs to connect. It is not only the gift of the experienced and the rational that Fionngas represents but also the gift of masculine energy represented in the Druid as hunter and sage.

And Fionn is attracted also to the magical waters of the River Boyne from which the Salmon has come. The river represents symbolically the importance of the feminine principle: flow, darkness, sinuousness, creation, source. So the rational and intuitive represent also the coming together of the masculine and feminine energies within the young man, symbolised in the eating of the salmon's flesh: itself a strikingly spiritual analogy.

***

Stories hold a great capacity to heal, to make whole, to bring together disparate parts of ourselves through integration. This may be through the coming together of our masculine and feminine archetypes, or the interconnection of the rational and intuitive, or the integration of the dual and non-dual aspects of ourselves.

Newspapers, TV, academics, integralists, psychotherapists, and a whole plethora of various other commentators draw attention to the high levels of isolation and separation experienced by many in the modern age and not only in the Western world. Commentators identify five main areas where a sense of disconnection is most fully and acutely experienced within individuals:

- Disconnection of self from the self.
- Disconnection of self from others whether individuals, groups, or cultures.
- Disconnection of self from one's work.
- Disconnection of self from the environment: our planet as a whole dynamic entity.
- Disconnection from our spiritual self.

Naturally, the force of this experience differs from person to person and is not felt equally across all five fields. Each of us can enquire for ourselves to what extent we experience disconnect, which of these areas requires more or less attention, and what we wish to do about it. After all, the pursuit of truth or true nature is above all the study of ourselves.

Like Newton standing on the shoulders of giants, I am acutely aware of the long and distinguished line of eminent scientists, philosophers, teachers, monks, visionaries, artists, writers, healers, and storytellers that have explored this road to integration before me and whose stories and ideas I have incorporated into this book. These are people who have long known, and skilfully expressed, the notion that the full integration of *all* aspects of the human mind is essential for humankind's health, progress, and well-being.

For myself, even though I spend what time I can exploring ways to develop deeper levels of awareness and consciousness across these fields of separation—through reading, writing, teaching, working, meditating, and enquiring—I still have a very long and winding road to travel.

One of my principle reasons for writing this book, and bringing together well over one hundred stories on the themes of wholeness, integration, connection, awareness, oneness, wakefulness, life, work, and the dark shadow was to offer to myself and others a wider range of perspectives on which to reflect, meditate, study, and—perhaps most of all—gently laugh at myself and my own very human ridiculousness.

Enjoy the read and enjoy the craic!

List of Stories by Theme

The themes of Work, Life, the Dark Shadow, and OneSelf are not displayed here, as symbols indicate their presence in the text.

The themes below may also include their opposites.

Abundance
1.7, 1.15, 2.1, 2.10, 2.11, 2.12, 2.20, 2.22, 3.6, 3.8, 3.14, 3.15, 4.8, 5.7, 5.18, 6.4, 6.6, 7.5, 7.9, 7.12, 7.16, 7.17, 7.18

Acceptance
2.4, 4.5, 5.9, 5.12, 5.15, 6.1, 6.2, 6.3, 6.5, 6.6, 6.8, 6.9, 6.10, 6.11, 6.12, 6.13, 6.14, 7.5, 7.9, 7.11, 7.12, 7.16, 7.17, 7.18

Alignment
1.5, 1.7, 1.12, 1.14, 1.15, 1.17, 2.1, 2.4, 2.8, 2.20, 3.2, 3.6, 3.7, 3.9, 3.10, 3.13, 3.17, 4.2, 4.3, 4.8, 4.10, 5.10, 5.13, 5.16, 5.18, 6.6, 6.7, 6.8, 6.11, 6.15, 7.1, 7.2, 7.4, 7.5, 7.6, 7.8, 7.10, 7.11, 7.13, 7.16, 7.17, 7.18

Anger
2.8, 6.6, 6.7, 7.7

Appearance
1.3, 2.6, 2.7, 2.13, 2.14, 2.16, 2.20, 2.22, 3.1, 3.3, 3.4, 3.8, 3.11, 4.4, 4.6, 4.9, 4.10, 4.12, 5.15, 5.17, 5.18, 6.2, 6.6, 6.7, 6.8, 6.9, 6.11, 6.13, 7.6, 7.7, 7.9, 7.10, 7.13, 7.15, 7.16, 7.17

Assertiveness
1.12, 1.13, 2.19, 4.6

Assumption
1.1, 1.3, 1.11, 1.14, 1.16, 1.17, 2.3, 2.5, 2.7, 2.9, 2.10, 2.12, 2.20, 2.22, 3.4, 3.11, 3.16, 4.4, 4.6, 4.13, 5.5, 5.8, 5.9, 5.14, 5.15, 6.2, 6.6, 6.7, 6.8, 6.10, 7.7, 7.12, 7.13, 7.14, 7.15, 7.17

Attachment
1.8, 2.2, 2.15, 3.4, 3.6, 3.8, 4.4, 4.7, 4.9, 4.10, 4.11, 5.1, 5.3, 5.4, 5.7, 5.9, 5.14, 5.15, 5.18, 6.2, 6.3, 6.4, 6.6, 6.8, 6.10, 6.11, 6.13, 6.14, 6.15, 7.3, 7.7, 7.12, 7.13, 7.14, 7.15, 7.16, 7.17

Attention
1.3, 1.5, 1.6, 1.9, 1.10, 2.3, 2.17, 2.21, 3.11, 3.12, 4.5, 4.14, 4.16, 5.3, 6.7, 6.9, 6.12, 7.1, 7.2, 7.4, 7.8, 7.9, 7.10, 7.11, 7.13, 7.17, 7.18

Awakened and Enlightened
1.1, 1.3, 1.7, 1.10, 2.1, 2.8, 2.22, 5.13, 6.1, 6.2, 6.4, 6.7, 6.8, 6.9, 6.12, 7.1, 7.4, 7.5, 7.6, 7.10, 7.11, 7.13, 7.14, 7.16, 7.17, 7.18

Awareness
1. 3, 1.7, 1.10, 1.15, 2.6, 2.11, 2.15, 2.16, 2.22, 3.2, 3.5, 3.8, 3.11, 3.12, 3.13, 3.17, 4.5, 4.6, 4.8, 4.14, 4.16, 5.3, 5.12, 5.13, 5.16, 5.17, 5.18, 6.1, 6.2, 6.8, 6.9, 6.12, 7.1, 7.5, 7.6, 7.9, 7.10, 7.13, 7.14, 7.15, 7.17

Beyond the Surface of Things
1.3, 1.7, 1.8, 1.10, 2.1, 2.4, 2.5, 2.6, 2.7, 2.8, 2.9, 2.10, 2.13, 2.14, 2.15, 2.20, 2.22, 3.2, 3.5, 3.6, 3.7, 3.8, 3.11, 3.12, 3.14, 4.2, 4.3, 4.4, 4.6, 4.9, 4.13, 5.16, 5.17, 5.18, 6.2, 6.6, 6.7, 6.8, 6.9, 6.11, 6.12, 6.14, 7.2, 7.5, 7.6, 7.7, 7.9, 7.11, 7.13, 7.14, 7.15, 7.17

Busy-ness
1.7, 2.3, 2.17, 3.1, 3.8, 4.1, 5.15, 7.4, 7.17

Courage
1.2, 1.5, 1.6, 1.13, 1.14, 1.15, 1.17, 2.21, 3.9, 3.10, 3.13, 3.15, 4.6, 4.7, 4.9, 4.10, 4.12, 4.16, 5.12, 5.13, 6.5, 6.6, 6.7, 6.8, 6.11, 7.7, 7.11, 7.12, 7.13, 7.17

Communication
1.12, 1.14, 2.5, 2.19, 2.20, 3.4, 3.9, 3.11, 3.12, 3.13, 3.14, 3.15, 3.16, 4.2, 4.7, 4.8, 4.10, 4.13, 4.15, 4.16, 5.4, 5.15, 5.16, 6.3, 7.13, 7.15

Compassion
3.9, 4.3, 4.10, 5.12, 5.13, 6.7, 6.9, 6.10, 7.13, 7.16, 7.17

Competition and Cooperation
1.14, 1.15, 2.11, 2.18, 2.20, 3.6, 3.14, 3.15, 4.5, 5.14, 5.16, 7.8, 7.13

Control
3.1, 3.2, 3.8, 3.15, 4.1, 4.4, 7.13, 7.15

Creativity
1.6, 1.9, 1.10, 1.13, 1.15, 2.6, 2.10, 2.17, 2.21, 3.9, 3.10, 3.13, 3.14, 3.15, 3.17, 4.4, 4.10, 4.16, 5.14, 5.15, 5.16, 5.17, 6.13, 6.15, 7.11

Death
2.13, 3.9, 4.7, 4.12, 5.8, 5.9, 5.10, 5.12, 6.4, 6.6, 6.7, 6.8, 6.9, 6.10, 6.11, 6.12, 7.11, 7.16, 7.17

Delusion
1.8, 1.16, 2.2, 2.3, 2.5, 2.7, 2.12, 2.14, 2.22, 3.1, 3.4, 3.8, 3.11, 4.1, 4.13, 4.15, 5.1, 5.4, 5.8, 5.9, 5.18, 6.1, 6.2, 6.6, 6.7, 6.8, 6.9, 6.10, 6.11, 6.14, 6.15, 7.3, 7.4, 7.7, 7.9, 7.12, 7.13, 7.14, 7.15, 7.16, 7.17

Detachment
1.4, 2.1, 3.2, 4.5, 5.13, 6.8, 6.9, 6.11, 7.1, 7.4, 7.11, 7.17, 7.18

Difficult Conversations
2.19, 4.2, 4.6, 4.7, 4.10, 4.13, 4.15, 6.11

Direction
1.14, 1.15, 1.17, 2.11, 2.18, 3.2, 3.5, 3.10, 3.15

Discrimination and Discernment
1.3, 1.8, 1.10, 1.13, 2.2, 2.3, 2.6, 2.7, 2.8, 2.12, 2.13, 2.16, 2.22, 3.3, 3.5, 3.6, 3.11, 3.12, 5.16, 5.17, 5.18, 6.6, 6.7, 6.12

Dreams
4.9, 5.16, 6.11, 6.14, 7.7

Education
1.1, 1.2, 1.3, 1.9, 1.10, 1.16, 2.12, 2.16, 2.22, 3.4, 3.12, 3.13, 3.14, 3.15, 3.16, 4.1, 4.2, 4.8, 4.16, 5.3, 5.6, 5.8, 5.10, 5.15, 5.16, 6.15, 7.9, 7.11

Ego
1.4, 2.14, 3.8, 4.6, 5.4, 5.8, 6.7, 7.8, 7.15, 7.16, 7.17

Expectation
1.2, 1.16, 2.9, 2.20, 3.6, 4.6, 6.2, 6.14, 7.3, 7.7, 7.13

Experts
3.1, 3.4, 4.8, 4.12, 5.4, 5.5, 5.14, 5.15, 7.8

Fear and Doubt
1.14, 2.5, 3.4, 4.7, 4.12, 5.4, 5.7, 5.8, 5.9, 5.10, 5.11, 6.1, 6.2, 6.4, 6.6, 6.7, 6.8, 7.1, 7.7, 7.12, 7.14, 7.16, 7.17

Finding One's Own Path

1.1, 1.6, 1.9, 1.13, 1.15, 1.17, 3.12, 3.15, 4.8, 4.10, 4.16, 5.10, 5.16, 6.6, 7.9, 7.11, 7.13, 7.17

Flow

1.7, 2.2, 2.21, 3.1, 3.2, 3.6, 3.7, 3.10, 3.13, 3.15, 3.17, 4.5, 5.3, 6.11, 7.4, 7.5, 7.6, 7.10, 7.11, 7.12, 7.16, 7.17, 7.18

Happiness

2.1, 5.10, 5.18, 6.1, 6.5, 6.6, 6.9, 6.11, 6.12, 6.13, 7.13, 7.14, 7.17

Healing and Health

1.6, 1.11, 1.12, 2.8, 2.21, 3.8, 3.9, 3.17, 4.7, 4.9, 4.12, 5.12, 5.13, 5.18, 6.9, 6.10, 6.11, 7.12, 7.16, 7.17, 7.18

Honesty

2.3, 2.7, 2.19, 3.11, 3.16, 4.3, 4.6, 4.10, 4.13, 5.15, 6.12, 7.13

Illusion

1.4, 1.8, 1.10, 1.11, 1.16, 2.5, 2.7, 2.9, 2.12, 2.22, 3.4, 3.8, 3.11, 4.1, 4.3, 4.4, 4.6, 4.10, 4.13, 5.1, 5.2, 5.3, 5.4, 5.8, 6.1, 6.2, 6.6, 6.8, 6.9, 6.10, 6.11, 6.12, 6.14, 6.15, 7.3, 7.7, 7.13, 7.14, 7.15, 7.16, 7.17

Inner Captain

1.6, 1.12, 1.16, 1.17, 2.4, 2.11, 2.19, 3.9, 3.15, 4.2, 4.7, 4.8, 4.12, 4.13, 4.14, 4.16, 5.8, 5.10, 5.12, 5.15, 6.6, 6.7, 6.11, 7.13, 7.17

Inner Critic

1.11, 1.14, 4.9

Impermanence

2.2, 2.4, 3.1, 4.9, 5.6, 6.1, 6.4, 6.6, 6.9, 6.10, 6.11, 6.12, 7.6, 7.16, 7.17

Inclusion

2.11, 2.20, 3.13, 3.14, 3.15, 3.17, 4.5, 4.8, 5.13, 5.14, 5.16, 6.6, 7.12, 7.17

Integrity

1.7, 1.17, 2.1, 2.4, 2.19, 3.10, 3.13, 3.15, 3.16, 3.17, 4.3, 4.5, 4.6, 4.8, 4.10, 4.13, 5.1, 5.10, 5.12, 5.16, 5.18, 6.6, 6.8, 6.11, 7.4, 7.10, 7.11, 7.13, 7.16, 7.17

Intuition

1.6, 2.2, 3.9, 3.13, 4.5, 4.9, 5.15, 5.17, 7.17

Investment
1.15, 2.6, 2.22, 3.3, 3.6, 4.3, 7.17

Leadership
1.1, 1.2, 1.3, 1.10, 1.15, 2.3, 2.5, 2.6, 2.11, 2.18, 2.19, 2.20, 3.5, 3.12, 3.13, 3.14, 3.15, 3.16, 3.17, 4.3, 4.5, 4.6, 4.7, 4.8, 4.10, 4.11, 4.12, 4.16, 5.6, 5.12, 5.14, 5.15, 5.16, 5.18, 6.11, 6.13, 6.15, 7.8, 7.12, 7.13, 7.15

Letting Go
2.1, 3.2, 3.6, 4.9, 5.3, 5.7, 5.9, 5.17, 6.1, 6.4, 6.7, 6.8, 6.9, 6.10, 6.11, 6.12, 6.15, 7.1, 7.4, 7.5, 7.6, 7.10, 7.11, 7.12, 7.14, 7.16, 7.17, 7.18

Listening
3.11, 3.13, 3.14, 4.15, 5.4, 6.7, 7.17

Love
2.4, 2.21, 4.5, 5.12, 5.13, 5.18, 6.10, 7.1, 7.16, 7.17, 7.18

Mastery
1.1, 1.5, 1.6, 1.7, 1.9, 1.13, 1.17, 2.1, 2.11, 2.21, 3.2, 3.8, 3.10, 3.12, 3.13, 3.16, 3.17, 4.1, 4.2, 4.4, 4.16, 5.13, 5.18, 6.1, 6.4, 6.6, 6.8, 7.1, 7.4, 7.8, 7.10, 7.11, 7.13, 7.17

Maturity
2.19, 3.1, 3.10, 3.16, 3.17, 4.1, 4.7, 4.8, 4.11, 4.13, 4.16, 5.10, 5.12, 6.6, 6.7, 6.11, 6.14, 6.15, 7.12, 7.17

Mid-Life
1.4, 2.14, 4.16, 5.18, 6.5, 6.6, 6.7, 6.9, 6.11, 6.14, 6.15, 7.11, 7.17

Multiple Perspectives
1.3, 1.4, 1.10, 1.15, 1.17, 2.6, 2.11, 2.16, 2.22, 3.1, 3.5, 3.11, 3.14, 4.6, 4.11, 4.15, 5.12, 5.16, 5.17, 6.1, 6.4, 6.6, 6.7, 6.8, 6.9, 6.10, 6.11, 6.12, 6.13, 6.15, 7.5, 7.6, 7.13, 7.16, 7.17

Natural World
1.3, 1.7, 2.1, 2.2, 3.1, 3.2, 3.8, 5.7, 5.9, 5.12, 6.10, 6.11, 7.5, 7.16, 7.17

No-Self
2.1, 6.8, 7.2, 7.4, 7.6, 7.8, 7.10, 7.14, 7.16, 7.17, 7.18

Ownership and Responsibility
1.1, 1.10, 1.12, 1.16, 2.4, 2.19, 3.7, 3.9, 3.12, 3.15, 3.16, 3.17, 4.5, 4.6, 4.7, 4.11, 4.12, 4.13, 4.14, 5.8, 5.10, 5.12, 5.13, 5.15, 5.18, 6.1, 6.5, 6.7, 6.9, 6.11, 6.14, 6.15, 7.7, 7.12, 7.13, 7.17

Pace and Lead
1.7, 1.10, 3.14, 4.2, 5.12, 5.14, 6.7, 6.8, 6.11, 6.13, 6.17, 7.17

Passion and Enthusiasm
2.21, 3.10, 3.13, 3.15, 3.17, 4.3, 4.5, 4.8, 6.1, 6.12, 6.14, 7.11

Perfection
3.1, 5.5, 6.2, 7.5

Possibility Frame
1.10, 1.15, 2.11, 3.5, 3.15, 3.15, 4.2, 4.5, 4.10, 5.17, 7.6, 7.12, 7.17

Presence
1.3, 1.4, 1.7, 3.11, 3.17, 4.16, 5.13, 6.4, 6.8, 7.1, 7.10, 7.13, 7.17, 7.18

Projection
1.11, 1.16, 2.7, 2.22, 3.4, 3.11, 4.9, 5.8, 6.14, 7.7, 7.12, 7.17

Purpose
1.14, 1.15, 1.17, 2.5, 2.11, 2.21, 3.8, 3.10, 3.12, 3.13, 3.14, 4.5, 4.8, 5.16, 5.17, 5.18, 6.5, 7.8, 7.11, 7.16

Quality Questions
1.11, 2.3, 2.4, 2.9, 2.20, 3.12, 4.2, 4.8, 4.11, 4.15, 5.16, 6.7, 6.11, 7.7

Quiet Mind
1.3, 1.5, 1.7, 2.2, 2.3, 2.4, 2.17, 3.8, 3.17, 4.1, 4.5, 5.3, 5.13, 6.1, 6.4, 6.8, 6.9, 6.10, 7.1, 7.3, 7.4, 7.10

Rationality
2.2, 3.1, 3.8, 7.14

Seeking
1.2, 2.9, 2.15, 3.8, 6.1, 6.2, 6.10, 6.11, 6.14, 7.3, 7.14

Self-Belief
1.6, 1.14, 1.17, 2.5, 4.8, 4.10, 4.16

Self-Organising Systems
1.7, 1.10, 2.10, 3.2, 3.6, 3.9, 3.17, 6.1, 6.5, 6.6, 6.11, 7.5, 7.7, 7.8, 7.12, 7.17

State Management
1.5, 1.6, 1.7, 1.9, 1.14, 2.4, 2.5, 2.17, 3.2, 3.10, 4.5, 4.16, 5.3, 6.1, 6.4, 6.7, 6.8, 6.9, 6.10, 6.11, 6.13, 6.15, 7.2, 7.4, 7.10, 7.13, 7.17

Status
1.13, 3.14, 4.3, 4.4, 4.6, 4.7, 4.9, 4.10, 4.12, 4.15, 6.11, 7.13

Straight Talking
2.19, 3.16, 4.6, 4.7, 4.13, 5.18, 6.11, 7.13

Strategy
1.12, 1.15, 2.18, 2.20, 3.5, 3.12, 3.14, 4.2, 4.5, 4.8, 4.10, 4.16, 5.16

Stuckness
1.2, 1.10, 1.12, 2.8, 2.14, 2.15, 2.19, 2.22, 3.4, 4.1, 4.11, 4.12, 4.13, 5.1, 5.2, 5.3, 5.4, 5.5, 5.7, 5.8, 5.9, 5.14, 5.17, 5.18, 6.1, 6.2, 6.3, 6.8, 6.10, 6.11, 6.14, 7.3, 7.9, 7.13, 7.14, 7.15, 7.17

Suffering and Loss
2.13, 2.15, 2.21, 2.22, 3.6, 3.8, 3.9, 4.9, 4.11, 5.11, 6.1, 6.2, 6.3, 6.4, 6.6, 6.7, 6.8, 6.9, 6.10, 6.11, 6.12, 6.13, 7.7, 7.13, 7.14, 7.15, 7.16, 7.17

Surrender
2.1, 2.4, 2.21, 3.2, 3.8, 5.13, 6.2, 6.4, 6.5, 6.8, 6.9, 6.10, 6.11, 7.1, 7.4, 7.5, 7.6, 7.11, 7.16, 7.17, 7.18

Sustainability
2.11, 2.20, 3.3, 3.9, 3.12, 3.13, 3.14, 3.15, 5.14, 5.16, 7.13, 7.17, 7.18

Systems
1.6, 1.7, 2.2, 2.4, 2.6, 2.10, 2.18, 3.1, 3.2, 3.4, 3.5, 3.7, 3.9, 3.12, 3.13, 3.14, 3.15, 3.16, 3.17, 4.7, 4.14, 5.6, 5.13, 5.14, 5.16, 6.6, 6.11, 7.15, 7.17

Transformation
1.15, 2.5, 2.8, 2.21, 2.22, 3.8, 3.9, 3.15, 3.17, 4.5, 4.11, 5.13, 5.18, 6.6, 6.7, 6.9, 6.11, 7.1, 7.4, 7.5, 7.10, 7.11, 7.13, 7.16, 7.17, 7.18

Unconventionality
1.6, 1.17, 3.5, 3.7, 3.15, 3.17, 4.4, 4.10, 4.16, 6.13, 7.13

Vision

1.3, 1.15, 2.6, 2.11, 2.16, 3.15, 4.4, 4.5, 4.8, 5.6, 5.16, 5.18, 7.13

Youth

4.1, 6.1, 6.2, 6.5, 6.14

The Seven Chautauquas

The stories in this book are divided into seven sections or Chautauquas entitled:

1. Finding One's Own Path
2. Beyond the Surface of Things
3. Flow
4. Difficult Conversations
5. Stuckness
6. All Things Must Pass
7. Not Knowing Mind

I've called them Chautauquas because that seems to describe them well. The original Chautauquas were North American in origin, named after the county in New York State where the movement began in the nineteenth century. They were travelling cultural events that combined lectures with music and theatre. That's not quite what you get here, but it's close enough. You can add your own singing and dancing.

I first came across the Chautauqua in Robert Pirsig's *Zen and the Art of Motorcycle Maintenance* which I first read in the mid-seventies when it was first published. I've revisited that book many times since, as well as Pirsig's other excellent Chautauqua: *Lila*. Each time I read these books I continue to find greater depth in them, and that is exactly what should be the case in a Chautauqua.

Pirsig announces his intention to entertain and edify his readers early on in *Zen*. In true Chautauqua fashion, he says he aims to 'improve the mind and bring culture and enlightenment to the ears and thoughts of the hearer.' And he goes on to lament the demise of the Chautauquas, abandoned to the ever-increasing pace and glitz of radio, TV and movies. Not entirely an improvement, he wryly observes.

I've got a huge amount from Pirsig's probing and insightful enquiries into values and quality over the years, as well as his thoughtful and provocative way of communicating, so my Chautauquas are a kind of homage to the man.

These Chautauquas are all organised within a particular format. They start with a brief introduction of the main theme followed by a short story from life as an example of that theme. The story may offer a particular perspective or something to reflect upon.

Then there is a brief explication of each of the stories in the Chautauqua in terms of its particular themes and messages. These descriptions are merely thumb guides to help direct a reader who is looking for something specific. There is a great deal more to most of the stories than I have touched upon in these sections; and the discerning reader may wish to skip these altogether and draw his or her own conclusions about the deepest meanings and ramifications of each story. There are also further notes on some of the stories at the end of the book.

Another short narrative based on a personal experience follows, and then the main event: the stories themselves.

Chautauqua 1

Finding One's Own Path

Stories on the Themes of Awareness, Presence, and Direction

Reading the newspapers and watching TV these days, it can often seem that an agenda has been decided for us by others. The great theme in the media as I write this is of doom and destruction in the financial markets. It's as if I'm being told that my life will inevitably be poorer and more diminished whether I like it or not. Well, I'm not prepared to go along with that, not one little bit. I'm the star in my movie and I just don't buy the fact that I can't be happy simply because I might have less material wealth than before. Wealth for me includes important other things such as health, contribution, relationships, self-mastery, creativity, the arts, appreciation of the natural world, and many other things besides money and material possessions.

The fact is that the media are in the entertainment business. They focus on the past and the future and mostly have nothing at all to do with deep and informative analysis of the present. Above all they want to scare us through drama: the anxiety of a foreboding future, a gloomy comparison with the good old days. If it's a financial crisis today it will no doubt be something else tomorrow.

We need to put ourselves at the centre of our lives and take full responsibility for whatever it is we do: to make our own way, to carve out our own path, to star in our movie. It's so easy to get knocked off track, to lose confidence in ourselves. This can particularly happen when we entertain the delusion that people who have wealth, status, or position actually know what they're talking about. Of course, some of them do. My point is not to *assume* that they do, and not to lose sight of what our own deep instinct and personal wisdom tells us.

Some twenty years ago I was asked to run a two-week professional development programme for a group of fourteen teachers from a variety of international backgrounds. I was fairly new to the institution that had organised the programme and eager to do well. At the end of the first week I invited feedback from the group as to how the first five days had gone. Twelve had loved it and two trashed both the programme and me personally.

The feedback went to the Director of Studies who summoned me to her office: 'What the hell have you done to these two students? You better turn them and the programme around next week!'

The following week I did as instructed. I changed my style. I played it safe. I spent a huge amount of time on my two nemeses. At the end of the programme the feedback was collected once again. This time everybody hated the course, and twelve highly motivated teachers from the previous week couldn't hide their disappointment or surprise at how it could have been so different.

It was a sobering but crucial learning experience for me. Never again would I sacrifice the majority for the minority in a similar situation; never again would I trust 'authority' implicitly. And from that time on I began to trust my own gut, my own inner voice, my own direction, my own wisdom. I don't always get it right, but it is always my choice and my responsibility.

***

The stories in this section pursue these themes. The first four *Mastery, Shake the Tree, Clear Vision, and Detachment* (1.1–4) are stories from the Zen tradition. Zen has always been celebrated (or slandered) for its unconventionality and iconoclasm—qualities which certainly endear it to me. These stories exhort us to find courage in our own convictions, to find our own pathway, to look beneath the surface of things, and not to defer to the conventional views and opinions of others. Above all, these stories challenge us to take leadership of our own life, and to look for guidance rather than leadership in others.

Stories 5 and 6 turn our attention to the powers of presence and presence of mind. *Centredness* (1.5) explores composure and personal integrity—the centredness of the grounded individual. *Unconventional Methods* (1.6) explores the power of risk, surprise, the emotions, and the unconventional when working in tight corners.

Stop! (1.7) reminds us that finding one's own path requires nothing more than following the natural order of things, the natural systems that surround us.

The three stories on thievery (1.8–10) offer different insights on a theme. *The Swine* (1.8) warns against gullibility. This story mocks those who would wish to get rich without effort; who are easily persuaded by thinly disguised scams to part with their wealth and wits; who follow the latest fashion or fad without thought or judgement. This story, by the way, is at least eight hundred years old.

Praxis (1.9) has less to do with thievery than the importance of learning experientially and being practical when wishing to become a master in your chosen path. The path also requires some risk and creative thinking. *In Every Weakness, the Seeds of Strength* (1.10) indicates that whatever pathway you have chosen, no matter how mean and humble, no matter how dishonest and anti-social, it too is a road that can lead to illumination and enlightenment.

The three African stories (1.11–13) differ from each other in their themes. *The Inner Voice* (1.11) illustrates how we create our own reality, our own world, within our heads. No more, no less. Only when the farmer doesn't know the answer himself is his adversary defeated. As David Bohm, the theoretical physicist famously observed, 'We don't have thoughts, rather it is our thoughts that have us.'

Non-Violent Communication (1.12) challenges us to act with wisdom appropriate to context and to manage our power with sensitivity and assertiveness. *Uhuru* (1.13) shows how we can achieve our chosen path even when our access to status and authority is limited. In this case, the desire to experience a gentle reversal of power is done with humour and assumed artlessness.

The final four stories (1.14–17) look at contexts of performance in different arenas. *Tiny Frogs* (1.14) concerns being true to ourselves and our dreams, and refusing to listen to the doubts and denigrations of others. *Ringing the Changes* (1.15) is a real-life case history of a large internationally renowned organisation. It suggests that life and change become easier when we listen to those we have a relationship with, take their key values into consideration, and notice how the winds of change are operating in the world. Think differently, offer your highest quality, and stay true to your chosen pathway.

Wizards of Oz [1] (1.16) laughs at how we can be so easily derailed from our pathways when we make assumptions and are dishonest with ourselves and others. And finally *Wizards of Oz [2]* (1.17) calls us to move beyond our limiting beliefs about what can and can't be done, to look differently at whatever territory we occupy, to question and challenge conventional wisdom, and to be our own man ... or woman!

***

Sometimes the universe intervenes to support us in our struggles to stay true to our pathway and our innate sense of wisdom. Sometimes it seems that the universe genuinely *wants* us to win.

I had been asked to run a management development seminar for a group of Chinese managers in Hong Kong. My style of working has always been experiential and hands-on and I saw no problem working with this group of 120 people.

But I was still quite new to Hong Kong and, at that time, had little experience of working with Chinese cultures. On the morning of the seminar I travelled from my base on Hong Kong Island under Victoria Harbour to Kowloon on the MTR, Hong Kong's underground railway system. And as chance would have it, I bumped into an acquaintance, a British guy, who was 'an old China hand'.

He'd lived in the Territory for many years and was married to a Chinese woman. He asked me where I was going, so I told him about the seminar and what I planned to do.

He sucked in his breath and looked doubtful in that time honoured British way. 'I wouldn't do that if I were you,' he said. 'These Chinese, it's all about face. They won't want to get up and do activities in front of the others. Mark my words, they won't volunteer for anything. What you need to do is be the expert, and tell them exactly what's what. They'll listen because that's what they're trained to do. Years of conditioning, you see.'

I thanked him for his expert insight and concern before getting off at the interchange. A cold fear sank deeply into my belly. 'Looks like this could be a complete and utter disaster,' I thought to myself.

There simply wasn't time now to change anything. And, anyway, I wouldn't have felt authentic lecturing from the front. All I could do was console myself with the fact that at least I'd learn something even if I did crash in flames.

It went a treat. True, it took time to warm people up and build enough trust for the bravest to put a toe in the water. But step by step, more and more people joined in the exercises. And those who preferred to be observers grew more and more engaged in the 'theatre', increasingly offering their interpretations of what was going on from their observer perspective.

The universe, simply by refusing me sufficient time to change what I'd planned, proved to be my greatest ally and teacher—once again!

Four Short Zen Stories

1.1 Mastery

A seeker after wisdom arrived at a monastery and asked to become a disciple of the great Master who taught there.

'No!' said the Master, 'you may study with me, and you may stay at the monastery, but on no account are you to become my disciple.'

'Who should I follow then?'

'No one. As soon as you follow the path of another, you are no longer following the "Truth."'

'Then what is a Master for?' asked the perplexed seeker.

'To make you see the uselessness of having one.'

1.2 Shake the Tree

A man entered a monastery to study and meditate for a year in order to experience at least the seeds of enlightenment. At the end he felt nothing but disappointment and worthlessness.

He said to the Abbot, 'Why has my retreat failed to bear fruit?'

'Perhaps,' the Abbot replied, 'you never found the courage to shake the tree.'

1.3 Clear Vision

A monk asked his Master what kind of meditation he practised each morning.

The Master, who loved to meditate in the monastery garden, said: 'I look carefully and with clear eyes to see the rose bush in all its full glory.'

'Why would you do that? Why would you need to look carefully to see the rose bush in bloom?'

'In case I see not the rose bush, but my preconception of it.'

1.4 Detachment

The Master seemed completely unconcerned about the opinions of others. One of his monks asked him how he had reached this stage of egoless inner detachment.

He said: 'For the first eighteen years of my life I didn't give a damn about what others thought of me. After that I thought about nothing else. Finally, in my maturing years, I came to an extraordinary realisation. Everybody was so busy worrying about their own stuff that nobody was paying me any attention at all.'

Three Stories on the Theme of Composure

1.5 Centredness

At a tea house in ancient Japan, a short-tempered soldier believed he had been insulted by the Master of the Tea Ceremony. Although the incident was accidental, and the Tea Master apologised profusely, the soldier refused to accept and demanded that honour be settled next morning with swords at dawn.

The Master of the Tea Ceremony had no art in duelling or swordsmanship so he asked his friend, a great Samurai Warrior, 'What should I do?'

The Samurai observed the Tea Master as he poured tea for his customers. He was struck by the perfect composure and concentration of the man as he practised his art.

'When you face your opponent tomorrow,' said the Samurai, 'assume a striking position, your sword raised above your head, with the same composure and concentration you use when performing the Tea Ceremony.'

At dawn the next morning the Tea Master followed exactly the wise words of the Warrior. The soldier, preparing to strike, was in turn struck by the apparent composure and calmness of the Tea Master. He stared for a long while into the man's attentive and alert expression. Then he sheathed his sword, bowed deeply, apologised for his rashness, and left.

1.6 Unconventional Methods

A famous physician was attending a banquet at the palace of a great Sultan. A lady-in-waiting, a favourite of the Sultan, brought some delicacies on a tray to the physician. As she bent over to offer the food, something in her back clicked and locked, and she screamed out in pain. The Sultan was deeply upset and ordered the physician to cure her as he deemed him to be responsible for the incident.

This was something of a problem for the physician since he had, quite naturally, left all his remedies, medicines, and instruments at home. He experienced a brief moment of panic, but realising something would have to be done immediately if he were to maintain his reputation and pacify the Sultan, to say nothing of curing the unfortunate lady, he resolved to act with unconventional methods.

Taking a deep breath and trusting to Providence, he thrust his hands inside the woman's blouse and firmly squeezed her breasts. The woman was deeply shocked and to hide her embarrassment bent her upper body even lower. The whole court heard another loud click, and she screamed in even greater pain than before.

Before the furious Sultan could intervene, the physician expertly manoeuvred his hands beneath the woman's skirt and attempted to pull down her underwear. At this outrage the woman took a step backwards, straightened up and angrily delivered a mighty slap across the face of the physician. Only then did she realise that her pain had gone and she had complete freedom and mobility in her body once again.

The physician smiled and said, 'Challenging moments often require unconventional methods.'

1.7 Stop!

Why are you so busy?
Stop and look around.
These mountains and lakes,
these forests and glades
are at one with themselves.
They know what they are.
They are not lost. They invite you too
to pause, to breathe, to know
there is no other place but here
no other time but now.

Listen, watch, smell, feel.
If you cannot sense
the power, and magic, and rhythm,
and wisdom of the natural world
you are without hope. Stop!
Till you know how to be truly silent
you do not know how to speak.
Till you know how to be utterly still
you do not know how to move.
Your own True Nature knows who you are.
Let it live through you. Let it find you.

Three Takes on Thievery

1.8 The Swine

One fine morning a trickster was apprehended in a coastal village for passing off forged coins. He was sentenced to death, tied to a post in the village square, and left to contemplate the iniquity of his ways and his impending fate. Meanwhile the villagers went about their business on their farms and in their boats.

Sometime in the afternoon, a young farmhand passed through the town on his way to market with a herd of pigs. Seeing the trickster tied to the post he asked: 'Why are you tied up? What have you done?'

'Alas,' said the trickster, 'These are godless folk that live here. And because I am a simple holy man who wishes nothing more than to celebrate my God they have tried to tempt me.'

'How have they done that?' asked the curious farmhand.

'They have tried to force me to accept money, and corrupt me in a variety of different and lascivious ways so that I will break my holy vows and leave the true path to paradise. But I have refused, and so they have tied me here.'

The farmhand thought this was very unfair, and knew it was his duty to help the holy man. So he offered to take his place. As the trickster tied the farmhand to the pole, the good young man advised the trickster to hurry up and escape so he wouldn't be caught again by the godless villagers.

The villagers returned after dark. They immediately threw a sack over the farmhand's head, bound him tightly and threw him off a high cliff into the sea.

Next morning the villagers were very surprised to see the trickster entering the village with a herd of pigs. 'How did you survive and where did you get all those pigs?' they demanded to know.

'In the sea there are friendly water spirits who regard the cliff as a sacred place. Everybody who enters the sea by jumping from the cliff and drowning is richly rewarded as you can plainly see.'

In less time than it takes to think a thought the whole village rushed off to the cliff top and threw themselves into the deep waters below.

This is how the trickster took over an entire village.

1.9 Praxis

The son of a Master Thief asked his father to initiate him into the mysteries of the profession. The older man agreed to do this, and that night invited his son to accompany him on a mission to steal from a large villa. As the family slept, the two intruders silently entered and the father indicated that his son should enter a small room to see if there was anything inside worth taking. As soon as he did so, the father turned the key and locked the son inside.

Then he left the house by the route through which they had got in, went to the front door and knocked loudly enough to wake the whole household. Then he quickly and silently disappeared.

Much later, the son got home, very, very cross as you might imagine. 'How could you do that to me?' he bellowed at his father. 'It took me all my wits and ingenuity to avoid getting caught. If I hadn't been driven to the utmost extremes of creativity by my fear of being captured, I would never have escaped.'

'Well done, son. You've just completed your first lesson.'

1.10 In Every Weakness, the Seeds of Strength

A thief came to the great Buddhist Master, Nagarjuna. He said, 'Master, I want to study and learn from you, but one thing I must make clear is that I am a thief. Thieving is my trade, I love doing it, and I am extremely good at it. In the past I have tried to stop but now I know that this is impossible. So if you accept me as your disciple please understand I will do whatever you ask of me except to give up my thievery.'

Nagarjuna replied, 'What's the problem? Your being a thief is your affair. I have nothing against you being a thief.'

'Truly?' said the thief. 'Every time I have engaged with the company of monks and other holy men they have all told me to stop stealing.' So the thief was delighted that his behaviour was acceptable and Nagarjuna accepted him into his company.

'You can do whatever you like,' Nagarjuna now told the thief, 'I have only one condition to demand of you. Be aware! That is the condition. Be aware! Go and steal, rob, and break into people's houses. All this is no concern of mine. All I ask is that you do it with full awareness.'

A couple of weeks later, the thief came back to Nagarjuna and said, 'Master, you have a subtle mind and I have a big problem. If am aware, I cannot steal. When I steal, awareness disappears. You have trapped me.'

'You have trapped yourself,' said Nagarjuna. 'I want to hear no more talk of thieving and stealing. I am not a thief and I know nothing about these things;

they are no concern of mine. But you must decide. If you want awareness that's your choice. If you don't want it, then that's your choice too!'

The thief said, 'Master, now that I have tasted a little of the beauty of awareness I do not intend to lose it. Let me tell you a story. Last night I entered the palace of the Sultan. I made my way into the great treasury and I opened the royal chest. I was about to become the richest thief in the world, and then I looked up and you were there beside me, and instantly I became aware. The diamonds and rubies, the sapphires, and emeralds … I saw them clearly, for the first time in my life I saw through my blindness. I saw them as they are—stones, just stones. Then just as quickly I lost awareness and that vast treasure was there before me again, sparkling and gleaming, seducing my spirit, and greed shone in my eyes and clutched my belly tight. And many times, standing there like a fool, I passed between awareness and my lack of it … And when I was aware I became like a Buddha and serenity flowed through me … And then greed swept through me and made me her slave … until suddenly after so many rounds of illumination and illusion, I made my choice … those stones were just not worth it.'

'Now,' said Nagarjuna, 'you understand how thievery too is a road to the Truth.'

Three African Stories

1.11 The Inner Voice

The wife of a farmer lay on her deathbed. She said to her husband, 'Promise you'll not betray me when I'm gone. I don't want to leave you and I don't want you to spend time with other women after I'm dead. Promise me you'll stay faithful, or I swear I'll return to haunt you.'

For quite some time after she died, the farmer kept his promise. But then he met a woman and they fell in love. Sure enough, as soon as they became engaged to be married, the ghost of his former wife began appearing every night as he lay in bed. Not only did she accuse him of breaking his promise, but she would also taunt him and repeat back to him, word for word, all the conversations he'd had with his fiancée during the course of the day. So unnerved was he by the ghost's knowledge of his most intimate encounters that he could barely sleep.

So he went to see the Mganga, a traditional healer, who lived in the nearby village. 'She knows every last detail of my life,' the farmer told him recounting his misery.

'This is one very smart ghost,' said the Mganga. 'You should be v-e-r-y impressed by this ghost. But, do not fear, I will tell you exactly what to do.'

That night the ghost reappeared and the farmer did exactly as the Mganga had advised. 'Oh, Ghost of my former wife, you are so wise and intelligent. There is nothing I can hide from you. If you can give me the answer to one question, I will never see this new woman again and I'll remain a bachelor for the rest of my life.'

'What is this question?' the ghost responded, 'I shall answer it.'

The farmer plunged his right hand into a sack of rice that lay next to him on the floor. 'Tell me exactly how many grains of rice I'm holding in this my right fist.'

Without a word the ghost evaporated, and never returned.

1.12 Non-Violent Communication

A lion was terrorising the community. It had attacked so many people that few had the courage to attend to their farms. As a result the people were half starved. Then, by chance or destiny, a skilful Healer passed through that country, tamed the lion, and persuaded it to practise the discipline of non-violent communication.

Now that the lion was harmless it didn't take long for the villagers to return to their farms, and as their bellies and confidence grew again, so their courage returned. Soon they began to heap revenge on the lion for all the indignities it had caused them in the past. They would hurl rocks and insults at it. They would even tweak its tail and pull whiskers from its mane.

When the Healer passed through that country again the lion sought him out and complained how much he was now suffering.

'Well, you've stopped scaring people, that's your problem.'

'But it was you who taught me the principles of non-violent communication,' whined the great beast.

'I taught you to stop inflicting pain, not to stop roaring.'

1.13 Uhuru (Freedom)

A British general was due to visit his troops who were stationed in the remote north-west of Kenya. The Governor thought it would be a nice touch if all the local native women would stand at the edge of the road and greet him with ululations in the traditional way as he drove past in his Land Rover.

There was a rather major consideration however as the local women in this particular district of Kenya never wore a stitch of clothing except perhaps an amulet, or a necklace, or a wispy belt to accentuate the curve of the hips.

So the Governor had a little talk with the Headman and chatted to him about the great honour he was about to bestow upon him and his people. In passing he also made known his concerns about local customs and attire. The Governor wished to ensure that the women would be appropriately covered so as not to disturb the General's British sensibilities.

The Headman quite understood and said that he did not foresee a problem. Perhaps the Governor could arrange for sufficient skirts and blouses to be provided so the women could discreetly cover their glory for this onetime special palaver. *'Hamna tabu'*—no problem—stated the Headman with his big toothy grin.

The big day arrived and the famous British general was imminently expected. But then the Governor's aide-de-camp reported a glitch. Although the native women were dutifully wearing their skirts, they did not like the blouses and had left them in their huts. So now they were all lined up along the road, fully skirted but splendidly bare breasted and with not another stitch on, not even underwear.

The Governor was apoplectic. He was livid with rage. He summoned the Headman and made his views felt. The Headman replied, *'Pole, Bwana Kubwa, lakini hamna tabu sana'* (So sorry, Great Leader, but there is really no problem at all). He explained that the women had a clever plan to cover their breasts as the general was driven by.

'Are you sure?' fumed the Governor.

'Ndio, kweli sana sa-a-a-na' (Yes I'm very, very sure), the Headman replied confidently.

There was no time to discuss further. The motorcade was seen approaching in the distance. And as the great general's Land Rover cruised slowly past, with the man himself saluting and standing stiffly to attention, we can only guess at his inner process as woman after bare-breasted woman lifted her skirt and coyly covered her breasts with it.

Four Performance Stories

1.14 Tiny Frogs

Once upon a time there was a community of tiny frogs who decided to hold a running competition. The goal was to reach the summit of a very high tower. A huge crowd gathered to watch the contest and cheer on the runners. When the race began, and everyone saw how tiny the frogs were, nobody believed that they could possibly climb so high. So instead of shouting encouragement, the spectators took pity on them. So what the frogs heard as they began their ascent were comments such as: 'No way they're going to make it!' 'Impossible. It's far too high!' 'How could they be so dumb!'

And so, one by one, the frogs lost heart and dropped out. Except for a few, who with renewed vigour, climbed higher and higher.

The crowd watched in amazement as these tiny creatures forged on. They couldn't believe they'd make it against the odds.

'They haven't got a hope. It's way beyond their capacities.'

More tiny frogs lost heart and gave up … but there was one who just kept going. Higher and higher it climbed. It refused to give in. And on it went, lungs bursting, muscles pumping, until it achieved the summit.

Of course afterwards all the other tiny frogs, and most of the spectators too, wanted to know how the tiny frog had managed to achieve the impossible. So they asked it.

Turned out that tiny frog was deaf.

1.15 Ringing the Changes

For over a hundred years in many parts of the world, circuses have been a great source of entertainment to children and adults alike. Performed in great canvas tents, called Big Tops, audiences have been amused, entertained and enthralled by clowns, acrobats, and wild animals performing all sorts of tricks.

But by the late twentieth century the circus business was in worldwide crisis. Owners were competing for a dwindling market by cutting seat prices; yet the star performers were asking for higher and higher wages. At the same time customers were requiring more sophisticated standards of entertainment and comfort, and many had serious concerns about whether it was right to keep wild animals in small cages. The future seemed bleak for circuses everywhere.

In these hard and ultra-competitive times, a stilt-walking fire-eater had an inspirational idea. He listened to what the customers were saying and he created a completely new concept in circus entertainment. At a stroke he blew the competition away, and in ten years his new circus made as much money as his main rivals had turned over in the previous century!

Guy Laliberté cut all acts involving animals and instead employed the world's best talents to perform the traditional circus skills of juggling, clowning, mime, and acrobatics. He devised his shows around enthralling themes and exciting concepts with tremendous creativity and breath-taking audacity. He gave his audience what they wanted in the way they wanted it. Finally, he took the circus out of the tent and put it into comfortable yet inspiring venues for which he was able to charge London and New York prices … and his audiences were more than happy to pay.

Cirque du Soleil was a success because Laliberté listened to his customers, delighted them with his product, allowed them to feel comfortable with their surroundings and their consciences, and still found it possible to create an organisation of high profitability, sustainability, and unquestioned integrity.

1.16 Wizards of Oz [1]

It was April in a remote part of northern Australia, summer was coming to an end and the Aborigines wanted to know from their new tribal elder about the weather. Was the coming winter going to be cold or mild?

Since he was an elder in a modern community, and he had gone to college and all that, and spent much time in the big city before returning 'home', he had never been taught the old secrets. When he looked at the sky he couldn't tell what the winter was going to be like.

So, just to be on the safe side, he told his community that the winter was indeed going to be cold and that everybody should collect plenty of firewood and be prepared for the hardships ahead.

But being a practical leader and an educated one at that, the problem weighed on his mind. After a few days he had a brainwave.

He walked over to the pay phone on the highway, called the Bureau of Meteorology and asked, 'Can you folks tell me what winter's going to be like up here in the north?'

The meteorologist said, 'Well, from our current projections it looks as if the winter is likely to be quite frosty.' So the elder went back to his people and told them to collect even more wood and get ready for a freeze.

A fortnight later he called the Bureau of Meteorology again. 'How's winter looking now? What are those computers of yours saying?'

The meteorologist responded, 'Yes, we're pretty confident it's going to be a very cold winter.' The elder again went back to his community and ordered them to collect every scrap of firewood they could find in the vicinity and beyond.

Another two weeks passed and the elder called the Bureau again. 'Are you guys absolutely certain that this winter's going to be a real freezer?'

'No doubt about it,' the meteorologist replied. 'It's looking more and more like it's shaping up to be one of the coldest winters ever.'

'How can you be so sure?' the elder asked.

The weatherman replied, 'Our satellites have reported that the Aborigines up north are collecting firewood like there's no tomorrow, and that's always a sure sign.'

1.17 Wizards of Oz [2]

In 1983, an Australian sheep farmer named Cliff Young, entered the Sydney–Melbourne 'ultra-marathon'. It's an 875-kilometre endurance race that takes around six days to complete. Cliff was up against 150 world class athletes backed by some of the biggest names in sports sponsorship.

Cliff was backed by no one. In fact he turned up to race wearing his farm overalls and work boots. Nobody could believe it. That wasn't all. Not only had Cliff never run a formal race in his life, he was 61 years old.

After the start the runners left Cliff far behind. They'd all done their training and preparation meticulously. They all knew that to stand a chance of winning they had to run for eighteen hours a day and sleep for six.

But no one had told Cliff that he was supposed to do that. So with his unique shuffling style of moving, which many found ridiculous at the time, he just kept going. While the other athletes slept, he just kept on running. By the fourth night he'd caught up with and passed the leaders as they snored. He won the race, breaking the previous record by nine hours.

The man who did it his way, who didn't know what he 'ought to' or 'should' do, or what to wear, or how to train, who didn't compartmentalise life into separate stages of action, became an overnight hero. Cliff simply saw the territory for what it was. He saw what was needed. And he refused to give in to conventional wisdom, or limiting beliefs, or dualistic thinking about what could or couldn't be done. He was in a 'flow' state that lasted the best part of five days.

When he was asked how he overcame the need to sleep, he just replied that he imagined he was out on his ranch rounding up sheep in a storm. And that's not all. When presented with his cash prize for winning, he said he hadn't done it for the money and gave away every cent of it.

Chautauqua 2

Beyond the Surface of Things

Stories on the Themes of Appearance and Illusion

As a society we have learned to live on the surface. We have developed ways of thinking about things that have trapped us in the illusion of understanding because we think these are the only ways to see 'reality'. One example of this is the world of science where for many centuries scientists have seen *parts* as the primary organising principle and wholeness as secondary. More recent science, notably relativity and quantum physics, has disputed this mechanistic Aristotelian view, and takes *wholeness* as primary, backing this up with considerable evidence.

It's not that the mechanical view is wrong, it's just incomplete. It serves many functions and purposes well but it also hides deeper truths and more profound possibilities. It focuses on doing rather than being, which is like studying the nature of a wave while ignoring the context of its existence within a great ocean.

On a planet that seems increasingly separate and fragmented, perhaps changing our perspective may not be a bad idea. Working with our rationality need not preclude our connecting to the wisdom of our intuition, creativity, and imagination. Studying the whole need not preclude us from appreciating the parts and the contribution they make. From quantum theory we have as much to learn about indivisibility as we do from the contemplative wisdom traditions. Both the scientists and the spiritual masters suggest that it may be useful to enquire into our current perspectives and mindsets with a little more rigour.

Our learned inability to see below the surface of things arises in all contexts: some trivial, some important. For example, most of us recognise the importance of setting goals in our life. They give us purpose and direction in the exterior world. But if the future steps that need to be taken to achieve these goals demand so much of our attention that we lose awareness of the step we are taking now this moment, then we are missing the point of our *inner* purpose and *inner* direction. For the step we are taking now is actually all that exists. Our past is simply memory, sensory codings of past events; our future is simply a projection of our past experience imagined in a future moment which can never exist.

And the one step we are taking now, if we take it with full consciousness and awareness, holds within it every other step we will ever take, and the final goal or destination too. So that every step we take becomes an expression of the quality we choose to bring to each moment, and a recognition of our deep connection with everything around us.

Every time we lose this awareness we miss the depth and complexity of each moment that is available to us. Every time we fail to challenge conventional views of existence we lose sight of the true meaning and value of life. And we fall asleep so easily.

Some years ago I was living in Brittany, in northern France. My partner at that time was a painter and most mornings she would rise with the dawn to catch the quality of the morning light. Before or after breakfast, depending on the level of my hunger, I would stroll down the lanes to find her and observe her at work.

One late summer morning she was painting in oils. She'd applied the under layers of deep colour to give the painting depth and complexity and was starting on the surface application. I asked her what she was painting. She was sitting in the gateway to a wheat field but I couldn't make any sense of what she was up to. 'I'm painting the wheat field,' she said smiling. But to me it looked nothing like a wheat field. Everybody knows wheat is basically yellow.

'How is that a wheat field?' I said. 'I don't see any yellow.'

'Well take a look at *this* wheat field,' she replied patiently.

'Well, I'm looking at it and it's *yellow*!'

'No,' she said, 'really take a look at it. See it for what is there, not what you would like to think is there.'

So I looked and was silent.

'So what do you see now,' she asked gently.

'Purples, browns, greens, magentas, some blue, white, mauves, pinks, ochres ... I found several more ... and,' I added weakly, 'some yellow.'

And that's when I began to see more clearly and more deeply below the surface of things to find the richness and complexity that lies hidden from the superficial gaze.

***

The stories in this section explore what lies below and beyond the surface of things. The first four are Zen stories. The first story *Right Value* (2.1) explores life's priorities and the second *The Limits of Reason* (2.2) gently suggests that we might wish to consider the limitation of our human capacities. The third *Busy-ness* (2.3) chides us for our lack of rigour when we don't face up to our inner dragons with clarity and honesty; in particular the story notes that getting 'busy' is very often just an avoidance strategy that keeps us safe at the surface of things. The fourth story *Is That So?* (2.4) ironically accepts the surface situation while deeply acknowledging the complexity of what is truly happening.

The two Chinese stories (2.5 and 2.6) *The Coin* and *Perspicacity* investigate the nature of what is hidden from ordinary sight; how what appears simple and unremarkable to some, reveals deeper meanings and subtleties to the one who is prepared to look beyond the surface of things and explore other perspectives, relationships, and frames.

Four Sufi stories follow. *Temptation* (2.7) notes the extremes we can go to deceive ourselves, especially when tempted by desire and when we have become stuck in certain patterns of thinking about things or people. *A Stunted Tree* (2.8) suggests that it is not useful to generalise about emotional states. There is a world of difference between a mature and an immature manifestation of emotion, symbolised by the withered, stunted tree miraculously breaking into blossom. At the outset of the story, the man is controlled by his emotion. Later, informed by a deep and intuitive awareness of wrongdoing, he channels righteous anger and a deep sense of social justice to destroy evil in service of the community.

Time and Place (2.9) poses a question. What kind of quality of life can you expect if you don't enquire beneath the surface of things by challenging partial information and asking high quality questions? The quality of our life depends upon the quality of our questions. *The Genius of Simplicity* (2.10) suggests, contrary to what many believe, that simple and practical means are often the best way to the deepest truths.

Of the two Kabbalah stories, *Perfect Partnerships* (2.11) urges us to overcome the blindness we have developed towards each other through classification, coding, analysis, distrust, suspicion, and separation, and to see each other as true partners that can supportively engage with and enrich each other. How else can we navigate the dense forests and labyrinthine jungles of what we create in our heads and in our day-to-day constructions of reality?

MBA (2.12) mocks the modern tendency to treat education as a commodity rather than a life-long process.

Of the three Christian stories (2.13–15), the first *Beyond the Surface of Things* (2.13) explores the Buddhist concept of Karma as much as the Christian ones of charity, generosity, and consequences. *Dog Years* (2.14) is a humorous just-so tale adapted from the Brothers Grimm which offers some amusing truths about the human condition. *The Inner Gap* (2.15) holds a mirror up to our inner and outer perceptions of reality. Whatever we see in the outside world is nothing more or less than a projection of our own inner world.

Finally, six mindset stories. *Optical Illusions* (2.16) reflects how our personal values can so easily distort reality. Our values are filters through which each of us perceives and makes meaning of the world. Here three people use their different value systems to understand exactly the same thing in completely different ways. They are each right but only partially so, for our values are nothing more than the navigating systems we use to negotiate our path through life. And tomorrow—if our circumstances change or if we perceive the world differently—our values may change too to accommodate our new way of making meaning.

Fred (2.17) explores the importance of reflection, contemplation, and meditation as an antidote to busy-ness and as an opportunity to create better solutions to pressing problems. *Difference That Makes the Difference* (2.18) challenges the common business practice of packing teams and boardrooms with like-minded people who won't ask challenging or embarrassing questions.

Straight Talking (2.19) touches on the unhealthy culture that exists in many organisations whereby relationships between managers and their teams are often characterised as parent–child relationships rather than adult–adult. Once everybody in an organisation is seen as an adult and sees others as adults, and agrees to enter into adult–adult communications and relationships, what could that organisation not achieve?

Qualities of Greatness (2.20) considers arrogance and superiority as core blocks to seeing beyond the surface of things. Aspects of wisdom and greatness reside in every person, and each one has a contribution to make in his or her own particular way. *Passion* (2.21) explores how deep connection with our true passion sets us free: physically, mentally, intellectually, and spiritually. When the energy of creation flows through us what power can constrain us?

Finally *Life's Value* (2.22) points a finger gently at our general ignorance and our tendency to get easily distracted from whatever paths we may wish to tread. Since our energy flows wherever our attention goes, we shouldn't be surprised if lives lived in triviality can seem so meaningless and unsatisfying.

***

Learning to explore beyond the surface of things throws up some surprising revelations: revelations that often appear contradictory or paradoxical. I find I have more power available to me when I am ill than when I am well. Of course, this is not really true. It's just that I'm more aware of the power and energy that runs through me when I'm not one hundred per cent, especially when I really need it. When I am well it is too easy to turn off the tap, or put a kink in the hose, that connects me to the infinite flow of energy which—at least if my experience of illness is to be believed—is always accessible to me and, I would assume, everybody else.

Two instances come to mind. The first was many years ago in my late twenties. I was working as a professional actor. Our company was on tour and we were performing at the Leeds Grand, a beautiful and imposing Victorian theatre with five, maybe even six, tiers of seating. It is, by any comparison, a very large space to work in. And I had lost my voice. I had a strep throat—pharyngitis. All I could manage that day was an indecipherable croak.

There were no understudies, no one else was available to play my part, and over a thousand eager punters were out there waiting for the show to go on. When my entrance came, I walked to centre stage for my soliloquy. I had no idea what would happen. And I started to speak. And from the depths of my belly, pushed up from diaphragm and lungs was a voice so powerful, so rich, so sensuous that I could only wonder from where it had come. What I did know was that it was a voice in which something in me had arranged for every other part to get out of the way. It was a voice of complete and utter effortlessness.

I made my exit and went to the dressing room. All I could manage was a squeak.

Roll time on a couple of decades. It is spring of 1999. I am in Belgrade to run a four-day professional development programme for the British Council. Belgrade is a depressing place because the talk is of war and impending NATO air strikes. The mood somehow gets to me and within twenty-four hours of arriving I am struck down with a virus that knocks me flat, that keeps me awake all night in a fever of such intensity that in the morning the sheets are wet with perspiration.

But twenty or so people are expecting a programme—some have travelled from as far away as the mountains of Montenegro by bus, a sixteen-hour journey. So I drag myself out of my bed and my room and make an invalid's progress down the main street to the training centre. And I work. And I manage to repeat this process every day for the whole four days. I cover less than two thirds of the content of my four-day programme, but as in Leeds my body–mind instinctively knows just how to cut out anything superfluous to what is necessary. No jokes, no fripperies, no excess energy, and above all no 'charisma'.

I work with a quiet intensity that I have never known before. And it is sensational. It is not *me* though. Something deep within is running me. I am just an instrument for what wants to flow out and respond to whatever is coming back from the group, and for what each moment needs.

I have not yet got close to that intensity again as hard as I try. And that may be it. Trying too hard instead of just letting go with a deep trust that whatever is true will simply arise. That remains my work to do.

The day after the course I left Serbia and my health returned almost immediately. Three days after I left, NATO bombs struck Belgrade and other Serbian towns. The Avala TV tower just outside Belgrade was destroyed. There were many casualties. Energy works in mysterious ways, certainly in ways my limited rational mind can find hard to comprehend.

Four Short Zen Stories

2.1 Right Value

A Zen Master lived a simple life in a cave near the summit of a sparsely wooded mountainside. One evening as he fetched water from a distant stream a thief crept into the cave. But there was nothing at all to steal. Just then the monk returned and said, 'My friend, you have had a long journey and a fruitless one. You should not leave here without some token of my hospitality. Please take my clothes as a gift for you.'

The thief was embarrassed, but took the rags and ran off. As a full and beautiful moon rose from the east, the naked monk prepared for evening meditation and thought, 'Poor chap! What a pity I couldn't give him this marvellous moon.'

2.2 The Limits of Reason

The historian had a very clear view on human progress and development. And he didn't think much of 'non-scientific' ways of understanding the human condition. He said to a Zen Master, 'Have not the efforts of human beings changed the course of human history?'

'Indeed they have,' responded the Master.

'And does not human endeavour change the planet?'

'Without question.'

'Then how can you teach that human action is of little consequence?'

'Because when the wind drops, the leaves still fall.'

2.3 Busy-ness

A successful businessman asked a Zen monk: 'What do you do to make a living?'

'Nothing,' the monk replied.

'Isn't that laziness?'

'Not at all. Laziness is the art of finding countless ways to distract yourself. Usually, being "busy" is a strategy people use in order to avoid asking themselves the really difficult and necessary questions that need to be asked. Most often, laziness is the vice of people who are *too busy*.'

2.4 Is That So?

An attractive girl in the town became pregnant and her parents pressed her to reveal the name of the father. For quite a long time the girl resisted the pressure, but finally she pointed to the Zen Master, Hakuin. This caused quite a scandal in the community, as you can imagine, especially as—up to that point—Hakuin had always been considered as a man of integrity, and quite beyond reproach.

But when the irate parents confronted him with their daughter's situation, he simply shrugged his shoulders and said, 'Is that so?'

After the girl had reached her time and the child was born, the two parents presented the small, gurgling, dynamic bundle of illegitimate vitality to Hakuin. They demanded that he should take care of the child since it was, after all, his responsibility. 'Is that so?' said Hakuin as he reached out calmly to accept the child.

For several months Hakuin took expert care of the growing baby, until its mother, no longer able to hold back the truth, confessed that the real father was a young man from the next town.

The parents went straight to Hakuin, on their knees with apologies, and asked if they could please have the baby back. When they explained the full story to Hakuin he simply shrugged his shoulders and said, 'Is that so?' before gently handing the baby back.

Two Chinese Stories

2.5 The Coin

A major battle was inevitable, and the general decided that attack was his best strategy even though his troops were vastly outnumbered. He was confident that victory could be achieved, but his troops were filled with fear and great doubt.

At a shrine on the road to the field of battle, the general halted his men and prayed with them. Then he announced, 'Let us invite Destiny to reveal herself.' He took from his pocket a silver coin, and said: 'If, when I toss this coin, it should fall as heads we shall win; if tails, we lose.'

He tossed the coin high in the air, and the eyes of every soldier watched its gentle trajectory intently. In hushed silence they held their breath as it fell to the ground.

'Heads!'

A huge roar of self-belief and empowerment was raised to the skies. The soldiers were so convinced of their strength and invulnerability that in the battle they made short work of their enemy. It was a great victory.

When the fighting was done, the wounded bandaged, and the dead buried, a young commander remarked to the general, 'No force can change Destiny.'

'Very true,' said the general, showing him the coin with heads on both sides.

2.6 Perspicacity

For many generations a family from Sung had bleached silk. To prevent their hands becoming sore and chapped during the bleaching process, they had developed a balm which was marvellously good at protecting their hands. They guarded the secret formula of this balm jealously.

A warrior passed one day through the district where this family worked and heard about their miraculous balm. He offered to buy the formula for twenty ounces of gold. The family discussed his offer. 'How many generations have we been bleaching silk? And how much money have we ever made? Very little? Let him have it if he pays us fifty ounces of gold.' And so the recipe was sold to the warrior for the price they proposed.

Sometime later, the stranger arrived in the state of Wu. He had been summoned there by the King to give advice on the ongoing and protracted war with the State of Yueh. The stranger, who was skilled in the arts of warfare, was placed in command of the navy, and soon he had drawn up his fleet to strike a blow against the enemy ships.

It was midwinter, and cold, bitter blasts roared down from the north. The winds were raw and the sea foamed. The stranger distributed to his sailors and soldiers alike the balm so their hands would be protected from the biting wind and icy seas. And they won a great victory thanks to this decisive advantage. The warrior was lavishly rewarded by the King of Wu with titles and lands.

The man of foresight uses perspicacity to seize opportunity. The remedy for chapped hands remained the same. But the secret was put to different uses. One man still bleaches silk, his hands raw from the work. The other lives in luxury, and others do his bidding. While you focus on the inner world, do not lose sight of the outer.

Four Sufi Stories

2.7 Temptation

An enviously handsome young man was attracting the attention of three or four young girls at a disco. Not only was he good looking, he danced with the grace of a gazelle and the self-possession of a panther. His conversation was witty and charming. And he was respectfully attentive to each one of them.

'Can I tempt you back to my apartment for drinks?' he enquired gently.

It was late but the offer was enticing. 'But we don't know who you are.'

'My name is Satan. I'm the Devil,' he replied smiling.

The girls laughed. 'Don't be so ridiculous. The Devil is ugly, misshapen, and evil.'

'Then you must have been listening to my detractors.'

2.8 A Stunted Tree

There was a man whose anger controlled him. It caused much grief both to himself and to others. He knew that almost all his problems were to do with his anger, yet he seemed powerless to do anything about it.

One day he was told about a Wise Counsellor, so he went to see her. The Counsellor said, 'Give up your present ways.' And she instructed him to go to a particular crossroads where he would find a stunted, leafless tree. There he was to stand and offer water to every passing traveller.

Because he fervently wanted to make this change, and because he trusted the Counsellor, the man went to the appointed place. For many years he followed her instructions, and travellers on the road understood that here was a disciple, under instruction, learning the disciplines of charity and self-restraint. They called him the Water Giver—Giver of Life.

One day, the man greeted a passer-by in a friendly way and offered him cool, fresh water. But the traveller pushed rudely past him, knocking the cup from the disciple's hand, and continuing on his way.

The Water Giver was incensed. He called out to the traveller, 'Hey you! Who the hell do you think you are? Return my greeting. Drink my water! Hey you!'

But the man rudely offered him just one finger and continued on his way.

At this, all self-discipline was lost. The Giver of Life took his shotgun, from where it hung on the branch of the stunted tree, and fired one accurate and deadly shot. The traveller fell lifeless to the ground.

Immediately, the stunted tree burst into blossom and leaves appeared on all its branches.

As it turned out, the man was a serial murderer, on his malign way to commit the worst atrocity of his long and vengeful life.

There are two types of anger. One serves the narrow needs of the self without heed to wider consequences. The other serves noble cause and purpose; it brings health, security, and justice to the wider community. A wise person is one who can discriminate between the two.

2.9 Time and Place

Jafar, the son of a rich Portuguese merchant, was restless. The life of ease and luxury that his father's wealth offered was insufficient. He craved a more spiritual existence far from the secular pleasures of the salons of Lisbon. So, on a certain day, he left Lisbon and travelled to Mecca, to seek out 'the Great Teacher of the Age'.

When Jafar arrived in Mecca, a complete stranger, dressed in a flowing robe of white and green, approached him. Without any word being spoken by Jafar, the stranger said, 'You seek the Great Teacher of the Age but you seek him here in the East when he is in the West, in Lisbon from where you have come. And there is also something else that is wrong with your great mission.'

The stranger advised Jafar to return to his homeland and gave him the name of a certain family of a certain tribe living in the wide rolling plains of the Alentejo. He told Jafar that the Great Teacher he sought was the son of this family, and his name was Mohiudin.

Jafar returned to Lisbon eager to resume the search. He discovered that Mohiudin and his family had indeed been living in Lisbon at the very time he had left for Mecca, and that now they had moved into the broad rolling region south of the capital.

Jafar once again set off in search of Mohiudin. He followed his trail through the Alentejo, and further south still through the hills, flowers, and glistening blue bays of the Algarve. Then on into barren mountains of Andalusia, until finally he reached the city of Seville.

Jafar asked a priest whether he knew of Mohiudin, son of el-Arabi. 'There,' said the priest, indicating a young boy weighed down with scriptures and other holy books.

Thoroughly disturbed at discovering that the one he sought was not yet nearly a man, Jafar stopped the boy and asked, 'Who is the Greatest Teacher of the Age?'

'You must give me time to answer your question,' replied Mohiudin.

'And may I ask, are you really Mohiudin, son of el-Arabi, of the tribe of Tai?'

'Indeed I am,' he replied.

Realising now that the stranger in the white and green robe had misinformed him, Jafar apologised to the boy, saying 'I am sorry for taking your time. There is nothing more you can give me.' And Jafar returned to Lisbon.

Many years later, when Jafar had established himself as a successful man in his own right, he travelled to Alexandria. By accident, as he was exploring the city, he found himself entering the courtyard of a certain Mohiudin ibn el-Arabi, of the tribe of Tai, also known as the Greatest Teacher.

Mohiudin spoke as Jafar entered. 'I have been expecting you. Many years ago you put a question to me. Now that I am ready to answer it you no longer need to ask it. All those years ago you told me there was nothing I could give you. What is it that I could give you now? The one in the white and green robe told you that there was something wrong in your great mission. You simply failed to challenge what he meant. Now you understand the wisdom of seeking the truth below the surface of things.'

Hearing this, Jafar gave up his wealth and found a new direction.

2.10 The Genius of Simplicity

Mullah Nasruddin had a faithful donkey that had provided him with good and steady service over many years. One day the donkey fell down a well close to Nasruddin's house at the edge of the village. It was a particularly deep well, and despite the Mullah's best efforts, and the willing assistance of his neighbours, they were unable to extricate the poor animal from its predicament.

Every night from his upstairs window Nasruddin could hear the pitiable braying of the distressed animal. So every day for several days the Mullah organised expeditions to the well to rescue the donkey. None were successful. Nasruddin got no sleep and the donkey refused to die quietly.

In the end the Mullah decided he would have to put the poor beast out of its misery. The well would have to become its grave and, along with several helpful neighbours, he began shovelling earth into its depths. They started shovelling at dawn, but the donkey refused to go quietly. At noon they were still shovelling. Haunted by the pathetic and indistinct braying of the earth-covered beast, they redoubled their efforts. Even into the late afternoon they could still hear the donkey's feeble protests. It wasn't till sunset that the donkey surprised them all by walking over the lip of the well on the very soil the diggers had spent all day shovelling in order to bury it.

Two Stories from the Kabbalah

2.11 Perfect Partnerships

A man is lost in a great forest. As night falls he becomes more and more desperate. Then he sees a light in the distance and is joyful that he will be saved. He stumbles towards his saviour and when he is close says, 'Thank God I've found you. Now you can show me the way out.'

But the woman carrying the lamp high above her head says, 'I'm sorry, I'm lost too. But don't worry, we're so much stronger together. We know that where I came from and where you came from there's no way out. So together we have greater access to useful information. Now we have a better chance of finding a way out.'

The man is reassured by this, but not completely. He studies the woman more closely and suddenly realises she is blind. 'Hey! You can't even see. Why do you need a lamp?'

'So you can see *me*,' she replies.

2.12 MBA

A proud father came running to tell his Rabbi some great news. 'Rabbi, Rabbi! I've just heard on the phone. My son has passed his MBA, summa cum laude. Now he has finally finished all his learning.'

The Rabbi replied drily, 'Don't worry! I'm sure the Universe in its wisdom will soon send him some more.'

Three Christian Stories

2.13 Beyond the Surface of Things

Two travelling angels knock at the door of an expensive mansion. They ask if they can stay the night. But the wealthy family are rude and condescending; they refuse to let the angels sleep in the guest room. Instead they are shown into the cold, windowless cellar where they have to make do with sleeping on the concrete floor.

When they get up in the morning, the elder angel notices a small hole in the wall and repairs it. The younger angel asks him why he has done that. 'Look beyond the surface of things,' is the reply.

The following evening, the travellers approach the door of a humble country cottage. And although the farmer and his wife are poor, they are exceedingly hospitable and generous. They even give up their own bed so the angels can rest deeply and without disturbance.

But the next morning the angels find the couple heartbroken. During the night their only cow, whose milk was their sole income, has died.

The younger angel is furious with her companion. As soon as they leave the simple homestead, she rounds on him. 'How could you allow this to happen? These people shared everything they had, yet you allowed tragedy to visit them. The rich man yesterday was mean and ungenerous, yet to him you gave help.'

'Look beyond the surface of things,' says the elder angel. 'Had you looked through the broken wall in the cellar of the mansion you would have seen hidden gold and treasure. But as the owner was so unwilling to share his good fortune, I sealed the hole so he would not find it.

'And last night as everyone lay sleeping, the Angel of Death came for the farmer's wife. So I gave him the cow instead.'

2.14 Dog Years

After the World was created, God in Her wisdom decided to grant all creatures a thirty-year life span. But the Donkey, realising how much work that would mean, was horrified and immediately negotiated an eighteen-year reduction. The Dog was none too happy either, fearing it would be useless and unwanted in old age, kicked from pillar to post. So God agreed to reduce its life span as well. Then the Monkey also pleaded for a reduction and God agreed to remove ten years from its busy and precarious life.

But the Humans were shocked to have been given so little time, especially as they considered themselves to be by far the most superior part of creation. So God gave them the donkey's eighteen years. But still the Humans were dissatisfied, so God gave them the extra years taken from the Dog. And still they complained, so God added the Monkey's unwanted ten years too.

And that's why Human Beings live in health and happiness for the first thirty or so years of their long lives—for that's their natural span. But after that the serious work starts, and they carry the heavy burden of working from dawn to dusk to pay for their home, to bring up their children, and to service the pension that's necessary to sustain them through so many years of life. Slaves to their masters, they'll put up with almost anything to get through their Donkey years.

After that come the years of the Dog when they sit by the fireside, grumbling and grousing, irritated by their offspring, and scratching at itches.

Finally, they enter their Monkey years where, as everyone knows, they do whatever the hell they like.

2.15 The Inner Gap

At the retreat, a woman complained, 'Why is everyone here so joyful while I am so miserable?'

The answer she got was, 'Because everyone here has learned to see beauty and goodness wherever they look.'

'Well, why can't I see it too?'

'Because you can't see on the outside what you haven't learned to see on the inside.'

Six Mindset Stories

2.16 Optical Illusions

There were four people in an Irish pub: the innkeeper, a Scot, a Brazilian, and a Philosopher.

The innkeeper poured some whiskey into a tumbler exactly as far as the halfway mark and said, 'Gentlemen, how would you describe this glass of whiskey?'

The Scot said, 'It's half empty.'

The Brazilian said, 'Not at all. This glass is half full.'

The Philosopher said nothing. He simply took the glass, observed the richness of its amber colour, sniffed it to appreciate the fine peaty aromas, drained it, held and swirled the whiskey around his tongue, took time to allow his taste buds to extract the richness and oakiness of the flavours, and then put the empty glass back on the bar. 'Very good quality,' he finally said.

2.17 Fred

A young auditor from a large multinational consultancy had just completed an exhaustive audit of a manufacturing plant in the north of England. He reported to the CEO that everything seemed fine except for one thing.

'What's that?' asked the Chief Executive.

'Well, there's a man in working overalls sitting on a chair on the factory floor with his eyes closed. He doesn't seem to have done a stroke of work for four days.'

'Ah! That's Fred. Ten years ago Fred came up with an idea that saves this factory ten million US dollars a year. It also saves every one of our other forty-seven factories around the world ten million dollars a year. That's 480 million dollars per year by my reckoning—4,800 million beautiful greenbacks over ten years.

'As far as I'm concerned Fred can sit on his chair with his eyes closed for the rest of his working life just on the off chance he comes up with another brilliant idea!'

2.18 The Difference That Makes the Difference

William Wrigley Jr., who created the great global chewing gum company, was a great believer in the importance of drawing out the different and often contradictory ideas, opinions, and approaches in a team.

On this subject he famously said: 'When two people in a group *always* agree, you have to ask yourself whether one of them is unnecessary ...'

2.19 Straight Talking

'The trouble with my organisation, as with most business organisations,' said the respected Chief Executive, 'is that the people who work in them refuse to grow up.'

'How can one tell whether a particular person has indeed grown up?' somebody asked him.

'First is when that person can have a courageous conversation and speak their truth—even if it is an unpopular truth. And secondly, when he or she no longer needs to be lied to about anything.'

2.20 Qualities of Greatness

It was rumoured that a great and wise management guru had taken up residence in an unassuming cottage at the head of a remote valley. A Chief Executive, who was encountering serious problems with staff morale and motivation, decided to pay him a visit hoping that he might get some wisdom from the man.

So he made the long and arduous journey to the distant village and knocked at the door. A grey-haired servant opened the door, and the CEO rather brusquely demanded to see the great consultant. Smiling affably, the servant stepped aside to let him in, and the visitor entered the living area eagerly anticipating a life-changing and business-enhancing interview with the wise guru.

But in a very short time he found himself being ushered out of the back door of the cottage. 'But I want to see the guru,' he spluttered.

'But you already have,' said the grey-haired man kindly. 'Every person you meet, plain and insignificant as they may appear, has within them some of the qualities of greatness and wisdom that you seek, and the ability in some way to make a contribution. Perhaps there is a current situation in your life where you are not paying attention to the gifts of the people who surround you.'

2.21 Passion

A music journalist wished to visit the pianist Artur Rubinstein when the great man was well into his nineties. Telephoning Rubinstein's residence the previous day, the journalist had been told that he may or may not be granted an interview but he was welcome to turn up the following morning just in case. Early next day the journalist arrived at Rubinstein's villa on the French coast and waited.

Rubinstein eventually appeared moving with a shuffling gait, and the journalist could not help but notice how advanced the pianist's arthritis was. His hands were mottled and set rigid like bird claws. With a cursory nod to the visitor, Rubinstein made his way to the piano and sat down at the stool.

Rubinstein slowly and painfully held his two claw-like hands above the keys. And then something miraculous began to take place. Gradually the journalist saw the hands begin to relax, open, and spread. And the great man began to play. For two hours he practised, moving from scales to more and more complex and demanding pieces. As he moved through his repertoire, the hands gained more and more fluidity, elasticity, and speed. Until abruptly, Rubinstein stopped and closed the lid of his Steinway.

And then slowly the hands resumed their former claw-like nature, and by the time breakfast was served to him, he was unable to hold even a knife.

2.22 Life's Value

One afternoon the great Sikh Teacher, Guru Nanak, was relaxing with his companions on the banks of a great river. His close friend and disciple, the Muslim Bhai Mardana, was playing with a large pebble he had picked up along the way, and thinking about the many pilgrims who were flocking to hear the Guru speak. 'Master,' said Mardana, 'you teach a way for each person to attain liberation, but many of these people still engage in conflict, vice, and other distractions. Why do people waste their lives in such foolish ways?'

'Because,' replied Nanak, 'most people don't realise the value of life, although it is truly the greatest treasure on this earth.'

'So why is it that people can't see life's true value? Surely it must be obvious to them.'

'Sadly not, for each individual person puts his own value on things according to his thinking. Your stone, for example, the one you found on the dusty road, may offer us some insight. Go and take it to the market. See what you can get for it.'

First, Mardana went to a market stall where spices were sold and asked the trader what she would barter for it. The woman laughed and told Mardana to get lost.

Then he tried a greengrocer. 'I'm busy serving my customers,' said the stall-holder roughly. 'Here, take an orange and stop wasting my time.'

Mardana went from stall to stall without any better success. At last he came to a jeweller whose eyes opened in astonishment when he saw the stone. The jeweller apologized to Mardana saying he didn't have enough money to purchase the gem, 'But I will give you fifty rupees if you will just allow me to gaze on it a little longer.'

Mardana raced back to report his experience to the Guru.

'You see,' said Nanak, 'how in our ignorance we can think a valuable gem no better than a worthless pebble. Before you went to the jeweller, you would have laughed if someone had told you this stone was worth a fortune. And so it is with your life. Your life is a most precious jewel, yet whatever you've traded it for, that is the life that is yours.'

Chautauqua 3

Flow

*Stories on the Themes of Creativity, Complexity,
Strategy, and Systems*

In the seventeenth century, scientists used a powerful metaphor to explain the universe. They described it as a great clock whose workings could be predicted and controlled.

The assumptions built into this metaphor—in terms of organisational development and leadership theory—are that cause and effect are simple relationships, that everything can be discovered and known through man's rational intelligence, and that people and organisations can be manipulated into creating efficient solutions.

It is an extraordinary fact that this way of thinking about people and organisations as machines, conforming to the laws of mechanical engineering, still holds considerable sway today—over three hundred years later. A lot of people who should know better seem wedded to the idea that organisational success depends solely on their ability to respond to events, control people, and predict outcomes.

This mechanistic approach to organisations, leadership, and management needs to shift fast. It needs to move beyond the paradigm that everything can be controlled—beyond even the idea that everything can be negotiated—and accept the findings of more contemporary scientific discovery that people, and the organisations they create, are self-organising systems in which relationships and influence are the key factors that produce change appropriate to need and circumstance.

Complexity theorists have noticed the tendency of systems to organise themselves naturally. Order comes from within not without. As theoretical biologist Professor Stuart Kauffman has suggested, we inhabit a universe where 'order comes for free'.[17] It is naturally built in and any attempt to impose control from the outside often causes more harm than good. In modern times, this awareness has developed into a healthy approach to management known as 'leadership by getting out of the way'.

For centuries, scientists failed to understand the apparently complex ways in which birds flocked, insects swarmed, and fish shoaled. Who was the leader? How was it done? Computer simulations have recently shown that there are only two or three simple rules that need to be followed by the individuals in a group, and that those rules are to be followed *only by each individual in relation to its neighbours*. There is never a leader, and there are no rules about a direction.

One of the reasons why scientists took such a long time to 'solve' this puzzle was because of the stuck cultural frame of reference they inhabited. They could not conceive that there could *not* be a leader, therefore they never looked at the problem from that perspective. This reflects perfectly the ingrained need in Western belief systems for external planning, control, and authority.

In his groundbreaking book on systems thinking, *The Fifth Discipline*, Peter Senge directly challenged the narrow linear approach of much modern organisational thinking, and its basis in the clockmaker metaphor. Despite the great success of the book, and general agreement as to its validity, very little has changed in the twenty odd years since it was written. Organisations are still very much stuck in the old ways of thinking it seems. Our cultural paradigms are very hard to overcome.

Systems awareness invites us to take a step back from our busy, yet narrow, engagement with day-to-day reality and, from a more distant perspective, notice a 'bigger picture'. This helicopter view, or balcony vision, goes a long way to enabling us to see what is happening in the world around us, not as a series of discrete events, but as a complex set of interconnected relationships that play out across time and space.

From this more distant perspective we can notice that life is not so much about single important static events—as much of the media and many political and organisational leaders would have us believe—but much more about the continuous *flow* of longer term processes and interrelationships within and between people and their environments.

From high up in this balcony position we can notice a great deal more systemic complexity than we can when engaged in the daily minutiae of running our lives at ground level. Because we have access to more information, because we're more distanced from our emotional entanglements, because we can see the systemic relationships between things more clearly, we can more easily generate new choices to old problems from up here. We can be much more *creative* and we can be much more *strategic*.

From up here we can more easily step into our nature as self-organising systems and notice how adaptive, resilient, enquiring, flexible, generative, learning, intelligent, relational, and free-flowing we can be when we put our minds to it.

***

Since I became more aware of my own tendency to make things happen the way I wanted them to be and of my desire to control others, whether consciously or not, I have made some efforts to change. None of the changes have been as startling as the strategy I now use when attending seminars and workshops.

I used to make a mental note of the people I wanted to work with in the pair and small group exercises. My criteria for choosing them were varied, and almost certainly outside of my conscious awareness. They probably included such things as: physical attraction, nice smile, level of energy, resemblance to people I like, radiation of intelligence and discernment, attentiveness to what was going on, and no doubt many others. The pattern would be that an exercise was announced and I would go and proactively create a group which included me and my chosen object or objects of desire.

And I would always be disappointed! Every time something was never quite right. People would never live up to my expectations of them. And of course not! Why should they? They were just being themselves; but I was doing a huge amount of projecting. I was busy giving them qualities that I *wanted* them to have, whether they liked it or not.

So I stopped. I stopped being proactive and I stopped trying to control things. Now I simply stand and wait to be chosen by others. I wait to see what the 'universe' in its wisdom brings. The consequence is I now work with all kinds of people that I wouldn't have worked with before and I am *never* disappointed. I have no expectations and I'm constantly amazed how fascinating and diversely engaging everybody is. I learn a lot more because these people very often see the world from perspectives very different from my own. And because I'm not listening for what I want from them but for what they are actually saying to me, I actually *hear* it a lot better.

Above all, I've learned to just be with the flow of things, to trust that whoever comes along to invite me will be exactly the right person for me, at that time, and for that exercise. By learning to be in the flow, to be present to whatever is happening, and *whoever* is happening, I can just be open to nothing more than the flow of communication, energy, and relationship that emerges from moment to moment.

I learn so much more than I did before. And I still meet those others who I was so attracted to before, but it happens much more naturally and without any expectation.

***

The stories in this section explore themes of flow and influence, of creativity, strategy, and systems. They include a wide variety of perspectives that challenge some of the more stuck Western attitudes to these themes—especially through laughing, probing, and provoking.

The first three (3.1–3) are stories from the East. The first *Something Missing* (3.1) is a Zen story that gently mocks the attempts of the rational, ordered mind to have everything just so. It brings to my mind Cezanne's observation that 'there's no such thing in Nature as a straight line'. *Go with the Flow* (3.2) reminds the reader to do just that: to integrate into the system and become non-resisting mind when working with an irresistible force. However, there are plenty of other Zen stories which recommend swimming upstream in certain circumstances.

Sustainability is Not a Cheap Option (3.3) is deceptive in its apparent simplicity. A possible reading is the importance of investing properly in adequate resources for the task at hand. As such it is a story about systems and sustainability.

The first of the five Sufi stories *The Blind Men and the Elephant* (3.4) stresses the importance of grasping the bigger picture and not reducing information to its constituent parts, which by themselves are useless and misleading. At a deeper level the story expresses the Sufi concept that God or the Soul is unknowable through rational thinking. The approach of the elders represents the dualistic nature of the small self and its tendency to break down everything into parts. Our view as readers is neat: it allows us to acknowledge and experience the indivisibility of what the elephant represents.

The Wise Fool (3.5) is originally a typical Mullah Nasruddin story. The wise fool sees the truth from multiple perspectives and sees things in their proper context. *Giving for the Self* (3.6) warns against attempting to interfere with, or control, the natural systems of the universe. It also counsels against mixing generosity with expectation of reward: 'It is the heart that gives, the fingers just let go.'

A Virtuous Circle (3.7) illustrates that what goes around comes around. It's an amusing and highly improbable systems story that suggests that no one can escape the consequences of the actions they take—Sufi Karma. *The Inner Teacher* (3.8) is a longer and more complex story. It explores how our impatience, our desire, and our rational mind can prevent us from seeing beyond the surface of things. It urges us to listen to our inner voice and to recognise that true wisdom or enlightenment requires the development of both an inner and an outer awareness.

The previous stories in this section have their provenance in Eastern thinking. The remaining stories illustrate the ways that we are learning to appreciate and activate flow states and systems thinking a great deal more in Western thought and experience. In two stories of courage (3.9 and 3.10) *Masculine Compassion* (3.9)—a 'true' story—illustrates the extraordinary healing and reframing powers of metaphor, while *Enthusiasm* (3.10) demonstrates the power of passion and enthusiasm to overcome fear and false modesty. Both these stories celebrate human creativity at its peak.

Stories 11 and 12 are both about the importance of taking a helicopter view to appreciate the complexity of systems at work. *Digging Deeper* (3.11) also touches lightly on the tendency of some to underestimate the intelligence and awareness of those they wish to analyse. Here the 'natives' show a lot more complexity in their thinking than the anthropologist who has come to study them. *Working with Complexity* (3.12) highlights the nature of quality questions and the importance of recognising that the world exists not as a straight line but as dynamic flow.

In four organisational stories (3.13–16), the first *Hearts and Heads* (3.13) is a plea for the engagement of heart as well as head in business organisations, and the acknowledgement that metaphor and stories have a key role to play in this transformation. *Going on a Bear Hunt* (3.14) explores the necessity of seeking sustainable and systemically generated solutions for entrenched problems. This is especially the case whenever a silo mentality exists: when each person can only see the problem from within their own narrow frame of reference.

Management by Getting Out of the Way (3.15) offers a case history from an organisation that took the brave and creative step of operating as if organisations really are self-organising systems. The story describes what happened, the creativity generated, and the amount of business success that accrued. *Management Wisdom* (3.16) invites more openness and communication in the marketplace. It challenges old assumptions and invites more rigour, thoughtfulness, and straight talking.

The Post-Conventional Leader (3.17) enquires into where an aware, strategic, post-conventional leader of the twenty-first century might place his or her attention. It explores the nature of paradox and how conscious leadership seeks to embrace both 'ends' of the

paradox at one and the same time by maintaining the state generally referred to as 'flow'.

***

If we really wish to let systems naturally self-organise, then we
need to stand back and allow more space for things to flow and to
let energies take their natural course. This does not mean an abne-
gation of responsibilities; it is rather an ability to sponsor the space
in which change can happen from within, and to let go of the need
to predict how things will turn out.

Some years ago I was invited to run a two-day group dynamics
programme with a class of thirty-six engineering students at a
French university. They were a delightful bunch of people, full of
energy and enthusiasm. The first session went very well, but when
I returned to the seminar room after the first break I noticed that
all my coloured chalk had disappeared. The students had had a
chalk fight and now waited in keen anticipation to see how 'Le
Professeur Anglais' would respond.

I just said, 'How interesting!' and sent a student for more chalk.
I then suggested that we would spend the next session establish-
ing ground rules for the rest of the semester—rules that would be
entirely their responsibility. Small groups worked on generating
the rules which took the form of either: 'It's OK to ...' or 'It's not
OK to ...' Rules would only be endorsed if they were acceptable
to everybody and the class agreed they would collectively take full
responsibility for whatever was agreed upon.

Inevitably, the rule: 'It's OK to have chalk fights in class' was passed
unanimously. No student is going to go against the prevailing culture of 'challenge authority' in such situations unless they want a
seriously hard time from their peers. That done they waited to see
what I would say. I congratulated them on their work. And indeed
many other ground rules they established were both thoughtful
and conducive to developing an excellent learning environment.
Before we broke for lunch I suggested that the agreed rules be written up during the break and posted on the classroom walls.

I returned after lunch to find my chalk supply had again been used as ammunition and once again sent a student to restock my provisions. I continued as if nothing had happened. It was another good session. These were good people even if a little disappointed that they failed to get a rise from the authority I represented.

Another break, another chalk fight while I enjoyed an afternoon coffee in the staffroom. I sent my assistant for more chalk and asked her to inform the Principal and the cleaning staff that I would appreciate it if they would leave the room overnight exactly as it was. The final session of the day was again productive and excellent work was done.

Next morning I arrived early in the seminar room. Chalk was everywhere. Chalk dust covered the floor, chalk marks flecked the walls. In small groups the students entered. They were outraged. 'What is this?' 'Where are the cleaners?' 'This is disgusting!'

I pointed to the rule about chalk fights that was posted on the wall and simply reminded them that we had agreed we would take responsibility for whatever rules we made. We had another good working session.

I returned after the break to an immaculate classroom. The students had done it themselves. The silent majority had taken action to assert themselves over the few charismatic rebels who had initiated the chalk wars. There was never a problem with chalk fights again.

My French colleague Christine asked me what I would have done had my strategy not worked. I replied that I had no idea whatsoever except to keep exploring other strategies till I found one that did work. On the other hand, I hadn't considered the possibility that my strategy would fail because I did everything possible to ensure that I gave the system the space and support it needed to self-organise and correct itself.

Three Stories from the Orient

3.1 Something Missing

Once upon a time there was a gardener who was very proud of his horticultural skills. He took great pleasure in making the elegant gardens that he tended as perfect as possible. One day, expecting some important visitors, he took even more pains than usual to create the look he desired. He cut the lawns in neat geometrical patterns, dead-headed the dying blooms, pulled out the weeds, pruned the hedges, trimmed the bushes, cleaned the pathways, and raked up all the dead leaves. He gazed at his work with pride, the living proof of rational man's ability to harness and control the chaos of nature.

From across the wall, an old Zen monk watched with deep attention. The gardener spotted him and felt secretly pleased his labours had been observed. 'A work of art, don't you think?' he shouted.

'Something's missing,' was the reply.

The gardener was shocked. 'Really! What is it?'

'Open the gate and I'll show you.'

Curious, the gardener let the old monk in. He went to the large tree in the centre of the garden and shook it vigorously. Hundreds of leaves fluttered down and the wind distributed them artlessly across the lawns and flowerbeds.

'There you are,' he said, 'You can let me out now.'

3.2 Go with the Flow

A man accidentally fell into a fast-flowing river. A little downstream of the point where he entered the water were treacherous and turbulent rapids leading to a huge and powerful waterfall that dropped steeply down over rocky outcrops into a deep and dangerous pool.

Those who watched the drama thought he had no hope. So they were amazed to see him pop up from the murky waters of the deep pool and swim leisurely to the bank without an apparent care in the world.

Asked about his experience, and how he overcame all the dangers of the river, he said: 'I simply became one with the water. I behaved as if I was the water and the water was me. I did not try to overcome it, or fight it, or bend it to my will. I shaped myself to water, and the water shaped itself to me. I embraced its force and its force embraced me. And so I survived.'

3.3 Sustainability is Not a Cheap Option

It was a very hot day and Mr Hu desperately needed a fan to cool himself down. So he went to Mrs Ho's market stall. 'What kind of fans do you have?' he asked.

'Five dollar, ten dollar, and twenty dollar fans,' she replied. 'I'll take a five dollar fan,' said Hu and she gave him a thin Mongolian fan.

Ten minutes later, Hu returned holding the broken fan. 'You have sold me rubbish. What sort of fan is this?' he roared.

'It broke?' said Mrs Ho in surprise. 'How did you use it?'

'What do you mean, how did I use it? Like any other fan. I waved it up and down in front of my face.'

'Oh, no no no! That is not how to use a five dollar fan. With five dollar fan you hold it very, very still, and wave your face up and down in front of it.'

Five Sufi Stories

3.4 The Blind Men and the Elephant

A great travelling circus arrived at the outskirts of a town in which all the inhabitants were blind. Many of the citizens came to greet the travellers and also to find out what their business was for no circus had ever passed that way before. There was great curiosity and cries of wonder as the sightless people feasted on sounds and smells they had never experienced before. Of particular fascination was a huge elephant, an animal previously unknown in that part of the world.

A delegation of elders was sent to find out more about what the elephant actually was. And as none of them had any concept about what an elephant could be in size, shape, or form they each groped different parts of the elephant blindly in order to know it better.

When these elders returned to the eager and curious throng of their fellows and neighbours they each had their story to tell. The first, whose hand had explored the tail said, 'It is long and thin and smooth and tough like a great python.' The second, whose hand had explored a leg said, 'It is massive and thick like the pillar of a temple.' The third, whose hand had explored the trunk said, 'It long, heavy, and rough to the touch like a great water pipe.' A fourth, whose hand had explored the ear said, 'It is broad and soft, and smooth like an expensive carpet from Kashmir.' And a fifth, whose hand had explored a tusk said, 'It is pointed and hard and curved like a mighty scimitar, a dangerous weapon indeed.'

Each man had explored one part of the beast, and none had a sense of the whole. They each made assumptions based on a partial knowledge of the available information. Each quickly jumped to his own conclusions and passed these on to others as if they were the whole truth. Thus it was that when the circus left town, nobody had any real sense of the elephant at all.

3.5 The Wise Fool

The wise fool doesn't care for conventional thinking. In fact, it hampers him. He knows that any problem cannot be solved with the same kind of thinking that caused it in the first place. The wise fool takes the whole context into consideration and looks at every issue from every conceivable angle. Ask him, 'Which is better, a fast horse or a slow one?' He will say, it depends. 'It depends whether you and your horse are going in the right direction.'

3.6 Giving for the Self

A rich trader was pained to see how his neighbour, a poor monk, suffered. So he began to leave some money every day in the monk's collection box so that at least the monk's children would not starve.

From the day he began to do this, his own wealth began to increase. The more he gave, the more his wealth grew. Then one day the monk mentioned that his own Master was a great Pandit who lived in the capital city.

The trader considered: 'If I have become wealthy giving to the monk, then surely I will do even better giving to his master.' And so he began to send donations to the Pandit instead. No sooner had he done this than his wealth began to decrease. The more he gave, the more he lost until all the profit he previously made was lost.

Confused, the trader finally spoke to the monk and told him what had happened. The monk laughed, 'Of course, while you were making a generous contribution and didn't much care in particular to whom you gave, the Universe in its turn gave to you without very much caring to whom it was giving. But when you began to select certain particular people to give to, the Universe did the same.'

3.7 A Virtuous Circle

A thief, attempting to break into a factory, put his foot through a skylight, fell twenty feet, and broke his leg.

He went to court to sue the factory owner who said, 'Sue the company that made the skylight.'

The owner of the company that manufactured the skylight said, 'Sue the builder. He failed to install it properly.'

The builder said, 'I was disturbed in my work by an exotic parrot that flew overhead and kept insulting me.'

The parrot was found. It explained that it had escaped from its cage when the owner had left the door open.

The owner was found. She said that she'd got distracted. She'd been admiring herself in the mirror wearing a woollen cloak that she had just been given. 'Normally I'm not much interested in clothes but the wool in the cloak had been woven in such an intricate and elaborate design that I was totally distracted.'

'Finally we have the guilty party,' said the judge. 'Bring the weaver here and we'll force him to pay the rightful compensation.'

When the weaver was found, he turned out to be the husband of the woman with the cloak. He also happened to be the thief who had fallen through the skylight.

3.8 The Inner Teacher

As was the tradition in his country, at the age of 50 Ramchand gave up his profession as an accountant and decided the time had come to seek true wisdom and enlightenment. He set off, dressed in simple attire, with just a few nuts and berries as provisions, and a fierce determination to find enlightenment. As he walked, a monk fell in step with him.

'What's your business?' enquired the monk after a while. 'I'm in search of wisdom and enlightenment,' responded Ramchand.

'Ahh!' said the monk, 'that you can find only within your innermost self, and only if you pay attention to what the world is offering you.'

Ramchand shrugged his shoulders and marched on, but the monk kept in step. After a while, they came to an old and gnarled tree that was creaking loudly as the breeze buffeted it this way and that. The monk said, 'The tree is asking for your help saying something is hurting inside. It begs you to remove it so the tree can find peace again.'

'Ridiculous,' said Ramchand rationalising with his accountant mind, 'how can a tree speak? Besides I'm far too busy. I'm seeking enlightenment.'

A few kilometres later, the monk remarked that he thought he had smelled wild honey at the site of the tree. Ramchand responded, 'Why on earth didn't you say so?' Then his calculating mind added, 'We could provision ourselves for our journey and sell the surplus to passing travellers.'

They hurried back to the tree where they found a party of travellers collecting huge amounts of honey from a deep cleft in the trunk. 'Enough to feed a whole army,' they were saying. 'Now we poor beggars can become merchants and live out our days in peace and prosperity.'

Ramchand and the monk continued their journey together. After a while they heard a strange murmur as they edged their way up a steep rocky slope. 'Listen!' said the monk, 'The ants are calling for assistance. They say they are building their kingdom below the surface of the earth, millions of them. But they cannot connect their excavations because strange and immovable rocks impede their progress. Should we help, Brother Ramchand?'

But Ramchand was impatient to move on. 'I'm seeking wisdom and enlightenment; rocks and ants are nothing to do with me.'

'As you say, Brother, yet all things connect and our world has much to teach us.'

But Ramchand ignored the monk and pressed on with his journey. Not long after, Ramchand realised that he'd mislaid his water bottle. This was one necessity he couldn't do without. Retracing their steps they came upon a group of people shouting in triumph at the exact spot where the ants had been singing for help. At the side of the road jewels and golden coins were piled up high.

'We were travelling on this road,' said one of the miners, 'when a monk suggested we dig here. He told us, "What are rocks to some may be gold to others." And this is what we found.'

Ramchand couldn't believe his misfortune. 'Had we stopped,' he said to the monk, 'we would have been rich by now!' 'Funny thing,' said a miner, 'our monk looked very like the one with you.' To which Ramchand retorted, 'All monks look alike.'

A day or so later as dusk was falling, the two men came to a river. As they waited for the ferry, a large fish broke the surface of the water and fixed them with its eye. 'The fish is telling us,' said the monk, 'that is has accidentally swallowed a huge pebble. It asks us to find the root of a particular herb that will help it retch up the stone.'

But at that instant the ferry arrived and Ramchand, eager to get on with his quest roughly pushed the monk on board. They crossed the river and that night stayed at the inn on the far bank.

Next morning they met the ferryman who kissed the monk's hand and thanked him profusely. 'For what? What happened?' asked Ramchand. The ferryman explained that he had seen him and the monk on the far bank the night before and, though they looked poor, had resolved to make one last trip. After all, everyone knew that helping a traveller in need, and especially a monk, brings blessing on the giver. And it must be true, 'because as I was putting away my boat I saw a large fish on the bank, and it seemed to be reaching out to eat some plant, so I put the plant in its mouth, and then— Heaven be praised—the fish coughed and vomited up the biggest and most perfect diamond you can ever imagine.'

And suddenly Ramchand's calculating mind was blown apart. Finally he made the connections. He turned on the monk and his anger knew no limit. 'Who are you to cause me such suffering? You knew about all these treasures, yet not once did you make their presence clear to me. Thanks to you I know how much I have lost. At least without you by my side I would have been blissfully ignorant of all the wealth and treasures around me in plants, soil, and rivers!'

The monk waited until Ramchand was done. After a while he smiled and put his hand lightly on Ramchand's shoulder. 'Friend, I am your Inner Teacher and I have always been with you. When—as I told you before—you learn to listen to me and also to be attentive to whatever the world has to offer you, then you may begin to wake up. When you cease your striving and seeking, you will find in each unfolding moment all the wisdom and enlightenment you desire.'

Two Stories of Courage

3.9 Masculine Compassion (1)

Anthony lay on his hospital bed wracked by spasms of pain. He had been diagnosed with a particularly virulent strain of liver cancer and the oncologist had given a bleak view of his chances of survival. His parents sat by his bedside.

'How do you feel, Anthony?' asked his tearful mother.

'Ma, it's like I've got piranhas swimming in my guts.'

Anthony's mother put her face in her hands and wept.

Silence.

Then his father leaned towards his ear and quietly said, 'In that case, son, go fishing.'

Ten years later, having made a full recovery, Anthony is still very much hooked on life and the healing power of metaphor.

3.10 Enthusiasm

When the great cellist, Jacqueline du Pré, was only 6 years old she took part in her first competition. She was seen running along a corridor, her quarter size cello held high above her head, whooping with glee, squeezing her way past other competitors. An adjudicator who happened to be passing said to her, 'Oh, well done! You must have just finished playing your piece.' 'No, no!' replied Jacqueline rushing past, 'I'm on my way to play it now.'

Two Systems Stories

3.11 Digging Deeper

An anthropologist was studying the behaviours and customs of a people who lived in a remote part of a far country. At one particular village he asked the local people to identify for him the most truthful person and the biggest liar in their community. Once identified, he asked these two to tell him the best way to the next village.

The Truthful One said, 'The path over the mountain.'

The Liar said, 'The path over the mountain.'

Confused, the anthropologist asked various others. Some said the mountain path, others the river, and others still mentioned the path through the forest.

He took the mountain path and ruminated over all the answers he had received to his question. When he arrived, without trouble, at the next village he told his story to the people there. He told them he had probably made the mistake of asking the wrong people for information.

'Not at all,' said the Village Headman. 'In fact, the answers you got are completely logical. They were based on the fact that some of the people were taking much more complexity into account than you were aware of. They were seeing farther. For example, everyone knows the river is the best route but only if you have a boat. The Truthful One observed you didn't have a boat but did have a donkey. And so he suggested, truthfully, that the best route for you was the mountain.

'On the other hand, the Liar noticed nothing. He observed neither absence of boat nor presence of donkey. Had he done so, he would have said, "River."'

3.12 Working with Complexity

Isidor Rabi won the Nobel Peace Prize for physics in 1944. When interviewed, he said he owed it all to his mother. 'When I was at school,' he said, 'all the other mothers asked their children what they had learned that day. As a result, my schoolmates only saw each problem from a narrow and limited perspective. If the teacher changed any element in a test, they simply lacked the vision and flexibility to solve any new challenge.

'My mother never asked me that question. Instead she would always say, "Isidor, what did you ask in class today?" And so I learned to consider any problem within a complex set of contextual possibilities. I learned to consider all angles, and to experience the world as fluid and dynamic. I learned to find natural solutions which engaged all elements of a system in a creative and sustainable tension.'

Four Organisational Stories

3.13 Hearts and Heads

A CEO of a large corporation frequently gave key business messages to his board and senior managers in the form of stories and metaphors. They really enjoyed the stories, understood them, and acted upon them. But sometimes they longed for something a little more rigorous, analytic, and professional— more hard facts and less vagueness, more reason and less suggestion.

But the Boss remained adamant. 'You must understand that business is not just about the head alone. Great business is also about courage in the heart and fire in the belly. Great business is about contexts, and relationships, and situations, and the interplay of structure and uncertainty. All of these things you will find in stories.'

But some remained unconvinced. So he said, 'A lost jewel is discovered by the light of a simple candle; a deep truth is revealed by the telling of a well-chosen story.'

Then to the few who still did not get his message, 'Do you know what the longest journey in the world is?' There were many guesses, but none had the answer he had in mind.

'The longest journey in the world is from the head to the heart. That is why I tell stories in a business context. I tell them because they are perfectly equipped to make that journey in a way that spreadsheets and graphs and economic forecasts will not. And what I want more of in my organisation is heart. For it is heart that will give us the courage to survive together and realise the dream we are collectively pursuing.'

3.14 Going on a Bear Hunt

The Pacific Power Company provides electricity to large areas in the US West Coast region. Often in winter the over-head power lines ice up which requires that linemen go out in hazardous conditions to shake the ice free. They have to climb the slippery poles and injuries are frequent. One year things were so bad, strike action was on the cards unless management could come up with a better solution. As senior management couldn't think of any effective ideas, one of the more junior managers suggested a think tank be formed from all sectors of the organisation including management, administration, engineers, linemen, cleaners, and secretaries.

A meeting was held but it didn't seem to be getting very far. One lineman told the group that last time he had been clearing ice he was attacked by a big black bear who didn't want him on his territory. 'Bear chased me for a mile,' he said. After a pause someone half jokingly said, 'Hey, why don't we train the bears to climb the poles. Their weight'll surely shake the ice free.'

There was a lot of laughter. Everyone knew it was impractical. 'But,' added another voice more seriously, 'what if we put honey pots on top of the poles? We wouldn't need to train them—they'd climb for the honey anyway!'

'Yeah,' shouted a voice from the back, 'but we'd still have to climb the poles in icy conditions to put the pots there.'

One of the more cynical linemen stood up. 'Here's an idea. Let's take one of those fancy helicopters our fat cat directors use and have the choppers place the honey pots on the poles. We wouldn't have to go out in cold weather and the fat cats would have to get off their backsides and walk places.'

There was a lot of knowing laughter at this. The meeting was on the edge. The manager who had brought this disparate group together realised the way things were going. So he called time out for fifteen minutes.

When they came back the first person who spoke was a secretary who had served as a nurse in Vietnam. 'You know I got to thinking over my coffee,' she said quietly. 'In Nam we had choppers bringing the wounded into our field hospitals all the time. You know, they create a huge force of downdraught from the blades. So I got to wondering whether that could shift the ice!'

To this day, the Pacific Power Company sends out helicopters in winter to shift the ice. Linemen no longer need to climb icy poles or get chased by bears. It took a secretary to solve the problem, and she probably wouldn't have thought about it without the bears, and the honey pots, and the helicopters. When searching for sustainable solutions to difficult problems, it pays to involve as many perspectives as possible. And that means calling on all available resources. Experts may scoff, but most experts find it hard to think outside of their silo mentality.

3.15 Management by Getting Out of the Way

In recent years, one of the most striking and successful employee engagement projects has been the Oticon story. Lars Kolind, the CEO of Oticon, asked his employees 'to think the unthinkable and make it happen'. He also stated very publicly that the chief enemy of organisations is organisation itself: too many rules, regulations, and control. Control is the enemy of creativity and innovation.

Accordingly he decreed that projects, not functions or processes, would be the central units of work. Teams would form, disband, and reform. Project leaders—whoever had an idea—would compete for resources and people. Project owners—members of the management team—would provide advice, support, and resources but make very few decisions.

Kolind recognised that human beings naturally have an innate sense of order and structure that comes from within. He also sensed that people create and produce their best ideas when they operate near the brink of 'chaos' and are not over-managed. The best organisations move between these two parameters of order and chaos. As a result the employees are engaged and alive, creative and highly enthusiastic.

Kolind's experiments were recognised by *Forbes* magazine. In October 2000 his organisation was ranked among the top twenty of the world's best small companies, the criteria for which was annual sales of less than US$500 million and year-on-year growth over an extended period.

3.16 Management Wisdom

Peter Drucker, sometimes called 'the Father of Modern Management', was once invited to speak at a celebrated business school at a prestigious university in the US. The topic was 'The Secrets of Great Managers'.

He stood in front of 3,000 leaders, managers, and MBA students and said, 'People are not mind readers. There are just two secrets to great management: if you want something ask; if you need something say.'

He turned on his heel and walked towards the exit. But before he could reach the edge of the stage, a voice called out, 'Is that it?'

He paused. 'No. There is one more thing.'

The audience waited. Another pause.

'Be brief.'

Then he left.

A Flow State Story

3.17 The Post-Conventional Leader

1. Has a lot of energy *and* yet still needs to rest.

2. May be smart *but* naive at the same time.

3. Is playful *and* disciplined.

4. Is rooted in reality *yet* can be easily transported into fantasy.

5. Seems both extroverted *and* introverted.

6. Can be humble *and* proud at the same time.

7. Has a certain amount of rebelliousness and independence as well as being a traditionalist and part of a community.

8. Has passion *and* yet maintains an objectivity.

9. Seeks the enjoyment of creation at the expense that sometimes things don't go smoothly.

Chautauqua 4

Difficult Conversations

Stories on the Themes of Mastery, Honesty,
Leadership, and Personal Responsibility

There is a moment in every great Hollywood movie when the hero comes face to face with his or her nemesis, the potential agent of their doom. This is usually the key turning point in the story—it is the biggest hurdle the protagonist must overcome if he or she is to become fully realised as a worthy hero.

Nemeses can come in all shapes and forms. They can be other people, extraterrestrials, animals, insects, things, or natural phenomena like the Perfect Storm. They require the hero to reach deep inside, to find levels of skill, resourcefulness, and courage that before this moment they did not know they had. And we can all identify with this moment because in our own lives we have had many similar, though maybe not so heightened, moments of our own. These critical moments of realisation reflect the travails and trials we have faced on our own hero's journey.

The ability to confront and overcome that which we most fear—that which has most power over us—is the pivotal stage in any hero's journey. It confirms us in our quest for mature adulthood which in its healthiest manifestation is a state of fully grounded mastery over ourselves and whatever we encounter in our lives. We have slayed the dragon and are now at peace with ourselves and the planet.

Yet the greatest dragon, the most intractable nemesis, is not that which exists outside of ourselves, but that which lives inside us. To slay the external dragon we first have to be ready to confront our fear of our own deepest inadequacies. To be ready to slay the dragon we have to be ready to die ourselves. This is a critical step for the hero that lives within all of us. When we are prepared to risk all, and die if necessary, to overcome the dragons we face, we fully liberate ourselves.

When this occurs we shift from the dualistic, immature world of the child to the fully embodied, non-dualistic world of the mature adult who no longer sees enemies but friends, who no longer experiences separation but indivisible connectedness, who no longer feels resistance but acceptance. This is the timeless message of the classic story of the hero's journey, the monomyth, the Hollywood movie.[18] It is no more than a reflection of the psychological battle within.

In our day-to-day lives, it can be very challenging to be awake enough, and rigorous enough, and honest enough to have the difficult conversations that are necessary with other people and with ourselves. Something happens, someone says something or does something, or doesn't do something, and we notice we are hurt, angry, and upset.

Sometimes we can just let it go. It's really not important. But often it *is* important. And if we bottle it, hold it inside, it can begin to rankle and fester. Either it eats away at us, causing stress and bitterness. Or it comes out covertly, often directed at people who had no part to play whatever in the original situation.

Why have we not done some straight talking to the one whose behaviour triggered our reaction in the first place? 'Can I just say I feel … whenever you … (description of their behaviour).' This is a key aspect of what it means to be an adult: to be able to speak our truth honestly and openly, and then be ready to listen to whatever the recipient of our feedback has to say to us in return. This is how we can have honest, open conversations that allow us to drop old baggage, understand each other better, learn from feedback and, above all, *move on*.

Why don't we do it as often as we know we should? Often it's fear, our inner dragon. We don't want to upset the other—we might come out of it worst, they might hold a future grudge against us, we could be ostracised, the person might cry, or worse, have a nervous breakdown, or kill us! So we stay in our inner immature child space and say nothing.

We say nothing but we give out all kinds of non-verbal signals of our displeasure. Our adversary has no idea about the inner process of our thinking but does pick up on our non-verbals. They get confused about these mixed signals we're giving out: saying nothing but looking grieved. So they back off and an even worse situation is created in which both parties deliberately avoid each other. As a result the gulf gets ever wider and harder to bridge.

Straight talking, first with ourselves and then with others, is an act of love and an assumption of personal responsibility. It liberates us from our negative emotions, it strengthens our sense of self-esteem, it allows us to stand tall and speak our truth respectfully. It allows other people to hear and understand our inner process, choose for themselves how they will respond, and invites them to respond in kind.

It is not without risk and it requires the development of some skill and some preparation. But the risk of not sharing our inner process, of blocking communication, of dwelling in an interior landscape of negative emotion about the world, others and, most of all, ourselves, hardly bears thinking about. Yet this is exactly where so many of us can become trapped. At worst, it can produce the most tragic of consequences. At best, the unwillingness to have difficult conversations keeps us stuck and small.

***

Some years ago I was a partner in a successful learning and development consultancy. As often happens in business partnerships, rather like marriage, relationships can change. At the outset everybody shares similar dreams and aspirations, but over time each person shifts their focus and values and starts to see and experience the world differently.

The company was doing well—I was earning more than I needed and my colleagues were talented people. But after several years of great success something was missing for me and I couldn't put my finger on what it was. So I kept my feelings and thoughts to myself hoping that the issue would simply resolve itself. It didn't. I thought I was being helpful by not raising my inner process. I couldn't see at the time that my behaviour may have looked like withdrawal or even resistance. By not sharing my inner process, it is very likely that I muddied the waters.

Eventually I began to perceive that what was troubling me was that a lot of the work we were doing no longer excited me. I wanted the company to take on new and different challenges, to explore new directions. That would be good for me and, I thought, good for the company too. But that was not my colleagues' wish, or at least not in the way I wanted it. We were no longer seeing eye to eye. Issues of power and control began to emerge in our meetings. The atmosphere became increasingly tense and, of course, communication suffered.

I realised I needed to make a move but three things held me back. Firstly, it's not easy to extract oneself under British law from a business partnership. Secondly, I realised that I had got used to a materially comfortable existence. Lastly, I recognised within myself a great doubt about whether I could survive alone in a competitive world. Was I good enough? Did I have the networks? Would clients be interested in the ideas I had to offer?

I found myself well and truly stuck. And above all I was avoiding having any of the really important conversations I needed to have with myself about what was causing my stuckness and what it was that I really wanted. At the same time the issues around power and control were intensifying. I was beginning to feel rather powerless. I had no stomach for a fight. I was making myself smaller and smaller.

At this point a friend gave me some excellent advice. He said, 'Nick, in any difficult situation in life you have only three choices: accept it, transform it, or walk away from it. Choose only one of these. Anything else is madness.'

It was great timing: just when I needed it. I couldn't accept the situation and I would never be able to transform it. So I decided to walk away from it and do so with whatever dignity and strength I could muster.

So I took a leaf from Hollywood. I cast my partners not perhaps in the role of my nemeses but at least in the role of worthy adversaries. They would be the ones who I had to face up to in order to confront my own fear and doubt. I would have to have a series of heroic, honest conversations with them so everything could be clear and resolved and so that we could all move on.

And that's exactly what happened. Once I'd faced up to the fear in myself and decided on a clear course of action I was able to stand in my own power, to say what I had to say, and to listen to what had to be said in return. It was painful yet it was also liberating and it opened up the possibility of useful change for everyone involved in the movie.

***

The first of two Zen stories *The Tortoise and the Hare* (4.1) points to the wisdom that mastery has more to do with being than doing; the second *Presentation is All* (4.2) points to the wisdom that success depends on how we frame our conversations and manage our 'adversaries'.

The first of two Sufi stories *The Source* (4.3) speaks of the bonds of service, duty, and respect that exist between all people no matter what their status. The compassion and wisdom of the Caliph is counterbalanced and completed by the trust and loyalty of the Bedouin. Each is master of his integrity; both offer service to the other.

The Smuggler (4.4) offers everything one expects in a Mullah Nasruddin story. The Mullah cuts through the illusions in which conventional thinking traps us. He lives in the world of the obvious, of what is right before our noses, while our complicated monkey minds search for more and more sophisticated possibilities that don't exist.

St Kefyn (4.5), from the Celtic Christian tradition, is a great reminder not to lose sight of our dreams. Do not trust that they will prosper by themselves without our active support.

The first of the three Balkan stories *Alexander and the Turnips* (4.6) explores the nature of value and perspective. A turnip is compared to all of Alexander's great power and wealth—and Alexander is found wanting.

Difficult Conversations (4.7) demonstrates the consequences that can occur when people lack the courage to have necessary conversations no matter how painful or sensitive they might be. *Competence or Excellence?* (4.8) investigates the liberating and transformational power that honest conversations with self and others can bring. It also explores the relationship between operations, tactics, and strategy, achieving goals a step at a time, and the rewards that accrue from the constant pursuit of quality.

In five perspective stories (4.9–13), *The Dreamer* (4.9) draws our attention to the conversations we pay attention to in our dreams. It also indicates that a great deal of our learning is unconscious and non-rational, and that our actions have consequences.

The Lost Wallet (4.10) explores honesty, logic, greed, power, and justice. By skilfully using fuzzy—or multi-valued—logic, the Headman holds a conversation that confounds the bullying merchant and restores justice to the honest tailor. It is a difficult conversation brilliantly executed. The key theme of *Taking Ownership* (4.11) is about taking responsibility for one's actions: change yourself rather than blame others.

Rogoxin (4.12) invites us to draw on our own inner captain when those in positions of leadership fail us. When we disconnect from our own sense of wisdom and defer to power and authority by default we let down ourselves and others.

Straight Talking (4.13) offers a down-to-earth narrative about the consequences of not engaging in straight talking. It's about honestly owning our truth, communicating within an adult-to-adult frame, and recognising that going along with others for fear of offending them is usually the least best option.

Finally there are three stories of wisdom and experience (4.14–16). *A Stitch in Time* (4.14) recommends taking immediate action to address important issues. Don't put off till tomorrow what needs to be done now. *Communication Blindspot* (4.15) addresses a thorny and universal mindset. This occurs when an individual observes that a problem is occurring but omits to include him or herself in the problem space. This is the root cause of any blame culture and the single main reason why we get stuck. The simple and powerful message is: if the world needs changing, start by changing yourself and speaking your truth.

Don't F**k with the Poodle (4.16) is a celebration of mid-life. It's a warning to those who want to sideline grey-beards that mature experience and nous will always overcome youthful energy and strength. First-rate bullshit and brilliance take years to hone. It's a celebration of the kind of mastery that comes with confidence and the ability to improvise skilfully whatever the circumstances.

***

It is not always necessary to have conversations that can be heard. Sometimes the silent ones speak the loudest. I was in my early thirties and travelling to southern France. I was en route to meet up with friends who were renovating a town house in a village just about equidistant between the picturesque, turreted towers of Carcassonne and Castelnaudary, the garrison town famous for cassoulet and headquarters of the French Foreign Legion.

My means were modest at the time so I chose the cheapest travel option: midnight train from Victoria to Dover, 2 a.m. ferry crossing to Calais, early morning train via Paris to Castelnaudary. Very cheap and not so very cheerful. At least not at that time in the morning, not even in mid-August.

But I was young and fit and could look back on an exciting and eventful year. I'd worked as an actor in a couple of good British repertory theatres, playing some challenging roles, and I'd been out in Africa working on a variety of theatre-based projects for the British Council in Zaire, Congo, Cameroon, and Nigeria. I checked my passport and glanced at the imposing full page African visas, stamped and embossed with all the pride of their independence.

The train left Victoria on time and I sat back and reflected on these great experiences. I ran my hand over my head, enjoying the bristly feeling of a really close cut. It was unusual. I'd had my hair cropped a couple of days previously for a small film part. I thought too of the journey ahead. I love train journeys so this was something more to anticipate. How would the journey unfold?

There was a cold wind at Dover; the bus connection was late; the ferry was uncomfortable and not particularly clean; and I was tired and already getting grumpy. Fortunately the seat I found was right next to the gangplank so I was first off the boat in Calais. It was 4 a.m.

Now for those of you unfamiliar with the old customs hall at Calais, here are the salient points. The building is designed to impress upon any *etrangere* that France is a mighty nation with an imposing history and is not to be messed with. One enters the immense hall down a very long sloping walkway designed to make a person feel as small and exposed as possible. The wary traveller can feel the scrutiny of official eyes upon him as he or she makes his way down into the belly of the beast.

And as soon as I started down the walkway I could see an officious looking customs officer at the bottom and he had already fixed his beady eye on me.

It was clear even at that distance that he had decided to grill the first person who came down the slope. And that person was me, and I was cold, tired, and irritated. Moreover, I was ready for a fight.

'Passeport, M'sieur!' he sneered.

I gave it to him, fixing him with a steely eyeball-to-eyeball glance.

He offered a slight supercilious smile in return, knowing full well the power he wielded.

He opened the passport, right at the page of the huge Zairean visa stamp.

'Ou allez-vous?' There was a slight quaver in his voice.

He turned the page to the Congolese stamp just as I replied.

'Castelnaudary.'

His eyes flicked up to my close cropped hair, and then he made the connection: I was going to join the Legion.

He jumped to attention and saluted with a Gallic flourish.

'Passez, Monsieur!'

And he escorted me all the way to the train, had a word with the guard, and insisted I travel first class.

I'd only said one word, but what a conversation!

Two Zen Stories

4.1 The Tortoise and the Hare

A highly motivated student of martial arts went to a famous Sensei and said, 'I wish to work with you and commit myself fully to learning your system. How long will it take me to master it?'

The Sensei regarded him for a moment and replied, 'Five years.'

'But that's too long,' responded the student with some impatience. 'I want to attain mastery as soon as possible. And I'm prepared to work very hard. I'll practice twelve or more hours a day if necessary.'

'In that case,' replied the Sensei, 'it will take you ten years.'

4.2 Presentation is All

Two Zen monks were wondering whether it was OK to smoke and meditate at the same time. They decided to ask the Abbot individually.

'So what was his answer?' asked the second monk later. The first monk replied, 'He got really angry. He said I should be more respectful towards practice and prayer. He chased me out with his stick.'

'That's strange,' said the second monk, 'because he was more than happy to let me smoke. What did you say to him?'

'I asked him if it was OK to smoke while I meditated,' replied the first monk.

'Ahh!' said the second monk. 'I asked him if I could meditate while I smoked.'

Two Sufi Stories

4.3 The Source

Hamdi the Bedouin knew every inch of the desert. He caught snakes and rats and sold their skins to the trading caravans. He also searched constantly for water, desert shrubs on which his camel could graze, and sheltered locations where he could pitch his ancient and threadbare tent for a day or two.

Normally the water he found was muddy and brackish, completely unpalatable to folks like you and me. But one day he came across a spring which had not been there before. And he thought it a miracle because it was almost transparent and had—or so it seemed to him—only the faintest taste of salt. He called it 'the Nectar of Paradise' and said to himself, 'I must take this miraculous water to someone who will fully appreciate its qualities.'

And so, taking only a few simple provisions and two leather skins of water, one for himself and one for the Caliph, he set off for the great city at the edge of the desert. When he arrived after many days of travel he was finally admitted to the Caliph to whom he presented his leather bottle of water.

'Lion of the Desert, I am the Bedouin Hamdi and I know well the waters of the desert, although I am ignorant of almost everything else. I have discovered this Nectar of Paradise and have brought it straight to you, as one who will recognise its marvellous qualities.'

The Caliph sipped from the skin and managed to restrain a grimace at the extreme salinity of its contents. He then ordered Hamdi to wait with an escort in an outer room while he deliberated upon the appropriate course of action.

He then spoke to his Vizier. 'What to us is of no account to him is everything. Let him be escorted therefore, at dead of night, from our great citadel back to his own tent. Do not let him see the great river Tigris and do not let him taste fresh water. Then reward him handsomely with five hundred golden pounds and thank him for his great service to me.

'Tell him he is from henceforth to be known as "The Keeper of the Nectar of Paradise". Tell him that he is to give it freely—and in my name—to all travellers on the road that happen to pass by this miraculous spring of his.'

4.4 The Smuggler

In a small village on the border between Persia and Turkey lived Mullah Nasruddin. He was not only the poorest member of his community but also the most despised since no one had ever seen him do an honest day's work in their lives.

One morning, dressed in his long, dirty, threadbare robe, he crossed the border checkpoint into Persia with his donkey and cart. On the floor of the cart were a few old storage boxes. The customs officer lazily waved him through. He returned late in the afternoon with the donkey and cart and the boxes and wearing a white, clean, and rather stylish ankle-length shirt. The customs officer made a note and informed his superior.

Next morning Nasruddin passed through the border again. On his return in the early evening, Nasruddin was sporting a rather raffish silver-topped walking cane as he walked beside his donkey.

The customs officers discreetly noted every particular. 'OK, Mullah, what's your game?' demanded one of them roughly. But Nasruddin was a picture of innocence as he sweetly talked his way past all their questions. He'd found some long-lost wealthy relations was his explanation.

The local Commander of Customs and Excise was not going to see his men made a fool of, especially by one such as Nasruddin. So next morning when the Mullah arrived at the border post with his donkey, cart, and boxes he said to his men, 'OK boys, take all those boxes apart.' With great thoroughness they went through all Nasruddin's possessions which were loaded on the flat bed of the cart, but they found absolutely nothing incriminating. After a long delay, Nasruddin went on his way.

On his return in the late afternoon, his fingernails were beautifully manicured.

Next day, same thing. This time the Commander said, 'OK boys, take the cart apart.' They unscrewed, un-nailed, unhinged, and undid absolutely everything that could be separated and looked into. But they found absolutely nothing to incriminate the Mullah. So, after the cart was painstakingly reassembled again, he went on his way.

Later that evening returning from Persia, he was wearing a brand new pair of designer shoes in expensive Moroccan leather. The customs officers exchanged meaningful glances as Nasruddin passed them by.

By now the Commander was growing extremely frustrated. His many years of experience told him that the Mullah was smuggling goods across the border, and doing very well indeed by the look of it. But what exactly was he smuggling? He was going to win this battle if it was the last thing he did. The battle was about to become personal.

Next morning, the Commander says, 'OK boys, I want every orifice of the donkey examined.' A thorough examination is conducted by the local vet who finally pronounces the animal is 'clean'. So Nasruddin is allowed to cross the border into Persia once again, leaving the Commander and his men irate and very, very puzzled.

That evening, Nasruddin's smile was worth a million dollars. That morning, the few teeth that the Mullah still had were stained red with betel juice. Now a full set gleamed white and were topped with golden crowns. The customs officers watched him pass, mouths agape.

The following day, Mullah Nasruddin passes through the checkpoint with his donkey, cart, and boxes whistling innocently. 'OK boys,' says the Commander viciously, 'today we're going to search the Mullah's every orifice.' It's not a pleasant experience for Nasruddin. But, like the donkey, he too is 'clean'.

And so it goes on. Every day, week after week, month after month, the Mullah is squeaky clean as he crosses the checkpoint, yet his wealth is visibly rising. On the Turkish side of the border his wealth is modest, a little here, a little there. Nothing that the border police can take him to task for.

But across the border, on the Persian side, within full sight of their customs post, they can see all too visible signs of the Mullah's phenomenal rise to wealth and power. The Nasruddin Café is followed by the Nasruddin Pharmacy, the Nasruddin Hotel, the Nasruddin Casino, and finally the Nasruddin Shopping Mall.

Years pass, and finally the old Customs Commander retires. He has failed to nail the Mullah who has become immensely rich and respected. And of course, Nasruddin no longer has to work. He lives a life of luxury on both sides of the border, crossing freely whenever he chooses.

Even in retirement, the Commander's sleep is disturbed by nightmares which always involve the Mullah, the donkey, the cart, the absolute absence of evidence, and the whole populations of Turkey and Persia laughing at him.

One day as the Commander strolls through the leisure gardens in the centre of town, he sees Nasruddin sitting on a bench in the shade. He goes across to him and says, 'Please Mullah, put me out of my misery. Let me at least go to my deathbed in peace. For God's sake tell me, now that I no longer have any power or authority, what was it you were smuggling across the border for all those years?'

Nasruddin shakes him warmly by the hand and offers a sweet smile before replying, 'Donkeys.'

A Celtic Christian Story

4.5 St Kefyn

In early Christian days people used not to pray with their hands together as they do today but with their arms spread wide and their palms upwards. One day an Irish priest, St Kefyn, began to pray. He prayed very hard and he was very still so that his words would go directly to Heaven without anything to get in the way. And when he stopped praying he noticed a bird sitting on his right hand.

Not wanting to disturb the bird he went back to his prayers. And when he had finished them, he found the bird had made a nest. And not wanting to disturb the bird and its nest he went back to praying again.

When he opened his eyes, he saw that eggs had been laid in the nest. And not wanting to disturb the eggs, he went back to his prayers. When he finally stopped his praying he noticed the eggs had hatched into five little hungry nestlings. So in order not to disturb them he went back to his conversations with his Maker. It was only after all the birds had flown from the nest that St Kefyn finished his praying, got up, and went home.

The moral of the story is don't stop praying for the success of your outcomes until all your plans and projects have hatched and have an independent life of their own.

Three Balkan Stories

4.6 Alexander and the Turnips

The great Macedonian King, Alexander, conqueror of the world, was hunting alone in deep forests one day. He had been hunting unsuccessfully for many hours when, around noon, he came across an old woman outside her simple hut preparing some food in a blackened pot perched on top of a glowing fire.

He was ravenous and as it was already mid-afternoon, he introduced himself saying, 'Today you have as your guest the greatest King and Emperor the world has ever seen. What are you cooking in your pot? It smells absolutely delicious.'

'Turnip soup,' the old woman replied with studied economy.

'Excellent. And will you let me taste some, Madam?'

'No, I won't,' the old woman replied. 'This soup is mine. It's for me and nobody else. All your lands, dominions, and possessions are not worth a spoonful of what these turnips are worth. You, O Great Emperor, may want what is mine, but I have no desire for anything you have. Look around you, on every side you have enemies disputing the territories you have conquered. Yet no one disputes my ownership of these turnips. I am free while you, Sir, are beset by problems and plotters. On your way, Sir, and leave me to enjoy my turnips in peace.'

For a moment Alexander gazed at the undisputed owner of the turnips and thought of his own disputed territories and the battles that still had to be fought. He turned his horse away and slowly returned to his camp, arriving there with a little more humility and perspective than he had left with that morning.

4.7 Difficult Conversations

In 1920, King Alexander of Greece was bitten on the leg by his pet monkey. The bite became infected and the poison quickly spread into the royal bloodstream.

Eminent doctors and surgeons from far and wide across Europe were summoned to the royal bedside. They all knew what had to be done. The leg would have to be amputated. But this was a difficult conversation that none of the doctors was prepared to have. To suggest the removal of a royal limb was unthinkable.

Lack of necessary action tends to have consequences. In this case the course of modern history was changed. The King died, the Greek government fell, the Ottomans defeated the Greek army, and Kemal Atatürk was thereby able to create the modern secular state of Turkey.

Failure to engage in difficult conversations can have serious consequences far beyond what is immediately discernible. Willingness to engage in difficult conversations means that viruses and cancers in the system can be identified and isolated so that health can be restored.

4.8 Competence or Excellence?

A junior military officer was assigned to a new platoon. He was young and ambitious and very much wanted to succeed. The army he served in was among the biggest in the world at that time and it encouraged and supported—or at least gave lip service to—a culture of continuous change and improvement to keep abreast of developments.

The young officer considered how best he could serve and took time to reflect before taking action with his new platoon. He realised he had two choices. The first was that he could tell his soldiers what to do. Fortunately, he was wise enough to know that his men knew a lot more about soldiery than he did so early in his career. Or he could work with them to support their development into an effective and efficient fighting machine that would constantly strive to improve itself. The first route offered competence, the second excellence.

He assessed the skills, abilities, attitudes, and character of his soldiers and he took time to build a relationship with each one of them. To those whose abilities were practical and technical he gave the task of developing operational skills such as weapons training and assessment, hand-to-hand combat, navigation, and so on. To those who demonstrated the ability to think from the perspective of others, he gave the task of developing tactical skills: not only military tactics, but training, support, intelligence, and administration.

And for himself and one or two capable others he explored the task of developing strategic skills: How would his platoon operate effectively as a unit? How would it fit in with other platoons and the company as a whole? How would his platoon contribute to the requirements of the army overall?

He challenged and supported each soldier to take responsibility for their personal contributions and always ensured their successes were publicly recorded. And at the same time he took personal responsibility for any lapses and shortcomings that occurred.

In this way his platoon soon became the most highly motivated, efficient, and effective unit in the company. Many of the technical and tactical improvements made by his men revolutionised the way they went about their business and very soon platoon members were requested to offer training to other platoons. At a strategic level, the contributions of the officer and his team were also noted by more senior officers and soon he was running programmes at staff level so that the army as a whole could benefit from shared best practice and the ability to out-think and out-smart the enemy.

The differences and inventions inspired by this young officer and his team changed the course of history. The army transformed from an unwieldy, sprawling giant into a lean, professional, highly disciplined outfit. And the soldier himself became not only a highly respected general and brilliant strategist but eventually Head of State.

Asked late in life how he had plotted his rise to the top, he said, 'I only asked how I could serve. I also asked what steps were unnecessary in any particular procedure, and then I removed them. And I also asked what I could do that would delight my superiors and my men by making their lives easier, and what would dismay my enemies by making their lives more difficult.' His name was Kemal Atatürk.

Five Perspective Stories

4.9 The Dreamer

A rich merchant, wealthy as a king, demanded nothing less than blood, sweat, and tears from his servants. Every day he worked them harder and harder, and the money in his coffers multiplied. But at night he tossed and turned and his sleep was wracked by disturbing dreams. He imagined he himself was a lowly labourer, forced to carry out back-breaking and pointless tasks, beaten and cursed whenever he slackened his pace.

At the same time, one of the great merchant's lowliest servants, who bent his back each day to the strenuous and menial tasks set by his master, dreamed every night that he was a great lord ordering his own servants and slaves about.

The merchant heard about his servant's dreams and couldn't help but compare them with his own. What was their meaning? What did they signify? It did not take him long to find an interpretation that satisfied him. He halved his business projects, halved the amount of work expected from his servants, and slept twice as well as he had ever done before.

4.10 The Lost Wallet

One day a poor tailor found a wallet in the marketplace. Looking inside he found nine hundred shillings, a name and address, and a short note saying: 'If lost and returned to owner, one hundred shillings reward.'

The tailor took the wallet to the owner but instead of being thankful, the man said. 'I see you have already taken the hundred shillings due as your reward.'

The tailor insisted he had not; and the owner, a wealthy merchant, insisted that a hundred shillings was missing from the one thousand shillings that had been in the wallet. So they agreed to take their dispute to the village headman who listened to the stories of each man.

'So who do you believe, Headman, this uneducated tailor or me?' demanded the wallet's owner. 'You, of course!' said the Headman, but then he gave the wallet and all its contents to the tailor.

'What are you doing?' roared the rich man amazed.

'You said your wallet contained a thousand shillings. This man says he found a wallet that had only nine hundred shillings inside. So obviously this wallet cannot be yours,' the Headman stated with authority.

'But what about my wallet and cash?'

The Headman paused for a moment to give his judgement the more weight. 'We shall have to wait till someone finds a wallet with a thousand shillings in it.'

4.11 Taking Ownership

A man in Gandhi's entourage was forever complaining about this, that, and the other. Finally, Gandhi said to him, 'If it is a peaceful and calm life you are seeking, I think it will be easier if you change yourself rather than seeking to change others. Which will you find easier: to protect your feet with slippers, or to carpet the whole earth?'

4.12 Rogoxin

A sick child lies in a hospital bed. The child is barely 6 months old and suffering from congestive heart failure. A doctor passes by and gives the nurse a prescription to administer to the child. He prescribes the drug Rogoxin but when the nurse looks at the script it seems to her the decimal point is in the wrong place.

She asks a colleague, another nurse, who has the same opinion. Another doctor passes, as harried and pressured as the previous one. The nurse asks him to check the prescription.

'Who wrote this?' he asks, barely glancing in the direction of the white form.

'Dr Evans,' she replies.

'It's not likely that he's made a mistake, is it?' the doctor says confidently.

So the nurse, trusting the status of the white coat over her own blue uniform, gives the injection, which is ten times too strong, and the child dies.

At the subsequent inquiry the key questions that arise are: Who is responsible? How could this situation have been avoided?

4.13 Straight Talking

A man was engaged to be married to a woman who had grown up in the arid Australian countryside. And although the man had met his future in-laws several times in the big city where he lived, he had never been to the remote farm where they lived. One day the young couple decided to spend the weekend at this farm which was situated some eighty kilometres from the equally remote town of Nar Nar Goon.

The morning after they arrived was one of those baking Australian summer days so they spent the morning sitting in the cool shade of the veranda, chatting sociably. The father-in-law-to-be suggested to the young man that they go into Nar Nar Goon for lunch. The young man thought to himself, 'In this heat? You've got to be nuts!' But what he said was, 'Sure, Dad, that sounds like a great idea.'

He turned to his fiancée, 'What do you think, sweetheart?'

The fiancée thought, 'In this heat? Jeez. Anyway, the restaurant will be the pits, and I bet the aircon's not working in Dad's car.' But what she said was, 'Whatever you like, darling.' She shouted through the kitchen window, 'What do you think, Mum? We're planning to go to Nar Nar Goon for lunch.'

The mother thought, 'Oh no! I've made a beautiful salad. It's already in the fridge. We could have a lovely meal here on the veranda.' But what she said was, 'That's a lovely idea. If everyone wants to go, why not?'

They all got into the car and bumped and bounced the eighty kilometres into town. The aircon was bust, so the windows had to be wound right down, and by the time they got to Nar Nar Goon their perspiration had attracted so much dust and sand that they were each coated with a fine layer of red mud.

The food was even worse than usual. They drove home in silence bouncing over another eighty kilometres of rutted track.

Later that afternoon, as they sat on the veranda sipping tea and iced tinnies, the young man wryly whispered to his fiancée, 'That was an interesting experience!' She said, 'I just wish we'd stayed here. I knew the restaurant would be awful.'

He gave her a shocked look. 'Why the hell didn't you say so in the first place? I didn't want to go either.'

The mother added, 'I wish you'd both said your piece. I had a lovely salad in the fridge which took me ages to make.' They all glared at the father. He glared back at them. 'I didn't want to go either. I was just making small talk. I didn't reckon you'd take me up on it.'

Four intelligent, sentient beings went on a journey that none of them really wanted to take. Thinking to please others, thinking not to hurt feelings, and for the good of the group as a whole they all suppressed their own feelings and intuition. Any one of them, by speaking honestly, could have challenged the collusion they had all become trapped in.

The only strategy to avoid wasting time and energy in Nar Nar Goon is straight talking: the art of expressing clearly and honestly how we really respond to an idea, a proposal, an assumption, an action, or a behaviour. Of course, it carries some risk. But the alternative can be far worse.

Three Stories of Wisdom and Experience

4.14 A Stitch in Time

A sailor noticed a small tear high up on his main sail. It was a lovely day with a calm sea and a gentle breeze and he didn't want to disturb his peace of mind just to climb to a difficult place to sew one stitch. So he decided to leave it until later.

Unfortunately, that night as he was sailing under the stars a strong wind arose. Soon the tear was much larger than it had been before. He could see that if he left it till the morning, the sail might well be completely destroyed. He would have to do it now, but in the wind and rain, in the dark and in the rough sea it would be a much more dangerous and uncomfortable process than had he done what needed doing earlier.

It was then he remembered the old tailors' proverb: 'Sew it now and sew it fine; a stitch in time will save you nine.'

4.15 Communication Blindspot

A consultant had been called in by the senior leadership team of a large organisation employing 20,000 people across the globe. They told him they wanted him to pre-pare a communications policy for them so they could more effectively connect with their staff.

'Not a problem,' responded the consultant. 'All I need to know before I start is this: When you are attempting to communicate with your people, what is it you are not hearing?'

4.16 Don't F**k with the Poodle

A French diplomat and his wife want to make the most of their posting in Tanzania so they seize every opportunity to explore the country. They organise a week-long safari in the Serengeti taking their aging poodle, Napoleon, with them.

Napoleon gets rather bored while the diplomats enjoy their three-hour French lunch and starts chasing butterflies. Before long he's lost. As he searches for the trail back to camp he spots a young leopard heading in his direction, looking mean and hungry.

'Merde,' thinks Napoleon. 'This could be serious.' But then he notices a pile of large bones on the ground and, with his back to the leopard, begins to chew on one of the biggest. As the leopard is about to strike the poodle exclaims loudly, 'Magnifique! That lion was delicious. I could do with a leopard for des-sert.'

The leopard quickly aborts his leap and slinks away. Hiding in the undergrowth the leopard congratulates himself on his narrow escape. 'A moment later, and that old poodle would have had me for pudding.'

A monkey has watched all this from a nearby tree and quickly calculates a way he can profit from what he has seen. He reckons a word in the ear of the leopard about Napoleon's brazen and shameless strategy will win him protection and favour for months to come. So he drops down from his perch and chases after the leopard.

The leopard is livid that he has been made a fool of. He says to the monkey, 'Jump on my back and just watch me partition that poodle.'

But the poodle has observed this little tête-à-tête and senses something is afoot. As the leopard approaches with the monkey riding high on his back, Napoleon has chosen to sit calmly on the ground, without an apparent care in the world, looking in the exact opposite direction to that from which his foes are approaching.

When the leopard is within earshot, Napoleon yawns nonchalantly and then curses loudly, 'Where the hell *is* that damn monkey? I sent him off ages ago to bring me that leopard for lunch.'

Chautauqua 5

Stuckness

Stories on the Themes of Attachment, Fear, Ego, Shadow, Death, and Other Dark Matters

There is a very simple way to trap a monkey. You cut a small hole about the size of the width of a monkey's palm in the side of a coconut. Inside the coconut you put the kind of food that your monkey loves to eat. Finally you attach a strong rope or chain between the coconut and an immovable object. Now you just wait quietly and out of sight.

The monkey will slide his hand inside the coconut and grab the food in its fist. And now it has a dilemma: food or freedom. It cannot have both for the bunched fist is too big to slip out of the hole the open palm passed so easily through. It is well and truly stuck. As you approach to catch it, it will not let go of the food. It attaches greater value to food than to freedom and only later will it realise that this has consequences.

Most human beings are not unlike this monkey. We get trapped and stuck in all sorts of amazing and highly creative ways. We get attached to things and don't want to let go. When we are deprived of these things, or forced to let them go, then we suffer. We cannot imagine living without them. Things we get attached to include people, money, possessions, pets, books, toys, perks, traditions, drugs, and of course ourselves.

Stuckness is often a form of resistance. It is a refusal to recognise that the world around us is constantly moving on. It's just that we're choosing not to move along with it. We're expecting the world to change to suit us. And it doesn't. It can't.

Stuckness can be borne of fear. The risk of change, of moving into the unknown is too great. Safety and security are only to be found in what one knows, what one has grown accustomed to, what is acknowledged as conventional wisdom.

Stuckness also manifests itself in ego. The person most difficult to work with in a learning context is the one who, when given an activity or exercise to work on, says: 'I can't do that; that's not ME!' As if he or she had never changed since birth! As if to take even the smallest step outside the carefully constructed comfort zone was to invite ridicule and destruction! I go here sometimes when asked to dance …

But perhaps what keeps us stuck more than anything else is refusal to recognise and own our 'shadow'. Our shadow is all those parts of ourselves we don't like and refuse to acknowledge. Sometimes we've pushed them so far away from our consciousness that we can't even see them in ourselves. Even when our friends or enemies point them out, we remain blind to them and continue in our denial. This is a problem because we can't change what we do not acknowledge.

We can spend a lot of time and energy disowning or suppressing our shadow. It tires us, it drains us, it makes us dishonest with ourselves, and it keeps us stuck.

Only when I own a part of me, an inner voice, can I sublimate or transform it. Otherwise it will run me. If I deny my anger, for example, it will run me covertly and manifest itself in all sorts of unhelpful ways. I might become passive–aggressive or vent my anger on some unfortunate bystander who has nothing whatsoever to do with the cause of my anger. These behaviours are neither useful nor helpful. They keep me trapped. They prevent me from liberating my energy and spirit from the mire of denial.

***

I was recently in Salt Lake City in Utah, at a seminar retreat run by Zen Master Genpo Roshi. I'd worked several times with the Roshi, learning the Big Mind process he's developed—the fastest and most elegant practice I've discovered yet for entering deep and powerful states of self-awareness.

For some reason I found it hard to get into the swing of the work this time. Maybe it was because I'd joined this particular group late, maybe just because my head was in the wrong space. Anyway, my work felt forced and ungrounded; it was hard to stay present. I managed to secure a ten-minute interview with Roshi in his office towards the end of my week.

I stood at the threshold of the Roshi's study. 'Come on in,' he said, 'How's it going?'

I paused to collect my thoughts, and then seeing no escape simply said, 'Stuck.'

He nodded and paused. 'Tell me about stuck.'

It was that kind of stuckness when there seems no straightforward answer. Thoughts crowded in. Seeing my confusion he said, 'Just tell me about the one that rises to the top.'

I waited a while to see what arose and then, as if by magic, it did. 'Sometimes, I feel a complete fraud.'

'Good,' he said. 'Just sit with that a moment and own it.'

'You know,' he added after a little while, 'when I became a Master, a Roshi, I felt a fraud for the first ten years or so. It was only when I truly owned that part of me, that particular voice, that I was able to hold it and value it.'

And so I sat with my Fraud and began to make friends with it. After all, it wasn't telling me that I didn't know *anything*. It was reminding me that I didn't know *everything*. And that I would do well to balance knowledge with humility, understanding with curiosity, desire with patience. That was a real gift of wisdom. A wiser and more mature Fraud than I was used to was speaking to me.

What I was suddenly awakened to—through Roshi's deceptively simple intervention—was that I would never be able to achieve any kind of authenticity or integrity unless I accepted my own inner Fraud, and until I could recognise that this part of me exists within me every moment of every day. It exists when I'm learning to do new things which I haven't yet mastered, and it exists even when I'm doing things that I've done for years and that I know I'm very good at. It's that little voice that sometimes says, even when things are going very well, 'One day, Nick, you're going to get found out.'

I left the short interview feeling much more light-hearted and much less stuck. I left holding a space in which I could own both my fraudulent self and my authentic self without any contradiction. I realised that they are both parts of who I am: only when I own that I'm a fraud can I begin to be truly authentic; being truly authentic means owning that I am also, at one and the same time, a fraud. It was a paradox, of course, and like any paradox that I can begin to embrace both 'ends' of, it had a hugely liberating effect on me.

***

Three Zen stories kick off this Chautauqua. The first *Vast Emptiness; Nothing Holy* (5.1) reminds us that we can get as stuck in the spiritual mind as in the marketplace mind. In fact the suggestion seems to be that marketplace mind with its pragmatic freedom from bullshit is the more appropriate choice in this situation. *Tying Up the Cat* (5.2) explores lack of criticality and rigour; the kind of blind and unthinking follower-ship that true masters despair of. This is a version of the Rogue Monkeys story which makes the same point in a business context: we get too easily stuck in old ways of doing things.

A Nice Cup of Tea (5.3) stresses the need to let go of all attachment to old learning and to empty the mind in order to acquire something new. This is the Lapsang Souchong path to mastery and enlightenment.

The Peace Maker (5.4) is the first of two Sufi stories. Its message appears to recommend keeping one's nose out of the affairs of others unless they specifically ask you for advice. Your personal wisdom is only valuable when people are ready to listen to it. *Imperfect Partnerships* (5.5) is another Mullah Nasruddin story that counsels against seeking perfection in your pursuit of happiness and success: 'As ye judge, so shall ye be judged.' Perfection is one of the best ways of all to get completely and utterly stuck because perfectionists set goals they can never reach.

The first of three Oriental stories, *The Shadow of Success* (5.6) suggests that science is a divine gift and can transform the life of a community. It also suggests that it is important to educate your people in the value of science and how it works if you wish the former ideal to be sustainable. *Stuckness* (5.7) illustrates the abundance that may await us when we, or external agents, create a shift in our situation.

Tied to the Nest (5.8) warns us against any obsession with gurus or masters. Do not overestimate the powers of others—take personal responsibility for your own life and find your own path.

Five dark stories follow. The first, *Dutch Courage* (5.9) suggests we face up to the inevitability of death. *Three Companions* (5.10) examines some priorities for life. The themes are not dissimilar from Beowulf's rousing endorsement of the northern warrior code, which he delivers to King Hrothgar and his men before slipping into the reptile infested waters of the dark mere to seek out and destroy Grendel's mother. A fabulous metaphor for facing up to one's own inner shadow if ever there was one!

> Do not grieve, my wise lord. It is better that each man
> Avenge his comrades than indulge in mourning them.
> For each one of us must expect an end
> To life in this world. Let whoever can
> Achieve glory before death. After a warrior is gone,
> That is the greatest and only thing he leaves behind.
> *Beowulf*, ll. 1385–90

The Wolf (5.11) describes a world where all forms of harmony and governance have broken down. Where there should be order, harmony, and peace there is chaos, distrust, and menace.

Masculine Compassion (2) (5.12) offers a stark reminder that feminine compassion—love, nurture, gentleness—needs counterbalancing through its masculine equivalent. It can seem that many Western cultures have these days embraced the feminine aspect of compassion far more than the masculine and have got somewhat stuck there. Perhaps it's time for a correction. The Warrior Stallion makes the point that death is a natural process and that tough love is sometimes the more compassionate choice.

Owning Our Shadow (5.13) is an old Taoist story that challenges us to embrace our shadows. The fiercer and more intractable they seem, the more they are disowned and the more they need to be recognised and accepted. Once we befriend our enemy, it no longer has power over us.

The first of five modern stories is *The World's Biggest Digger* (5.14). The story explores both literal and metaphorical stuckness. Key themes are cultural blinkeredness and the huge energy of goodwill and camaraderie released by collective work and a really good party.

The Subject Matter Expert (5.15) reminds us that while these people serve a great need in any enterprise they do not necessarily know much beyond their craft. And sometimes they make mistakes like the rest of us. Never be afraid to challenge a subject matter expert; if it's a doctor or a lawyer, your life or wallet may depend on it! Experts are often stuck because they find it hard to see beyond their silo mentality; others get stuck because they take the expert's knowledge as gospel.

Irresistible Development (5.16) is a great example of how to get ourselves unstuck! This story describes Walt Disney's recipe for the marriage of creativity and quality. *The Idea That Stuck* (5.17) urges us to go beyond the confines of our conventional thinking and to change the frames we put around information. Just because this doesn't work in Context A, does that mean it won't work in Contexts B–Z?

Coffee (5.18) suggests that we get stuck whenever we turn the hose off at the tap, whenever we pay attention to the wrong things in life. Focus on what's important. Turn on the tap; then be the hose and also the sheer power of the energy that flows through it. That's what your mind and body are for … to channel and direct that energy, that spirit.

***

There is a saying that what doesn't kill you makes you stronger, which has to be taken, of course, with a pinch of salt. But there is deep truth within it. If I look back upon my life I can count many examples of times when I was down. Some of these times I was truly desperate, disappointed in my ambitions at work, or in love, or just plain humiliated by the feedback I received from others or the world.

At these times it felt as if there was no reason or purpose for my life, that there could never be a way out, that there was no way I could ever recover. I would be stuck forever in total mediocrity or failure.

And yet I survived, and looking back I could begin to see that what happened to me was exactly what I needed at that time. It was a necessary and powerful jolt that shook me out of the rut in which I was stuck and onto a brand new super highway of possibility. My greatest setbacks, I came to realise, were also my greatest learning opportunities. I had to recognise them, of course, make the effort to get out of my self-indulgence and victimhood (what pleasure it can be to wallow in those spaces!), and seize the opportunities that life presented me with. Self-organising resilience.

One such period of my life happened when I was a post-graduate student at Oxford and part of the university boat race squad. Ever since I was about 6 years old it had been my life's ambition, my greatest dream, to row in that extraordinary and anachronistic race. The oarsmen from both universities were heroes and demi-gods to me. And at the age of 24 I'd earned myself a seat in the Oxford boat.

I'd come through six months of punishing training, pushing myself to the limit day after day: pounding the roads of Oxfordshire on early morning runs, sweating through circuits and pumping iron in the Iffley Road gym, freezing in the trial boats as we disturbed the wintry waters of the Thames at Oxford, Wallingford, and Putney.

The final selections for the last two seats in the Blue boat were particularly tough. Seat racing pits man against man in different combinations of crews until you work out which one makes a boat go faster. It's gladiatorial and there's no place for friendship or camaraderie; just determination to drive oneself and the others in your boat towards ever greater performance.

Six weeks before the race I'd finally won my place in the Blue boat, and in another week the final crews would be officially announced in the press. Everything was gearing up for the showdown with the Cantabs, a show-down we Dark Blues were determined to win.

I bought a copy of the *Daily Telegraph* on the Monday morning of the official announcement. At first I thought there must be a mistake or a misprint for my name wasn't there. Not in the Oxford crew, nor in the Isis crew, the reserve boat.

But it wasn't a mistake. I'd been unceremoniously dropped. I think the most hurtful thing of all was that no one had had the guts to tell me personally. Not the President who was rowing in the crew with me nor any of the coaches.

Apparently the medical officer at the university sports centre had looked at my medical records and discovered that I'd suffered from childhood asthma. So strong is the desire to win a University Boat Race that this very slight risk was deemed sufficient reason to cast me down from the seat of demigods and return me to the world of ordinary mortals.

They were tough days. It was bitterly painful. But I got to thinking about it after some time, and began the process of reframing events and healing myself. What would ever get me out of bed again, I asked myself, if I had achieved my lifetime's goal at the age of 24? I'd had the experience and it was a great one. I'd deserved my place in the crew and I'd worked hard for it.

No one could take that away. I'd proved a great deal to myself. Not least, I suppose, that an asthmatic like me could achieve so much and survive one of the toughest training regimes in the sporting world. I was so fit that even three months later I'd book a squash court for three hours and arrange for six partners to play me for half an hour, one after the other.

Looking back it was a great turning point for me. I have no regrets. It would have been a great feather in my cap, as the saying goes, but only one feather of many I've gathered in other ways and at other times in my life since then. So it didn't kill me and it did make me stronger.

Oxford won the boat race that year, 1974, beating Cambridge by a huge distance, and with a strong incoming tide behind them broke the course record by a considerable margin. They truly were a first class crew.

End note. Synchronicity is an interesting phenomenon. One early autumn day in 2008 I was standing in the large reception area of a conference centre in rural Wiltshire telling a friend about my time at Oxford and I briefly recounted the story above. We'd known each other for many years and he was surprised that I'd never mentioned this story before.

'What's all the more amazing,' he said, his big eyes wide open, 'is that I was with Donald MacDonald yesterday, at an event in Sussex.' Donald MacDonald was the President of Oxford University Boat Club at the time of the so-called 'Oxford Mutiny' when five US Olympic oarsmen refused to row with him in the crew. The film *True Blue* has immortalised those events in celluloid.

And then something even more unlikely happened. As Martin and I were having this conversation, into the same room walked David Rendel, Liberal Member of Parliament for Newbury, and Oxford University rowing Blue, who had rowed in that 1974 crew with me. It was the first time I'd seen him since that time.

'Yes, I remember all that,' he said, 'and I nearly resigned from the crew over it.'

'I'm glad you didn't,' I said. 'I know how much it means.'

Three Zen Stories

5.1 Vast Emptiness; Nothing Holy

Three monks were on a long and tiring pilgrimage. To support themselves and each other they shared everything equally, including their high and low moments. But after walking many days across a vast and barren plain, they realised all they had left between them was a quarter loaf of bread and a single swig of water. And they were all very, very hungry.

They began quarrelling over who should have these. Should one have it all or should they divide it? They made no progress on either count. But as night fell they hit upon a solution. Whoever had the most extraordinary dream would be the one to decide what was to be done.

In the morning, the first monk said, 'I had an amazing dream. I dreamed I had become fully awakened and then I was introduced to the Buddha who told me I deserved the bread for all my many hours of meditation and devotion.'

The second monk said, 'In my dream I met all the great Masters of our tradition. They praised me for the depth of my Enlightenment and assured me that it was I that deserved the bread.'

The third monk said, 'I had no dream. But I woke up in the middle of the night and felt the spirit move me to get up, eat the bread, and drink the water … which I did without hesitation.'

5.2 Tying Up the Cat

Many years ago, the howling of a monastery cat disturbed the monks' morning meditation session. The Abbot, a great spiritual teacher, ordered that the cat be tied up and muzzled during the morning meditation hour.

Some years later the Abbot died, and the monks continued to tie and muzzle the cat. And when, in turn, the cat died the monks brought another to the monastery and performed the same morning rituals on it.

Five hundred years later scholarly monks, in the lineage of the former Abbot, wrote learned tracts about the deep spiritual significance of tying and muzzling cats during morning meditation hour.

5.3 A Nice Cup of Tea

A young manager longed to find a mentor who could help him discover the secrets of becoming a Great Manager. One day he heard there was such a mentor and determined to seek out her wisdom.

He knocked on the door of the mentor's office. She welcomed him. 'I've come to you for help,' he said. 'I'm determined to fulfil my potential as a brilliant manager.'

The mentor opened her mouth to speak but the young manager raced on. 'I've read all the books on leadership and management. I've read everything on personal and professional development.'

Again the mentor sought a pause. But the stream continued to flow. 'My own view is … What I think of … Again what Chan Kim says is … On the other hand …'

On and on the waves of enthusiastic thoughtlessness rolled until finally the mentor thrust a tea cup into the young manager's hand and began pouring tea into it. Like the waves of the young manager's thought process she poured. The cup filled and began running over the lip. It filled the saucer. It ran onto the carpet. It spilled over the young manager's trousers. Finally he noticed and stopped his sermon.

'What … What are you doing?' he said amazed.

'Your mind is like this cup of tea,' she said. 'It is full of stuff that is not useful, full of second-hand thoughts, full of facts and information that have no context, sense of situation, or relationship. If you want to learn something new, first you must empty your mind.'

Two Sufi Stories

5.4 The Peace Maker

A man learned the art of understanding the language of animals. Passing through a village he came across a donkey braying loudly and a dog barking furiously back at it. He immediately understood the meaning of their argument.

The dog was saying, 'All you ever talk about is fields of green grass and bales of winter hay, you're so ridiculous; talk to me about raw meat and bones then we'll have a proper conversation.'

The man couldn't stop himself from intervening, 'But you're both missing the point; you're talking about the same thing, food; there's nothing to argue about.'

At that both animals turned to face him. The dog howled so loudly the man couldn't be heard, while the donkey knocked him down with a fierce kick. Then they went back to their argument.

5.5 Imperfect Partnerships

An old unmarried Mullah was asked if he had ever come close to marrying. 'Ah yes! When I was young I was very eager to marry the perfect wife and I journeyed far and wide in search of her.

'In Asia, I met a princess who was beautiful, charming and wise, but far too independent and headstrong for my comfort.

'In Europe, I met a beautiful girl who was an exquisite musician and full of life's joys, but sadly she was poor and lacked a real education.

'Finally, in Africa I found her. She was delightful: wise, accomplished, educated, and modest. I knew I had found the perfect wife.' The old Mullah stopped and looked wistful.

'So did you marry her, Mullah?' one of his listeners enquired.

'Unfortunately, she was waiting for the perfect husband.'

Three Oriental Stories

5.6 The Shadow of Success

A sultan who was ambitious for his people brought home to them from his travels the gift of a sundial. Before this, his people had been ignorant of what time was. They just passed the hours of daylight in whatever succession of activities came to mind, without order or sequence.

With the introduction of the sundial however everything began to change. Now they knew how to cut time into portions and divide the day into ordered segments. They learned to be reliable, industrious, and prompt. And with this new knowledge came success and wealth. The people of the sultan's lands knew greater happiness and prosperity than any of their ancestors.

When the sultan died, the people considered how best they could pay homage to his generosity and patronage. As the sundial symbolised both the foresight of the sultan and the success of the people, it was decided to build a vast temple around the sundial topped with a glorious cupola.

Naturally, as soon as this happened the sun's rays were no longer able to shine upon the sundial. No longer did its shadow divide up the day. No longer could the citizens organise their time, be punctual, or commit to deadlines. Industry declined, reliability vanished, and things returned to the ways of before.

The kingdom collapsed.

5.7 Stuckness

In the centre of a vast and barren plain stood an old and withered tree. Each night a small half-starved bird would shelter in its decaying branches. One evening a huge storm swept across the plain and tore the tree clean out of the ground.

The little bird was forced to find shelter elsewhere. So it flew fast and high across the barren plain searching for a new place to rest and find comfort. It flew many, many miles until it arrived at a lush green forest where great clusters of fruit hung in abundance from every branch. The little bird had never imagined such wealth could exist. And it never would have found it had not a great force threatened its previous idea of comfort and security.

5.8 Tied to the Nest

Through a combination of strange circumstances, the egg of a song thrush was placed in the nest of a chicken. In the fullness of time the song thrush hatched and began to grow. As was its nature, it would often ask its mother, 'When will I fly?' And the chicken would respond, 'When the time is right.' For in truth it had no idea how to help. It had neither skills to teach nor wit to push the young bird from its perch on the low branch. And so the young song thrush continued to hop about waiting for the day of its liberation.

And the song thrush itself was also responsible for its stuckness. It felt enormous gratitude to the chicken which had hatched and nurtured it. The song thrush said to itself, 'This mother of mine has great knowledge for certainly without her I would still be in the egg. If she knows how to hatch, she must surely know how to fly, and one day, when I am ready, she will surely teach me.'

And so the song thrush waited day after day, month after month, for a magical release by the one it revered so much. And so it waited for the rest of its days to transform from its earth-bound stage of development to the release of its full potential. And it never did.

Five Dark Stories

5.9 Dutch Courage

A London-based manager at a large reinsurance organisation received an e-mail message from Death. The message was stark. It said: 'I'll meet you in your office tomorrow afternoon.' The manager took the early morning flight to Amsterdam thinking to escape his fate. Crossing over one of the canals he met Death on the bridge coming the other way. 'What a fortunate coincidence,' said Death smoothly. 'I had had been planning to meet you in London but an unexpected situation occurred and I had to come here instead!'

5.10 Three Companions

Three companions accompany you throughout your life, but they are not of equal value.

First are your possessions; the things you own. But when you need them most, they stay at home and will not appear at your graveside to give you support.

Second are your friends; but while they may visit your grave to bid farewell and speed your final journey, they will not be willing to travel with you.

Third are the deeds you do in your life; these will leap into your grave with you, they will follow you in all things; no one can separate them from you. People will speak of them, and remember you in them long after you have left this life.

Doing things right, acting with integrity, facing tough decisions, and speaking your truth adds value to you, to others, and to the world at large. Your good deeds are more important than your material success, and even more important than the friends you make.

5.11 The Wolf

An owl observed a wolf travelling at speed, a glimmer of fear in its eyes. 'What are you running from?' asked the owl.

The wolf replied, 'The humans are hunting down all the wild horses. They want them for forced labour.'

'What's that got to do with you? No one's going to mistake you for a horse.'

'And what if someone who dislikes me suggests to the authorities that I'm a horse in disguise? Tell me, who do you think would negotiate for my freedom?'

5.12 Masculine Compassion (2)

The mustang foal was born deformed. Every time it tried to stand, its back legs would collapse and it would crumple back into the dust. Its mother tried everything she knew, nuzzling, coaxing, even licking her offspring into a standing position. Other mares in the herd gathered round the helpless foal offering their assistance too.

Even though their efforts met with no jot of success, their compassion was endless. Not one gave up the struggle to support the suffering animal.

After a while, a stallion galloped towards the group, his hooves drumming on the hard earth. The mares gave way respectfully as he approached. When he reached the spot where the foal lay, the stallion reared high above it front legs raised. And then, with brutal and dynamic force, he brought his front hooves down hard and swift on the soft skull of the foal.

The mares understood. Better a quick clean death than a slow painful one in the spiteful jaws of wild cats and coyotes. The herd paid their respects and moved on.

5.13 Owning Our Shadow

There was, living in Tibet about a thousand years ago, a Meditation Master whose name was Milarepa. So as not to be disturbed in his deep meditation he would seek out remote caves high in the Himalaya Mountains.

He had not long settled into one such cave when a large host of Demons moved in too. Their heavy presence and animosity distracted him from his meditation.

At first he fought them, but they just fought back and stayed right where they were.

So Milarepa tried another strategy. He recognised and named them. He treated them with honour, dignity, and respect. He was friendly and considerate towards them. Half of them left.

Next he invited the remaining Demons to stay as long as they liked. If they went out, he would welcome them back with genuine pleasure. Within a week all had gone except one particularly vicious and fearful Demon.

So Milarepa walked right up to that Demon. With no thought for himself, yet with an open heart and deep compassion, he gently placed his head right into the Demon's gaping maw. And in that instant it disappeared and never returned.

Five Modern Stories

5.14 The World's Biggest Digger

A large construction company wins government permission to quarry stone on a remote Polynesian island. And to do that they first have to build a road. Not only does the government want this quarry, the people of the island think they probably want it too, *and* the road. It could mean work and prosperity and access to many of the things they've been dreaming about for a long time. But there are still some that are not so sure.

The company's project manager writes a memo to HQ suggesting they fund a big party for the whole population of the island. His thinking is that the community will get to learn more about the project, the benefits it will bring, have a good time, and then give it their blessing and active support. He wants to enrol them in this massive project with enthusiasm and goodwill.

But the company refuses. The accountants say that spending a lot of the company's hard-earned profits on booze and a band is a waste of company money. Just get on with the project, they say.

'OK, fine,' says the project manager, 'your choice.'

When the great digger arrives to start the process of clearing trees for the road it sinks in the mud of the estuary and it isn't powerful enough to dig itself out. So a second even bigger digger is dispatched from company HQ which also gets stuck in the mud.

The project looks to be heading towards disaster but at this point the company has a fortunate break. They hear that *the biggest digger in the world* is going to pass nearby, en route from Brazil to Australia. They hire it, confident that it will not only get the job done in double quick time but also remove the other two diggers from the mire.

But the world's biggest digger gets stuck too. And now the company is completely stuffed. Serves them right!

'Let me handle it,' says the project manager. The company has little choice but to agree. 'First thing is we're going to have that party.' Word gets round the island fast and thousands attend. Free food and liquid refreshments are not to be missed.

The project manager bides his time till the food and drink have engendered a real community spirit and a sense of obligation. Then he calls for attention and says, 'OK guys, you've have had some fun, now it's time to do a bit of work.' He sends for giant ropes and all the men and women from all the communities right across the island attach the ropes to the world's biggest digger and start to pull together. It's hard work but eventually, after a huge amount of effort and a great amount of mud-spattered fun, they pull the world's biggest digger free. And then the world's biggest digger pulls out the other two trapped diggers, one after the other.

And that's how the world's biggest diggers got freed and the road and the quarry got built. Most important of all, it was how the whole community of a remote Polynesian island got fully enrolled at the start of the project, gave it their support, got involved in its development, and made sure—as time went by—that they got their fair share of the benefits from it too.

 ## 5.15 The Subject Matter Expert

A senior business leader arrived at Geneva airport to deliver a talk at a conference. The conference hotel was in Evian, an hour's drive away on the south side of the lake. He was met by a taxi driver in uniform and settled into the reassuring comfort of the large BMW. And they set off.

Looking up from his notes from time to time, he took note of the countryside and architecture as they drove along. He felt some unease but couldn't quite put his finger on it. About twenty minutes into the drive it dawned on him that the environment looked very Swiss. And where he wanted to go should be looking very French. And quite clearly he was on the north side of the lake, the Swiss side.

But of course he was in a reassuring BMW driven by a reassuring taxi driver in a reassuring suit. Surely this man would know a short cut or take a ferry. So the business leader settled back and reread his notes. He was, after all, in the hands of a subject matter expert.

Ten minutes late he glanced up. He noticed sweat on the brow and upper lip of the driver. And then the chauffeur switched on his GPS. And then he performed a smart U-turn.

The business leader was left to reflect on some key issues. After all, he had an extra hour to do so. Why had he, a respected leader of a large multinational organisation, denied all his experience and trusted the taxi driver against his own instinct and intuition? Why had he not expressed his concern much earlier? Why had he trusted the man when he had so much former organisational experience of subject matter experts getting it so completely and utterly wrong? What did he have to learn from this misadventure?

So he did what all great leaders do. He incorporated this story into his presentation which happened to be on the topic of leadership. With humour and humility he talked about his own responsibility for this misdirected journey and shared his learning with his audience: see the wider picture, engage with your experience, trust your intuition, and remember that subject experts, indispensable as they usually are, can be very often trapped in a very narrow view of 'reality'.

5.16 Irresistible Development

Walt Disney's success was built on a very simple but very powerful formula. It was a formula that encouraged both rigorous discipline in terms of planning on the one hand, and extraordinary creativity and opportunity to think out of the box on the other. This combination of structure and imagination, logic and creativity, reason and intuition was irresistible. It was, by any stretch of the imagination, a formula for success.

Whenever Disney wanted to develop a new movie he would divide his people into three teams. The first team were called the Dreamers. Their job was to dream the impossible. When the Dreamers had their scenario they took it to the next stage in the process. This was the Realist team.

The Realists were not allowed to criticise the Dream or the Dreamers; their job was to say how much of it was doable given the available resources. The Realists took the Dream and made it practical. The Dream was intact but now it had a plan for realisation.

The project was then presented to the last team: the Critics. The Critics were not allowed to criticise the Dream or the Dreamers or the Realists. But they *were* encouraged to test the project against the harsh light of practicality. They were invited to be critical. But rather than make destructive statements that de-energise any project meeting where ideas are up for debate, the Critics were encouraged to ask questions to get to the root of issues. 'Have you thought about ...?'

After this stage, the project went back to the Dreamers who, still holding to the essence of their Dream, now made changes in the light of the contributions of the Realists and Critics. When they were done, the project passed on to the Realists again to refine the practicalities further, and then again to the Critics for further challenging and questioning.

This cycle would continue until the Dreamers felt the essence of their creativity was still intact, the Realists knew they could make it happen, and the Critics had no more questions.

Next time you watch a classic Disney movie ask what you can learn from the strategies that brought such vitality to your screen and how you might apply it in your teams and family projects.

5.17 The Idea That Stuck

The story of Post-its, 3M's best known and most successful product, is a curious one, because originally the basic ingredient was seen to have been a disastrous failure. The basic ingredient was a glue that didn't stick! So it was rejected.

Some years later, a colleague of the failed glue inventor was singing in his church choir. He didn't like to dog-ear the pages of his hymn book and wondered how he could easily mark the pages that he needed to turn to. It was then he realised a not very sticky glue would be perfect. And so the idea of the Post-it was conceived, resurrected from the product that had previously been ridiculed.

Even then it took a lot of convincing to persuade senior management to run with this 'ridiculous' idea. But once the product was perfected and marketed there was no looking back. The Post-it was one of the great inventions of the twentieth century.

5.18 Coffee

A group of graduates, fully established in their successful careers, came together to visit their old university professor. Conversation soon turned into complaints about the huge amount of stress they experienced in their busy, achieving lifestyles.

The professor took the opportunity to offer his guests some coffee, went to the kitchen, and returned a while later with a large pot of coffee and an assortment of cups—porcelain, plastic, glass, crystal, pewter, some plain, some decorative, some cheap, some expensive, some exquisite. 'Help yourselves,' he said with a wave of the hand.

The professor waited till everyone had taken a cup, then spoke. 'Just take a look around at the cups you and others have chosen. You've all chosen the best ones; no one has touched the cheap and cheerful ones, the plain, the slightly chipped. Now while it's perfectly normal to wish for the best for yourselves, that is also the source of your anxiety and stress.

'Think about it for a moment. The cup adds no quality whatsoever to the coffee. It just adds more expense and, in addition, often hides or disguises what it is we are drinking. What you really wanted was coffee but without thinking you automatically chose the best cups … and then—here's my guess—you started looking around to compare the quality of your cup to those of others around you.

'So here's the deal. Life is the coffee. Your jobs, your income, your status are the cups. But these are just forms or tools to hold and contain life, and the type of cup you have does not create, or define, or change the quality of life that you have.

'Notice how often it may happen in your life that by focusing overly much on the cup you fail to appreciate and enjoy the coffee. So fully savour the coffee. You don't have to have the best of everything to feel fulfilled and happy; you just have to engage with the coffee and appreciate it in the moment. Enjoy it while you have it and drink deeply of it. Live simply. Love generously. Care deeply. Speak with wisdom and kindness.'

Chautauqua 6

All Things Must Pass

*Stories on the Themes of Impermanence,
Acceptance, and Letting Go*

It is a sobering thought to realise that everything we value, every-thing we love, including ourselves, will die. Sobering and also very liberating. For the more we recognise this truth, the more we can make the most of the time we have, appreciating in each passing moment the extraordinary and precious gift of life. Death is the antidote for taking things for granted.

But it does take a shift in mindset. Above all it requires acceptance of the fact that things are, well, just as they are. We cannot change what is. We can seek to improve the future although that is not guaranteed. But whatever is now, at this very moment, is. And it's already gone. There is only now and now and now and …

We can't change events in the past either. We can't wish away things that have happened that we don't like or approve of. It is a lot easier and much healthier to accept things as they are and work with that. Work with what the situation actually is and what it demands rather than what we would like it to be.

It's not healthy or wise to resist things that one does not have the power to change. I have friends for whom the mere mention of the name George W. Bush, during his years at the White House, would raise their blood pressure, set their pulse racing, and dispatch all rational thinking to the stratosphere. Really not helpful. For them or anyone. We have to work with what is.

As Buddhists say, 'Stop wanting it other than the way it is, that's where suffering lies.'

We also have to accept that death and loss are an indispensable part of the natural cycle and flow of things. Of course we need to grieve but we do not need to get stuck there. Of course there is injustice in the way we are dealt our hand by the Sisters of Fate but is there anything we can actually do once a life is taken? Yes, we can work to create a better future but we can never get that life back.

It can be helpful to see the great cycles of life and death as mentors that teach us proportion. Magnificent as we can be in the life we are given, in the great scheme of things, the development of the universe over millions of years, we are totally insignificant. Yet as members of the human race we do take ourselves so terribly seriously. It is easy to think we are *it*; that we've arrived at some kind of pinnacle of civilisation. If we do succeed in wiping ourselves out in the next hundred years or so, as could easily happen, then it will be the rats and cockroaches that will govern the earth. Will they think they've reached a pinnacle too?

Death, loss, and impermanence give us a healthy sense of proportion, a reminder that we are merely stewards of this planet—hopefully protecting and nurturing a space for future generations of *all* living things to find it in a better state than we did. And there is plenty of work to do.

We can start by acknowledging that life is not so much about what we do know but being willing to recognise how much we don't know. And we need to let go of a lot of the old baggage we are carrying. We need to question and challenge our existing mindsets, to discover and free ourselves from whatever stuckness we find ourselves in. And first of all we have to recognise just how stuck we actually are.

***

In a sense we're always stuck. Of course, we need to stay in any particular place long enough to learn about and integrate whatever it is that space has to teach us. Sometimes we can stay in a space a long time. There's much to learn and it may well be a valuable and generative space to be in. But there comes a time when we realise we've got too comfortable there and gotten stuck. We need awareness to remind us of the need to move on when the time is right; and if we're really smart, just *before* the time is right.

A good analogy is the monkey rungs, the fiendish contraption I used to play on as a boy in the simple, sparse playgrounds of the 1950s. Monkey rungs are simple: a set of twenty or so wooden rungs, set some forty centimetres apart, suspended rigidly about two metres above the ground. Like a ladder laid horizontally on supports. You start at one end and make your way—hand over hand—to the other end ... if you can.

You start on the first rung, holding on to it with your right hand. Right now you're stuck on that rung. If you want to get to the next, to move on in your life, what have you got to do? First off, you need to take some action. You need to find some energy to swing, to impel the whole of the left side of your body towards the next rung, reaching out for it with your left hand. And as you do so, as you swing towards the next target in your life, you now have to do the most important thing of all. You've got to *let go* of the place where you were. And you've got to trust that it will all work out.

This is the most natural of all processes. Letting go is one of the great secrets of life. Ask any actor, singer, or athlete about what is most important in their breathing and they will all say 'letting go of the previous breath before taking the next'.

***

It Will Pass (6.1) is the first of three Zen stories. The title carries the theme. *Enlightenment* (6.2) suggests that each of us is already enlightened, already connected to the source of all energy. It's just that we've found all kinds of ways to block that awareness. We're seeking for what we already have. *Loquacity* (6.3) touches on prioritisation and proportion.

The first of two brief Sufi stories is *Acceptance* (6.4). Its key themes are shadow and presence. *The Teacher of Truth* (6.5) is about ownership, a wry acceptance of the rewards of following your own path.

Two mid-life tales offset the brevity of the previous stories. *Lotte's Journey* (6.6) picks up a theme discussed in the previous section. It recognises that our road never runs smoothly, that fate and destiny can appear to deal us the worst of hands in the game of life. And yet all will pass. Nothing stays the same. Lotte learns in mid-life to accept that our greatest learning can emerge from our greatest suffering; that what we railed upon in our youth as unjust and unfair was nothing less than an essential process for gaining the tools and techniques to succeed in later years through the integration of all our experience.

The Wisdom of Solomon (6.7) is another story that describes the journey from youthful idealism and egotism to mid-life acceptance. The dead body on the doorstep is a wake-up call to the young man who has considered neither death in his life nor that he could be anything other than central to such a significant event. So he flees, literally, from the last of his youth. Over the years he learns many things. But it is Solomon who gives him at last the wisdom to see all things in proportion, to let go of his need to change the world and instead acquire mastery over himself and his impulses.

The first of five stories on life as a near-death experience is *Serenity* (6.8). It is a story of acceptance of our human fragility and of how most of us refuse to see how thin the veneer is between this life and the next.

The Shattered Goblet (6.9) invites us to see own our impermanence and recognise that since everything we love will be lost, it makes sense to appreciate it all the more while we have it. *The Cardamom Seed* (6.10) finds liberation and even serenity in the fact that death is inescapable. *Sweet Darkness* (6.11) laughs at our ridiculous dream of immortality and enumerates the awful consequences of living for ever. More mid-life wisdom!

Go for the Burn (6.12) is a story I heard from a sometime teacher of mine. It reflects his experience on a spiritual retreat in California some years ago. It invites us to laugh at how pain and death can bring such insight and meaning into our life ... while we have it.

The first of the three stories on perspective is called *Relativity* (6.13). It describes how the simple act of merely changing perspective and making a small intervention in one's life can bring about extraordinary relief—although nothing is actually different. *Wondrous Sounds* (6.14) is another story that describes the journey from the relentless seeking of youth to the acceptance of mid-life. The emptiness and desire of youth to find all the answers is replaced by an acceptance that there is only change and impermanence and that ultimately nothing can be truly known. The journey of life, the story suggests, is the gentle peeling away of layers of understanding, represented by the embedded doorways.

Rule Number Seven (6.15) reminds us to laugh at ourselves and our great capacity for self-importance.

***

One of the biggest obstacles that can be found on the path of one's own development is arrogance. And I speak with plenty of experience on this matter. Some years ago, definitely this side of the Millennium, I started experiencing lower back pain. Well, it wasn't so much pain as discomfort, especially doing those inelegant things like getting in and out of low-slung saloon and sports cars. And it was there all the time.

I tried everything. I saw my GP, had massage and deep heat treatments, visited chiropractors, lay on beaches in the sun, meditated. Nothing worked. My last hope was to see a specialist and I was sent to one of the best in the UK. He was thorough. My blood was drawn, I was X-rayed, and put through all kinds of hoops. The results came back; nothing to be found.

I awaited the great man's judgement. 'Wear and tear,' he pronounced sagely. I was furious. He was telling me I was getting old! And that wasn't all. I know medical people. I grew up in a household in which my father was a doctor and so too is one of my brothers. And believe me, most doctors will never tell you that they don't have an answer. What they will do is blame you for your problem.

It was then that I remembered the book. When the pain first started, some three years or so earlier, I had been attending a seminar and the trainer had recommended a book for anyone with back pain.[19]

I had listened politely, after all this concerned me, but how on earth could a book heal my pain? So I dismissed it.

Now I had no alternative. I'd run out of options. I searched on Amazon and found it: *Healing Back Pain* by John Sarno—£6.99 plus postage and packaging. I was still sceptical but at least I could afford it.

Now Sarno's take on back pain is straightforward, and I'm simplifying here because I'd like you to go and buy his book if you are similarly afflicted. He asks: Just what is going on? Why is back pain such an issue in the world today? It never used to be. The spine is one of the strongest and most flexible parts of the body; it's served us well for thousands of years. What's happening?

Before I share his view with you, I need also to share his caveats. His ideas will work with about eighty per cent of back pain issues, including upper, mid, and lower back pain, shoulder pain, tennis elbow, and sciatica. It won't work if you've had surgery on your spine.

What Sarno says is that most back pain is caused by the unconscious mind suppressing anger or fear. He says go back to the time when the pain started and notice what was happening in your life. Recognise it, articulate the anger or fear, let it go and within four weeks the pain will be gone. 'And of course pigs might fly,' I thought in my continuing arrogance.

So I floated back along my timeline to the period when the pain started. Oh my word! Yes, I was angry. Very angry. Very angry with two women as it happened. One in a professional context, the other in a personal context. And being a good and typical Brit I had bottled it all up. I had said not a word. I had gone passive–aggressive in the worst possible way.

So I took a breath and articulated my anger. Just to myself. I just let it all go. Let … it … all … go.

Within three weeks the discomfort in my back had completely and utterly gone. I was free. But here's the interesting thing: sometimes it comes back. And every time I feel the first twinge in my lower back, I just ask myself what it is that I'm getting angry about. I recognise it, own it, articulate it, and let it go. And I'm free once again.

The body is the most wonderful and finely tuned biofeedback mechanism. John Sarno, MD, healer! Hats off to you!

Three Zen Stories

6.1 It Will Pass

An apprentice monk said to the Abbot, 'My meditation practice is a disaster. I can't concentrate, I get pins and needles in my legs, and worst of all I fall asleep. I even cracked my head once on the floor.'

'It will pass,' said the Abbot.

Two weeks later, the apprentice told the Abbot, 'My meditation is incredible. I can sit for hours. I feel so awake, so enlightened, and so full of love and compassion.'

The Abbot smiled, then added, 'It will pass.'

6.2 Enlightenment

A pilgrim had been seeking a Teacher for many years. Some inner truth, some deep awakening was somehow eluding her that only the insight and wisdom of a Special One could unlock. She knew that if only she could find the right one, true enlightenment could finally be within her grasp. So she searched and she searched and she searched.

One day she was told about a Teacher who lived on an island not far from where she happened to be. She wasted no time in seeking him out. She arrived at a strip of sandy beach and saw the Teacher sitting on a small stool across the strip of water that separated them.

He looked completely serene. This was the One, she knew. But she couldn't swim and she could see neither boat nor bridge.

'How do I get to the other side?' she shouted.

He looked at her and laughed.'Pilgrim,'he yelled back,'from where I'm sitting you're already there!'

6.3 Loquacity

A man applied to become a monk at a certain monastery. It was a silent order but each monk was allowed to share two words with the Abbot every ten years.

After the first ten years, the monk was admitted to the Abbot's office.'Speak!' said the Abbot.

'Bed hard,' replied the monk. At which the Abbot picked up his stick and chased the monk out.

Ten years later the monk was again admitted to the Abbot's office.'Speak!'

'Food dreadful.'At which the Abbot picked up his stick and chased the monk out.

Another ten years passed and the monk returned once more to the office. Before the Abbot could speak, the monk said,'I quit!'

'I'm not surprised,' retorted the Abbot, 'ever since you arrived you've done nothing but complain.'

Two Brief Sufi Stories

6.4 Acceptance

A man was obsessed with the fear of death.

The Master said,'Why waste time on that?'

'How could I not?'

'By living in Paradise in the present moment.'

'And where can that Paradise be found?'

'Here. Now!'

6.5 The Teacher of Truth

A young man wished to become a Teacher of the Way.

'Are you sure?' asked the Master. 'Are you ready to be ignored, ridiculed, and totally impoverished till you're 50?'

'Yes, absolutely! But I'm curious, what will happen once I get to 50?'

'You'll have got used to it.'

Two Mid-Life Tales

6.6 Lotte's Journey

Once upon a time, near Athens, there lived a young woman named Lotte. She was the daughter of a successful and prosperous rope maker. When she was not attending to her studies or household chores, she would often watch with fascination as her father's employees wove long strands of fibre to create the strong hemp ropes that formed the basis of her family's fortune.

One day her father said, 'Lotte, I want you to travel with me for I have business with some of the islands in the Great Sea. It's time you saw something of the world, and who knows,' he paused and winked, 'maybe we will find you a rich and handsome husband to bring home.'

And so they travelled from island to island, selling rope and taking orders, until one fateful day, as they sailed towards Tripoli, a huge storm blew up and the boat was wrecked. Lotte barely made it ashore but she had lost everything. Of her father and his boats there was not a trace.

As she lay crumpled and exhausted on the sand, bewailing her fate and cursing heaven, a poor family of cloth makers found her. They took her in, fed and clothed her, and brought her back to good health. Time heals many things and within two or three years she could smile and laugh again. She had even learnt the art of making good strong cloth.

And then one day as she walked to fetch water from a distant well she was taken by slavers and hustled aboard their ship. They sailed for many days until they reached the port of Tyre where she was taken to be sold at the slave market.

Once again, Lotte had lost her world and the people she loved and trusted. She thought she must be the unluckiest woman in all history. She cursed the day she was born. Yet even in adversity there is still some light for at the slave market that day was a man looking for strong young men to work in his sawmills and factories. He was a kindly and compassionate man whose business was the making of tall masts for great ocean-going ships. He took pity on Lotte, and fearing what might become of her if left to other hands, bought her to save her from further humiliation.

But fate works in mysterious ways. On reaching home, the mast maker discovered that his fortune had been lost. Pirates had taken all his fleet of cargo ships which had been carrying masts to different parts of the world. So instead of giving Lotte to his wife as a servant-companion, he set her to work with himself and his wife making masts.

So thankful was Lotte for her rescue from a miserable fate that she worked hard and assiduously for her employer. Over time she impressed him so much with her attention to quality and her ability to select exactly the best timber that he granted her freedom and installed her as supervisor over the work teams as his fortune once again flourished.

So it was that Lotte, in the third phase of her life, began to recapture some of that inner happiness and belonging to community that she had known in former years.

One day the mast maker said to her, 'Lotte, you have proved yourself worthy and able to manage yourself and others. I want you to travel to Japan as my representative with a cargo of masts. I have no doubt you will return with handsome profits.'

But off the coast of China, the ship was struck by a *Tai Fun*—a Great Wind— and once again Lotte found herself washed up on the seashore of a strange and unknown land. Again she cursed her fate. 'How is it,' she sobbed, 'that every time when my life seems to hold promise of so many good things, Fate dashes down all my hopes and expectations? What have I done to deserve this pain and suffering?'

But Fate wasn't listening. At least no answer came to her on that desolate shore. So Lotte began walking.

Now as it happened, a legend existed in China, since many centuries past, that a female stranger would one day arrive and make the Emperor a sumptuous tent. And since no one in China at that time had the faintest idea what a tent actually was, this legend created annual excitement and curiosity in the general population, not to mention the Emperor himself.

So every year the Emperor sent his ambassadors around the villages of the Empire to see if any female strangers were known to be in the land. And it was just as an Ambassador entered a small coastal village on the road from the east, that Lotte entered it on the road from the west.

Through a translator at the Emperor's great palace, Lotte was asked if she could make a tent for an emperor. On reflection she thought she might be able to achieve such a thing. Although there was no rope to be had in the kingdom, she remembered her days watching her father's men weave strong hempen ropes, so she collected thousands of strands of raw silk and showed the Emperor's servants how to weave it into strong and beautiful ropes.

With the ropes made, she asked for sturdy, durable tent cloth. But no such thing was to be had in the whole of the Empire. And so she remembered her days with the cloth spinners of Tripoli and created exactly the kind of cloth that would make a tent fit for an Emperor. Then she needed poles to support the tents, but the Chinese had no idea what she was talking about. So calling on all her experience with the mast maker of Tyre she selected certain trees and had them skilfully cut, planed, and carved into tall and decorative tent poles.

With all the necessary materials to hand, she now took time to sit in calm contemplation, recalling all the many and varied tents she had seen while on her travels. And so it was Lotte produced and designed a tent fit for an Emperor.

The Emperor, as one might imagine, was mightily delighted by this wonder as well as by the fulfilment of the ancient legend. He granted Lotte any wish she might have. She chose to remain in China, where she married that handsome prince promised to her in her father's day. She gave birth to enough children as well as becoming a very successful tent maker and entrepreneur.

And she often took time, during her evening meditation, to reflect on how it was that so much grief and suffering in her past actually held the very keys to her success and contentment in the present moment of her later years.

6.7 The Wisdom of Solomon

One bright morning, a shopkeeper was horrified to find a dead body lying in the entrance to his store. Fearing he would be wrongly accused, he fled. He left behind his wife and two small children. He travelled many days to put sufficient distance between himself and those who might pursue him until finally he reached a far distant country.

He found work as a servant with a man whose name was Solomon and who was considered to be a wise and learned man in those parts. People would travel huge distances to seek advice from him even though his fee was always astronomically huge.

For a full twenty years the servant worked for his master. He worked hard and diligently and not once did he ask his master for wages. But in the fullness of time, the servant began to yearn again for his former life, to see his family and return to the land of his birth.

So he spoke his mind to his master saying, 'My Lord, after all these years I wish to return to the land from which I came. I have given you many years of service and would ask you now to recompense me in whatever way you think right.'

Solomon invited the man to follow him into the Treasury of his villa. There he gave him with hearty thanks three hundred golden dinars, a huge sum, as reward for his long years of service.

The servant was overcome with gratitude, but just as he was leaving to commence his journey, Solomon said, 'Surely you don't wish to leave until you have asked me for some of the advice for which I am so famous?'

The servant, with years of acquiescence to his Master ingrained in his behaviour, meekly acceded but barely managed to conceal the lump of anxiety in his throat.

'I have three pieces of advice to offer you,' continued Solomon, 'and I shall charge you no more than the usual fee.'

Solomon held out his money box and the servant, overcoming considerable inner reluctance, poured into it one hundred golden dinars.

'Here is your first piece of advice. Go back home the way you came. Don't abandon the old road for a new one.'

'And this advice costs me a hundred golden dinars?' the servant couldn't help blurting out.

'Indeed, yes, and all the more memorable for it being so expensive.'

The servant felt the vast weight of despair sink upon him. Meekly he invited the second piece of advice as he handed over another hundred golden dinars.

'Keep your nose out of the other people's business. Don't judge; let them put their own house in order.'

'Any marketplace crystal ball gazer could have told me this for a fraction of the price.'

'True, true,' murmured Solomon, 'but it is the very pain of parting with such a sum that will keep this advice fresh in your mind.'

The servant bowed to the inevitable. 'And the third piece of advice?'

'Indeed,' nodded Solomon as he graciously accepted the last of his servant's hard-earned fortune. 'Guard against your anger. Save it till tomorrow.'

'My ANGER!' fumed the servant, barely exercising what last vestiges of self-control remained with him, 'You ask me to save my *anger*?' And then he stopped, rendered speechless by a crushing sense of disbelief and a deep sense of defeat.

Solomon continued in his normal smooth and urbane way, 'And of course we can't send you on your way without something to remember us. Please, take this cake as a gift for you and your family, to share and celebrate together once you have safely returned.'

The servant received the heavily wrapped box. Weighty though it was, he paid it little attention but stuffed it straight inside his travel bag. Then, with all the dignity bestowed by twenty years of service, he thanked and bade farewell to his former Master.

And so our shopkeeper set off on the long journey home; his only wealth, three pieces of advice. Inside he was livid. 'Twenty years of hard labour for a cake!' he fumed.

He hadn't been going long when he fell in with a company of young travellers. Their energy and exuberance were contagious and soon he began to feel better. At least he was alive and the stories and songs he shared with his companions encouraged him to taste once again the delights of free speaking and great conversation.

At length they came to a fork in the road. The young company were set on taking the high road. They knew of a village, nestled in the mountains, famous for its hospitality and annual storytelling festival. This was their destination and he was more than welcome to join them.

As the former servant opened his mouth to accept he suddenly remembered Solomon's first piece of advice. 'Go home by the way you came. Don't abandon the old road for a new one!'

'I've paid dearly for this advice, I might as well use it,' he muttered grudgingly to himself. So he made his apologies and continued on his way. He'd not been walking long when he heard gunfire and shouts. And as he looked up towards the mountain road that his companions had taken he saw that a posse of bandits had ambushed them. 'By Solomon's beard!' he exclaimed, 'They don't have a chance!' He sank to his knees, 'Master, had I not heeded your advice I'd surely be dead. I thank you, Master, thank you.'

He suddenly saw his former master in a different light. Surely Solomon was the wisest man that ever lived. With some satisfaction he realised that his first hundred golden dinars had been money very well spent after all and he continued on his way in a much better frame of mind.

Some days later found him in a wilderness. The trees were strangled by creepers and the vegetation allowed very little light to penetrate as far as the surface of the road. He was tired and hungry and not a little anxious. He sorely needed somewhere to rest and restore his spirits when through the gloom he espied a light, and as he approached he saw it came from the window of an old cottage overgrown with weeds.

He knocked on the door and a tough thickset man, full of baleful energy, opened it. Somewhat nervously, the traveller asked for shelter and the man indicated with a curt nod that he should come inside. The man set another place at the table and served the traveller from a huge cauldron of goulash soup that hung above the fireplace. Both men ate in silence. When they were done, the man lifted a huge trapdoor in the floor and from the cellar below a frail blind woman appeared. The man took a skull from the shelf above the fire and poured soup into it. Then he thrust it into her hands and watched impatiently as she sucked the liquid through a thin tube.

Once finished, the woman retreated down the stairs and the man slammed the trapdoor shut behind her. He turned and glared at the traveller, 'What do you say about that then?' The traveller was about to give him a piece of his mind when he suddenly remembered Solomon's second piece of advice, 'Keep your nose out of the other people's business. Don't judge; let others put their own house in order.' So instead he swallowed hard and said, 'I'm sure you've got perfectly good reasons for doing as you do; reasons I can't even begin to fathom.'

'Too bloody right, my friend, too bloody right. That whore you just saw is my wife. Caught her at it I did with another man. That's his skull she was sucking her soup from and that metal pipe she was sucking on is what I used to gouge out her eyes. So what do you think about that?'

'I say that you acted according to the way you experience your reality,' said the traveller quietly.

'That's right, my friend, that's bloody well right, and any who sees things different gets their neck broke, their bones used for fertiliser, and their flesh fed to my pigs.' The traveller slept fitfully that night and set off as early as was polite next morning, grateful to be back on the road in one piece.

'Thank you, thank you, Solomon,' he said, savouring his second piece of advice. 'Cheap at ten times the price,' he thought to himself.

A few more days of hard walking brought him to the edge of the town he had fled from so many years before. Where before there had been hurt and fear, now there was anticipation and joy. But dusk was falling fast as he arrived at his house. He peered through the part curtained window into the gaily lit interior of the living room. He saw many people, trays full of food and drink, heard the sounds of music and celebration. Then he noticed his wife, older but still attractive and full of vitality.

He watched as his wife rose and was greeted by a much younger man. They embraced. Both were smiling. They began to dance as the guests cheered and applauded. Our traveller was furious; rage and the thirst for revenge rose in his breast. The twin voices of shame and jealousy screamed in his head: 'Both shall die,' he vowed as his hand felt for the pommel of his dagger. And then another voice, firm and very expensive, spoke too. It was Solomon's third piece of advice. 'Guard against your anger. Save it till tomorrow.'

The traveller's hand relaxed its grip on the knife and he slunk off to spend the night in the woods. 'But tomorrow,' he renewed his vow, 'both will feel the edge of this blade.'

He slept hardly at all and soon after dawn, red-eyed and stubbled, he emerged onto the streets no less vengeful and with the craving for vengeance still etched in his heart. By chance, an old friend was the first to meet him that morning. 'Waldo, is it really you? After so many years! And what good timing! Just imagine, only last night we were celebrating your eldest son's ordination as a priest. And your wife so happy for him. The two of them were dancing together half the night.'

And now he felt the tears sting behind his eyes: tears of relief and thankfulness as full realisation hit him. 'Oh Master, how wrong was my anger with you for the cost of your advice. Lord Solomon, surely you are the kindest and wisest of all men.'

Waldo hurried home. The door opened and there was a long moment of silence before recognition. And then, pandemonium, cries of joy and delight, embraces and kisses. And much, much talk. Then Waldo shouted, 'Stop. Stop. I have a gift: a present from my Master, Solomon the Wise.' He took out the cake from its box and with his dagger cut the first slice. And the coins began to fall. Hundreds of gold coins showering around the feet of family and friends. And when they were all collected, there were three hundred golden dinars, a fine reward for years of work and a lifetime of learning.

Five Stories on Life as a Near-Death Experience

6.8 Serenity

A blind Seer on a pilgrimage boarded a ship to his destination. As was the custom in that country, other passengers asked the blind seer for a blessing or a word of wisdom before their voyage began. All he said was, 'Without death, life has no meaning. Be grateful for the gift of your mortality.'

The passengers, being much the same as everybody else, didn't much care for the darkness of this message and consequently forgot it as soon as they heard it.

But once out at sea, a huge storm blew up. It was so severe that not only the passengers but even the crew and Captain fell to their knees and begged God to save them. Sometimes they screamed; sometimes they prayed and made promises about all the good works they would do if spared; sometimes they would simply sit helplessly and submit to their Fate. Meanwhile the blind Seer sat calmly with a smile on his face and, so it seemed, not a care in the world.

After the storm abated and everyone had regained their composure, some of the passengers asked the Seer how it was that he had remained so serene: 'How could you remain so calm during that hell when all that existed between us and death was the thickness of a plank of wood?'

'That is true,' responded the Seer smiling, 'and on dry land we don't even have that.'

6.9 The Shattered Goblet

The Tibetan master held up a sparkling crystal goblet for all to see. 'For me,' he said, 'this beautiful goblet is already broken. I admire it. I drink from it. It contains water perfectly, just as it is. Sometimes the rays of the sun shine through and the glass sparkles with brilliant colours. If I flick it with my thumbnail—so!—it rings out with clarity like a wind chime. But someday a gust of wind will knock it over or in a moment of clumsiness I'll brush it with my robe, and it will fall to the floor and shatter into thousands of tiny pieces. 'That's it,' I say, 'it's inevitable. When I truly accept that this glass is already broken, I awaken to the knowing that every moment with it is precious.'

6.10 The Cardamom Seed

A woman came to a Great Teacher carrying her dead baby in a shawl on her back. Refusing to accept that the child was gone she had wandered from village to village begging people for food and medicine to restore the child to health and strength. Finally, she came to the Great Teacher and asked if he had the means to save its life.

'That I do,' the Teacher replied, 'but first you must bring me a cardamom seed from a house that has never known a death.'

With renewed energy, the woman began her task. But by the end of the day, having asked every household in many villages, she had found not one that had escaped death. And finally she awoke to the realisation that sickness and death are inevitable and inescapable. She buried the child with dignity. And as she let go of the need to hold on to that which cannot be held on to, she was able to find once again some sense of inner peace.

6.11 Sweet Darkness

A king was out riding with his earls and lords. They rode hard and well and soon found themselves atop a high elevation. The king looked out over his territory: the fertile plain, the well-kept farms, the highly organised system of roads and canals, and felt a justifiable pride in his achievements.

At that moment a cloud obscured the sun and just as suddenly a dark thought struck him: 'Death will come for us all someday and I shall lose all my power and possessions.' His companions nodded assent. They too had much to lose. 'Yes,' they agreed, 'dying is hard.'

But one among them said nothing. A slight smile played on his lips and a sparkle flashed in his eye.

'To overcome Death and live forever,' exclaimed the King, 'that would be something: to send Death packing!' The silent lord smiled once more and the King's entourage sent uncomfortable glances in his direction.

The King warmed to his theme, 'Just imagine what hunts we could organise, what battles we could fight, what feasts we could devour. And we'd never fear grey hair, lack of teeth, or growing old.' The nobles could picture it too and nodded their assent. But the quiet lord became bolder. He laughed aloud this time.

'What's so amusing about Death,' the other lords chided him.

Meanwhile, the King continued in his reverie. 'Here we are, twenty men at the height of our powers. What is it that we could we not achieve, you and I together?' The earls and lords cheered their approval. But the lone dissenter laughed long and hard.

The King fixed a steely gaze upon him. 'What is the reason, pray, for your laughter? I see nothing amusing in our theme of immortality.'

'My Lord, forgive me, I have no desire to disrespect you. But your talk triggered my imagination. I got to wondering what life would be like if we were to live forever as you are suggesting.' He paused. Nobody spoke, waiting to see how things would turn out.

'Imagine how crowded this kingdom would be. Imagine how the great heroes of our history would still live: the first king who unified us, the great generals who gave us peace, the philosophers who taught us wisdom, the holy ones who brought us joy and harmony. Compared to them we would be as nothing, maybe serfs or peasants. And you, my lord,' he turned to the King, 'you would be a bureaucrat in the provinces.'

The silence deepened.

And then the King threw back his head and laughed. 'You are a wise and brave man, my friend. And you also speak the truth.'

'And as for you lot, you great bunch of flatterers,' he shouted, smiling at his entourage, 'for aiding and abetting me in my vanity, I fine you all three barrels each of your best wine.' He turned again to the laughing lord. 'And as for you, my wise friend, ride close beside me from this time on, and whenever you hear me again overestimating my talents and powers, whisper quietly in my ear: "There is business for you in the bureaucracy, My Lordling!"'

6.12 Go for the Burn

At a spiritual retreat, where a core pathway to awakening was through the repetitive process of hard physical labour known as 'Life Practice', participants were expected to engage fully in the exhausting process of maintaining the grounds and the overall infrastructure of the monastery.

After a long, hard day working in the cold and wet, digging ditches and chopping wood, feeling miserable, irritated, grimy, and aching, one participant forcefully expressed his feelings to a colleague.

A passing monk overheard and with a broad grin slapped the man on the back saying, 'Feel it all, my friend, feel it all. And be sure to appreciate it for what it is, for once you're gone, you won't feel a thing.'

Three Stories on Perspective

6.13 Relativity

A man came to the Village Headman and pleaded for help. 'I can't stand it any longer. My life is sheer hell. There's me, my wife, my children, and my in-laws all living together in a single room. We're arguing, and complaining, and constantly at each other's throats. It's destroying us all.'

'I can help if you promise to do as I say,' said the Headman.

'Anything. Whatever you say, I'll do it. It can't be worse than what I'm living with now.'

'Very good. What livestock do you have?'

'Two goats, a pig, a donkey, five chickens, and a turkey.'

'Bring them all into your single room and come back to see me in a week.'

What could the man do? He had promised to do as the Headman asked. He came back a week later in a terrible state. 'The stink! The mess! The noise. I'd be better off dead. It's like living in a mad-house.'

'Good!' said the Headman. 'Go home and throw out all the animals. Then come see me tomorrow.'

The next day the man returned with a wide smile on his face and his eyes sparkling with happiness. 'Thank you. Thank you. It's paradise. So clean, so quiet, and so much space to live life for me and my loved ones.'

6.14 Wondrous Sounds

A man is driving his car late one evening along a deserted mountain road when it breaks down. He starts walking and discovers around the next bend a monastery. He knocks on the great wooden door and explains his situation. The monks invite him in, provide him with dinner and good red wine, and offer him a bed for the night. They even send out Brother Pete to fix his car.

As the man dozes into sleep he hears an intriguing sound. It is a sound unlike anything he's ever heard; utterly seductive, utterly beguiling. He remembers stories from his youth of the Sirens luring Odysseus and his crew towards the rocks and utter destruction. He doesn't sleep at all that night, so enthralled is he by the mysterious music.

In the morning he asks the monks to tell him the source of the wondrous sounds but they reply, 'Sorry but we can't tell you. This is a mystery that can only be shared among us monks.' He leaves the monastery in frustration.

Years later, still unable to rid his mind of the sounds, the man returns again to the monastery and begs them to tell him about the source of the mystery. The monks shrug their shoulders. 'Sorry! We can't tell you. You're not a monk.'

'If the only way I can have the mystery of this beautiful sound revealed to me is by becoming a monk, then so be it. Please tell me how to become one.'

The Abbot says, 'You must travel the wide earth and discover exactly how many grains of sand there are and how many blades of grass. When you have found answers to these questions, and returned to inform us, then you will have become a monk.'

The man sets out on his journey and years later returns as a grey-haired old man. He knocks on the great wooden door of the monastery and is taken into the great hall where he stands before all the assembled monks.

'Brothers, in my quest to discover the source of that beautiful sound, I have travelled the wide ways of this great world. I have found the answers to your questions. By design, the world is held in a state of perpetual change. Only God knows what it is you ask. All a man can know is himself, and only then if he is honest and reflective and willing to strip away all self-deception.'

'Congratulations,' the monks roar. 'You have become a monk. Now we shall initiate you to the mystery of this sacred sound.'

They take the man to the bedroom where he had slept so many years before and behind a curtain show him a hidden wooden door. The Abbot says, 'The sound is beyond that door.'

The monks hand him a key. He opens the door. Behind the wooden door is another made of stone. He is given a key to the stone door and opens it. Beyond is a door fashioned from ruby. And beyond that are doors of agate, emerald, pearl, and diamond.

Finally, he finds himself in front of a great door crafted from pure white gold. The wondrous sounds are totally intoxicating him now. He can hardly bear it. The Abbot says, 'This is the last door,' and hands him the key.

His greatest desire is no more than centimetres away. Barely breathing, he unlocks the door, twists the handle, and gently pushes it open. Falling to his knees, he is utterly astounded as he is embraced by the source of that haunting and seductive sound ...

***

But, of course, I can't tell you what it is because I heard this story from a monk and he refused to tell me.

6.15 Rule Number Seven

A police chief and a senior politician were holding a meeting on the top floor of police HQ. About twenty minutes into their meeting, the door burst open and a uniformed policewoman entered completely oblivious to the two men. She was shouting and raging. She was cursing and swearing and quite clearly rather irritated about something or someone.

The police chief intervened. 'For goodness' sake woman, pull yourself together. Remember Rule Number Seven!'

At these last three words, the policewoman stopped as if awakened from a trance. She looked at the senior officer and said, 'I'm terribly sorry, Sir!' She straightened up, took a deep breath, and with a smile on her face left the office with calmness and dignity. Not forgetting to close the door quietly behind her.

'Impressive,' said the politician, as the two men continued their conversation.

Some twenty minutes later, the door burst open again and a plain clothes detective entered completely oblivious to the two men. He was shouting and raging. He was cursing and swearing and quite clearly rather irritated about something or someone.

The police chief intervened. 'For goodness' sake man, pull yourself together. Remember Rule Number Seven!'

At these last three words, the detective stopped as if awakened from a trance. He looked at the senior officer and said, 'I'm terribly sorry, Sir!' He straightened up, took a deep breath, and with a smile on his face left the office with calmness and dignity. Not forgetting to close the door quietly behind him.

'Truly impressive,' said the politician. 'Tell me, what *is* Rule Number Seven?

'As you see, Rule Number Seven is transformational,' replied the police chief. 'And it's really very simple. Rule Number Seven is: Don't take yourself so goddam seriously.'

'I see.' There was a pause, 'and what are the first six rules?'

'There aren't any others.'

Chautauqua 7

Not Knowing Mind

Stories on the Themes of Self, No-Self, and OneSelf

It seems to me that all pathways direct us towards the same place; they all flow in the same broad direction. They may take different routes to get there, and have different way-stations where the tired pilgrim may stop and rest, but there is *in essence* precious little difference between them. All the great spiritual pathways—Christian, Sufi, Kabbalah, Taoist, Buddhist, and also the great secular and pagan wisdom pathways—speak the same truth: Study yourself if you want to know God/the Buddha/Truth.

I don't *know* that this is true—there is after all so much I don't know. It is simply what, at this moment in my life, makes sense to me. And that is the only perspective I can honestly write from. And it is certainly not facts I am relying on here but a deeper sense of what really matters.

Studying oneself is what this book has been all about. The stories and commentaries between these covers have, I hope, offered insights and perspectives that may have informed and entertained, illuminated or provoked you on your own journey. I want to lead into this final section with an exploration of the deepest knowing of ourselves that is often beyond words.

I came across the following elegant and eloquent description of 'true self' in the *Big Mind* newsletter of August 2008. It is written by Bruce Lambson, Executive Director of the Western Zen Center in Salt Lake City, and describes in a few short paragraphs what many great scholars have written whole books to explain.

True self is that which embraces both our small egoic marketplace place self (human) and our extended universal indivisible self (being). When we recognise that it is our inescapable nature to inhabit these two realms of existence we can put the human together with the being and claim our birthright as a fully embodied, mature *human being*.

He begins by quoting the seemingly innocuous but very famous haiku by the great Japanese poet, Basho.

> Year after year
> On the monkey's face
> A monkey face.

I thought I would share my thoughts on this with you. This morning I just laughed out loud about it while I was shaving and thinking about this funny little haiku. Of course, I know I'm the monkey, I see that goofy face every day.

This poem points directly to the heart of Zen, to my own heart, my own self, my own face. What a funny thing is my life. I don't know how I got here, I don't know where I'm going after this, but while I'm here I'm a witness to the spectacular display of life on earth. It's all reflected in my monkey face, this face that is constantly changing and yet still uniquely, perfectly mine.

Dogen Zenji said, 'to study the Buddha Way is to study the self'. So, I study the self, my self, my heart, my face.

I'm very attached to my face. But what am I really attached to? I can call it a face but it's much more than that. It's skin, eyes, nose, mouth, etc. I use it to communicate, to see, smell and taste the world. I twist it around in a million expressions to try and manipulate the world around me. I couldn't survive very well without it. But no matter what I do with my face, I won't live forever, and I won't always be happy while I'm alive. I don't always like this face but it's the only one I've got.

Or is it? In Zen we talk about our Original Face. There's a Zen koan that asks, 'Show me your Original Face before your parents were born.' How do I answer this question? What is that face?

From the Big Mind work developed by Genpo Roshi, we can look at this koan using the apex triangle.

On the bottom left of the triangle, I see my regular physical face, my small self face. This is the one I was born with. It's temporary, impermanent, ever changing. The other day I saw a picture of my face when I was a baby and another when I was a teenager. Now I'm 56 it looks quite a bit different. I put my picture into a software program that ages you and I'm telling you, you might not recognize me when I'm 86. This is the relative face.

On the bottom right side of the triangle is my Original Face. This is my absolute face, the one that has never changed and never will change. It is unborn and undying and is the face I share with all sentient beings throughout space and time. It's the one that is reflected back to me in everything I see and experience. It's the face of oneness.

At the top of the triangle, the apex, is my True Face, the one which transcends and includes both my temporary, physical, relative face and my Original, Universal, Unborn Face. This really is my True Face, the face of my enlightened self, manifested in the world and in this body.

When I deeply realize that my life is the combination of both faces, and that my true face is both temporary and universal, then my monkey face laughs at my monkey face. And my monkey face cries for my monkey face, and for all the monkey faces of the world, because I see we are all truly one, both permanent and temporary, sharing our joys and sufferings as sentient beings in the mysterious and ungraspable reality of our life.

The first story *The Double Bind* (7.1) is a double bind, a stark message on which to contemplate. Four Zen stories follow—all good starting points for meditation and enquiry. The first, *I Do Not Know* (7.2) points to the profoundly changed quality that is to be discovered when we stop our projections and quieten our thoughts. *A Taste of God* (7.3) gently mocks the seeking mind and lightly reaches out towards the unknowable. *Silence* (7.4) explores the profound space of No-Self. *One Spirit* (7.5) points to the unity of all pathways and traditions.

Who Am I? (7.6) is a story from the Taoist tradition on themes of indivisibility, oneness, and cross-dressing. That's a joke to see if you're paying attention, yet there's also some truth in it.

Two stories follow on the theme of how as humans we construct our reality. *Lost the Plot* (7.7) explores the dramas and tensions we create for ourselves through the busy inner workings of our thought-laden anxieties. The story *Cathedrals of Clay* (7.8) indicates what can be achieved if only we could let go of our ego for just a while and build faith and trust in a common purpose with one another.

In four stories of oneness, the first, *The Bowl* (7.9), invites us to seek wisdom in ourselves rather than the external world. *Float Like a Butterfly; Sting Like a Bee* (7.10) highlights the advantages of an awakened mind, while *The Master Potter* (7.11) reveals the exquisiteness of the outcome when we fully merge ourselves with everything we do and with the universe around us. *Embrace Everything* (7.12) suggests that we turn away from the old metaphors of adversarial combat—usually metaphors of war or sport—and offer only what is good and pure towards our adversary. Whatever you give, you will always get back with interest. So choose what you give out wisely.

Three master–servant stories follow. *Mastery* (7.13) explores the dynamics of personal freedom. Being a slave or master is a question of mindset. Own what is yours and take responsibility, challenge convention, and partake freely of the free flowing energy that runs through us all. Above all be the star in your own movie.

Misery (7.14) is a short text. It gently mocks the idea of an ego and how much energy we uselessly use to serve it: the lights are on but nobody's home. *The Lunatics are Running the Asylum* (7.15) is a metaphor that illustrates how many of us have lost touch with our true master, our indivisible, undying, spiritual self. When the master is away, the servants—our short term needs and desires, the parts that make up who we think we are—compete for power and attention in their wish to run the show. No wonder our lives may sometimes feel incoherent and poorly directed.

Three stories for OneSelf conclude the section. *The Wave* (7.16) offers a metaphorical sense of our wholeness, oneness, and indivisibility. *Water, Sand, and Wind* (7.17) urges us to let go, to trust that we can embrace the One without losing connection to our temporary self; then as we merge the two, we can find our unique self at the apex.

Beyond Words (7.18) is a translation of a poem by the great thirteenth century Sufi poet Jalal ad-Din Rumi. Like all the previous stories it needs no interpretation when you trust your soul to intuit what you, at the very deepest level, already know.

***

In 1982, long before I began to explore many of the themes that have emerged in this book, I was offered a clear choice between life and no-life, between self and no-self. On a permanent basis.

I was in my room at the Kibo Hotel in the small village of Marangu, on the lower slopes of Kilimanjaro in Tanzania. I was lying in my bed, drenched in sweat, and close to death. I had contracted malaria. In fact, it was only my body that was lying on the bed, for my spirit, my soul, my energy, my chi—call it what you will—was hovering in an upper corner of the room.

From that vantage point, connected by a single, slender gossamer thread, I looked down on my fever-wracked body with utter serenity. I could stay or I could go. I looked towards no-life and it held no terrors. I looked towards life and all the challenges and opportunities it offered. Both were absolutely fine.

So I went to a higher place, an apex above those two essential aspects of myself, the human and the being, and I chose to return to earth. And from that apex space I realised that I could actually have 'being' any time I wanted, any time I could consciously remember to get out of my busy marketplace self and just sit in contemplation, with quiet and attentive mind, and just connect with that part of me that just always is.

One Stark Message

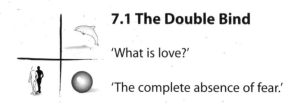

7.1 The Double Bind

'What is love?'

'The complete absence of fear.'

'What is it that we fear?'

'Love.'

Four Zen Stories

7.2 I Do Not Know

A great teacher was passing through Japan. The Emperor, a devout Buddhist who had spent a great fortune on temples and ceremonies, had his guards request his presence at the imperial palace.

'What is the noblest and highest truth of Buddhism?' enquired the Emperor, eager to learn more.

The Master paused then said, 'Vast emptiness; nothing holy.'

The Emperor was a little surprised to hear this.

'If there is just emptiness and no holiness, then who or what are you?'

'I do not know,' the Master replied.

7.3 A Taste of God

A mischievous Spiritual Master let it be widely known that he possessed a book that contained everything that could be conceivably known about God. He had shown it to nobody until one day, a persistent scholar persuaded him to lend it.

The scholar took the tome to his library where he opened it with fervour and excitement, only to find that every single page was blank.

'The book says nothing,' complained the Scholar.

'I know, I know,' said the Master, 'but consider how much it indicates!'

7.4 Silence

Very often visitors to the monastery would not respect the conventions. In their eagerness and curiosity, they would charge noisily from place to place: the tranquillity of the monastery would be shattered.

The monks protested at this intrusion but the Abbot was unperturbed. When the monks complained, he merely said: 'Silence is not the absence of sound, but the absence of self.'

7.5 One Spirit

The great Zen Master Gasan was one day visited by a well-travelled monk. During the course of their conversation, the monk asked Gasan whether he had ever read the Christian bible. 'No,' said Gasan, 'I have not. Please tell me something of it.'

So the monk recited a short passage from the Sermon on the Mount. 'Jesus said ... Why do you take thoughts to clothe you? Consider the lilies of the field, how they grow; they toil not, neither do they spin. And yet I say to you that even Solomon in all his glory was not arrayed as one of these.'

Master Gasan was silent for a while. 'Yes,' he said, 'these are the words of a Buddha. This is the essence of everything I am endeavouring to teach my monks at this monastery.'

A Story from the Tao

7.6 Who Am I?

One sunny afternoon Chuang Tzu, the great Taoist Master, dreamed that he was a butterfly. He fluttered from flower to flower, carried freely by wind and wings across a wide expansive meadow. In his dream he had no consciousness of his individuality and identity as a human being; he was pure butterfly.

In an instant he awoke and found himself sitting once again in the sun of the monastery garden, a man once again. But then he paused for a moment and began turning in his mind the thoughts that were arising: 'Was I a man before that thought he was a butterfly; or am I a butterfly who thinks he is a man?'

Two 'Constructing Reality' Stories

7.7 Lost the Plot

Every night a woman dreams that she is being chased along a dimly lit and never-ending corridor by a great and fearsome monster. Full of anxiety and a fevered imagination of actions and consequences, she feels the rancid breath and malevolent intentions of the beast, hard and hot on the back of her neck.

Every morning she awakes exhausted and fearful. It all seems so real, so life-like ...

Then one night the ghastly creature finally traps her. Just as it's about to rip off her clothes and tear her apart, she finally finds her rage and with it her voice.

'Who and what are you?' she shouts. 'Why are you following me? What are you going to do to me?'

Instantly, the great beast stops and straightens up, an incredulous expression on its face. 'How the hell should I know?' it says crossly. 'It's your dream.'

7.8 Cathedrals of Clay

There are certain species of termites, found in Africa and Australia, that build intricate towers up to ten metres high, great cathedrals of mud and clay. These amazing constructions are the largest structures on earth proportionate to the size of their builders. The engineering of the towers demonstrates a remarkable level of adaptive intelligence. You will find not only tunnels, arches, and intricate interconnected chambers but also air conditioning and even humidifying capabilities.

And yet there are no architects, no engineers, not even a queen termite to give instructions or boss anyone about. What's the secret?

All termites have an innate awareness that their purpose is to be termites and do what termites do best. This gives them a deep sense of collective identity. Then they share information and build effective relationships with each other. All the termites actually do is move around as they see fit, interact with one another, and react to what is actually going on around them. They closely observe what others are doing and with that information coordinate their own activities. Without blueprints or engineers their tunnels always meet in the middle. It probably also helps that termites do not appear to possess an ego.

Four Stories of Oneness

7.9 The Bowl

There was once a precious antique bowl that sold at auction for a small fortune. The previous owner had been a tramp who had no idea of its real value. He wandered from town to town begging food and small coins with it. He died in poverty completely unaware of the wealth he possessed.

A monk was struck by this story. He asked his Master what the bowl represented. 'Your True Nature,' she replied. 'People pay attention to the wisdom they find in books and in their teachers. They would do better to pay attention to the bowl in which they hold that wisdom.'

7.10 Float Like a Butterfly; Sting Like a Bee

The Buddha was wearing his transparent cloak of non-seeking Mind. He seemed to float across the ground, moving with the grace and elegance of a panther.

People noticed. 'Who are you?' asked a group of bystanders.

'Wrong question,' he replied. 'The question you want is: What are you?'

'Oh! I see,' said one of the group. 'In that case, *what* are you?'

'Awake!'

7.11 The Master Potter

For decades a Master Potter sought ways to bring his glazes to perfection. Every day, as he fired his kilns to white heat, he would experiment with temperature and chemistry to achieve the quality and beauty that he passionately believed was possible for his pottery and his porcelain.

There was no question that his work was of the very highest standard, yet he himself felt something was lacking. For all his technical creativity and ingenuity, for all his experimentation and passion, he could never quite reach that elusive standard which he had set himself.

And so believing his life's meaningful work was over, one day he simply walked into his kiln and evaporated in the molten heat.

When his apprentices opened the kiln again, once it had cooled, and looked at their Master's work, they had never seen anything so fine and so exquisite. The Master had finally become one with his life's work.

7.12 Embrace Everything

A shopkeeper received news that a huge shopping mall was to be constructed in the vacant lot opposite his general grocery store. Deeply upset and worried he poured out his troubles to a wise and trusted uncle 'What shall we do?

The shop has been in our family for generations. I will be ruined. All I know is shopkeeping.'

'Patience,' counselled the uncle. 'Your fear will lead you into anger and hatred. And these emotions will destroy you.'

'But what can I do?' wailed the anxious man.

'First thing every day, go stand on the pavement in front of your shop and wish your business joy and prosperity. Then turn around and do the same for the shopping mall.'

'Are you crazy? Offer good wishes and blessings to the enemy that will destroy me?'

'Whatever good that you offer him will return to you with interest. Whatever evil you wish him will also return to you with interest.'

A year later, the shopkeeper paid his uncle a visit. He reported that, just as he had feared, his business had been undermined and he had had to close down the shop. On the other hand, he was now General Manager of the shopping mall and successful and fulfilled beyond his wildest dreams.

Three Master–Servant Stories

7.13 Mastery

Maximus was his own man. In the prime of his youth, he was both attractive and physically powerful. He did things his own way and took orders from no one.

One day, a group of slave traders saw him as he rested beside a tree in the cool of the evening. 'This is a prize specimen,' said one. 'We could demand whatever price we wished for a slave like that.' 'But,' responded another, 'are we enough to subdue him? He looks fit enough to kill us all.'

But Maximus overheard them. 'Come,' he said, 'Fear not. I won't fight you. I do not harm my fellow beings. I won't resist. What is there to resist? So! I understand you want to sell me at the slave market. Is that the case?'

Rather shamefacedly, the group admitted that this had indeed been their plan. 'We're poor, you see,' they said shuffling from foot to foot. 'I mean, if you're willing, it would help us feed our families and insure us against old age.'

'Put away those shackles,' commanded Maximus, 'you'll not be needing them. I have nothing to escape from. I'll just walk on ahead of you. In fact, I'm rather looking forward to this adventure, standing tall on the stage in the marketplace, the centre of attention, rich people bidding for my services. Bring it on! And if I can help relieve you chaps from poverty at the same time, so much the better.'

The slavers were very nervous by now. Not only was this young man very physically powerful, he seemed to be completely mad as well. But there could be no backing down. 'Just follow me and do as I say,' commanded Maximus, 'or it will be the worse for you. And thanks, guys, I think I'm rather going to enjoy this piece of theatre in which I have chosen to take the star part.'

So it was that Maximus stood at the centre of the marketplace. All eyes were on him. Never before had such a beautifully proportioned representative of manhood been seen in those parts. Silence descended as the auctioneer stepped up to the podium. But before he could begin, Maximus intervened and in a commanding voice declared, 'Listen well to what I say. I am a Master ready and willing to be sold to any slave who chooses to buy me. I choose this destiny because these poor slavers need money to feed their children. Let the auction begin, but never forget … you are bidding for a Master.'

The bidding rose higher and higher. Never before had such sums been heard of at the slave market. Finally he was purchased by a great prince and the money was passed to the slavers. 'Are you satisfied now?' said Maximus. 'Go, feed your families and good luck to you.' He turned towards the prince. 'I will now accompany this slave to his palace.'

The prince laughed. He mocked Maximus as they rode with the princess towards the castle. 'You seem to have no sense of place or proportion. Are you completely mad? I am a great prince, yet you speak of me as your slave!'

Maximus replied, 'It is not I who am mad, but you. I am free, while you live within walls. Consider your princess, for example. I could certainly take her if I wished. She no longer desires you but me. You no longer interest her. It is you who are mad to think you can own a master or a slave ... or a wife.'

The prince was furious. He turned towards his wife, 'Is this true,' he demanded. 'Speak truly or, by Heaven, you will die.'

'In truth, then,' she stuttered, 'beside him you seem a pale apparition. I am obsessed, enthralled, and enchanted. It is all I can do to stay in control of myself. This is my truth as you have required of me.'

Shocked and hurt, the prince ordered Maximus to dismount. 'I free you; I'll not have my authority challenged in my kingdom or my personal affairs.'

Before dismounting, Maximus gazed levelly into the prince's eyes. 'I thank you. As I choose to take responsibility for everything I do, and everything that comes my way, no man can make me a slave. I chose to come to the market, I chose to be sold, I chose that the slavers should take your money, and I chose to come this far with you. As you own this horse, you have every right to ask me to dismount. I have no issue with that. And now I wish you, and your good wife, good day.'

And with that he went on his way, following his own path.

7.14 Misery

'Why am I so miserable?' enquired the monk.

'Because,' said the Master, 'just about all your actions and almost every single one of your thoughts is for yourself ... and there's no such thing.'

7.15 The Lunatics are Running the Asylum

There was a deeply wise and compassionate man who from time to time would travel to far-flung lands. Often he was away for many years at a time. On these occasions, he would leave his house in the hands of his servants.

Over time, while the master was away, the servants would sometimes confuse or muddle their duties, or forget what the true purpose of their different functions was. They would squabble and fight amongst each other and a few even harboured the delusion that the house actually belonged to them.

When the master began his travels, he had left instructions for the running of the house in his study. But over time this room had become sacrosanct amongst the staff and no one was allowed to enter it. It became to some a place of extraordinary holiness and deep mystery but from which they were eternally excluded; while to others no such apartment existed. They explained away the doors as simply being a part of the internal decoration of the property.

When the owner finally returned, many of the servants were unable to recognise him, some thought him an imposter, and others just a figment of their imagination.

It took the master a great deal of heart and mind to reassert his true nature and his true function.

Three Stories of OneSelf

7.16 The Wave

A wave had been travelling for a considerable time. Unaware of the influence of the currents and the wind on the direction it was taking, it considered itself very much in charge of its own destiny. It felt … important.

Until, looking up one morning, it noticed its neighbours up ahead crashing forcefully onto the shore of a vast continent.

'Oh my God!' it cried, 'Look what's to become of me.'

But another wave, travelling along behind the first, sensed the anguish of its neighbour and gently asked, 'Why so sad?'

'Look out there, dead ahead. We're heading for oblivion, for nothingness.'

But the second wave said, 'Wake up! Take a good look around and see yourself as you truly are. Not as a wave whose form will inevitably change but as an integral part of the mighty ocean that holds you in its vast embrace.'

7.17 Water, Sand, and Wind

From its distant source in the high mountains of the East, a river ran through all kinds of terrain and habitat, until it reached the dry sands of the desert. And here it found to its astonishment and bitter disappointment that no matter how generously it poured itself into the sands, its waters could make no headway.

Yet it truly felt its destiny was to cross this vast expanse and find release in a great sea. It was not a big river, but it felt important enough to have a strong sense of its own identity. So it continued to flow in the vain hope that somehow, someday it would succeed.

One day as the river lay exhausted in the marsh of its own making, it seemed to hear a voice—the soft and sibilant sound of the sands. 'The wind … the wind crosses the desert and so can you,' it sighed. 'Let go, embrace the wind, let it carry you far and free across the sands.'

But the river didn't want to give up its identity. It feared to lose its individuality. 'How can I trust the wind? How can I know that if I ever lose my self, my form, that I can find it again?'

And the sands said, 'You can remain as you are, stuck in this marsh, or you can give yourself up to the wind and trust in the natural way of things.'

'But can I not remain as a river, as I am?'

'You mistake your true nature,' sighed the sands. 'You do not distinguish between your solid self and your essence. Let yourself go.'

And hearing this, the river began to notice a certain sensation, a long forgotten feeling arising from within. A memory had been rekindled, a long forgotten spark from a time when it, in some shape or form, had been carried in the arms of the wind. And ever so slowly it willed itself to let go, to allow its vapours to rise up as mist, which the wind collected and bore swiftly and gently high above the sands, as if one substance, to the far distant mountains of the west, where once again upon the high plateau it fell as gentle rain.

And because of the Great Doubt that the river had experienced, it paid close attention to its transformation. And so it finally came to recognise its true nature: that there was indeed truly no contradiction in being both itself and the one. One-Self.

7.18 Beyond Words

Out beyond the realm of
wrongdoing and rightdoing
you'll find a meadow.
I'll meet you there.
When the soul settles down in that lush grass,
the world is too full to speak of.
Ideas, words, even the phrase 'each other'
Makes no sense at all.

Rumi

Epilogue

Pre-flections on Work, Life, the Dark Shadow, and OneSelf

Far Beyond the Surface of Things

Recently, I had the great good fortune to make several trips out of Cairo into the Sahara Desert. Not the tourist desert nearby, but the real desert several hundred kilometres to the south west, traversing the longest continuous sand dune in the Western world, Abu Maharriq, Father of Shifters.

It's been called Abu Muharriq for centuries for the simple reason that it's changing all the time, blown by the wind, one element of the complex dune system merging into or separating from another, refiguring its contours, shifting its shape. Yet its general line of direction, roughly north–south, remains constant. For centuries, camel routes ran either side of it, carrying precious loads from the oases of the south to the metropolises of the north. All that remains of the routes today are the stone cairns on the rocky outcrops that mark the way, shards of discarded pottery, coins, clay stoppers from shattered amphorae, and the tracks of Toyota 4x4s, the modern ships of the desert.

Each time I've crossed the dune, and the vast tracts of land either side of it, it's different, depending on the time of day and the quality of light. Different, yet interminably the same: bleak and awesome, benign yet unforgiving. The desert is unlike any other place on earth: a vast, silent, implacable witness to eternity and the insignificance of the deeds and pretensions of humankind.

The desert surrounding Abu Muharriq has been around for five million years. Billions of fossilised sea shells bear witness to the Mediterranean's several incursions to this far-inland region, as do the shark's teeth and odd bones of aquatic dinosaurs. Beside them, scattered liberally on the desert floor, lie the abandoned artefacts of long forgotten African ancestors: arrow heads, cutting tools, grinding stones, decorations, and pottery.

With good preparation and equipment, plenty of water, the ability to read sun, stars, and compass, even a handy GPS, it is not difficult to survive the desert. It just requires common sense, a modicum of fitness and humility and, above all, a willingness to enter into the spirit of the place. It takes an enormous lack of imagination not to sense the desert's spirit.

For walking in the desert, good sandals are far superior to good boots. While sandals allow the spiritful walker to feel the texture and ground of the desert, boots stoutly insulate the traveller from the experience. Sandals don't hold the sand; the sand, dry and fine, pours out quickly from under the soles. Boots and socks accumulate sand and debris and require frequent emptying. The desert is a place to let go: of assumptions, of self-importance, of immortality, of ego. All around, the fossilised bones and vast expanses of arid emptiness mock our frailty and short span of fevered activity between birth and death.

The desert is quite simply itself; it has nothing to prove. Forget whatever is written in our imagination or the hyped incantations of travel magazines. The desert is neither romantic, brutal, beautiful, nor vengeful. It just is. And it challenges us, at least through the lens of my own experience, to strip away all cultural and personal accretions and to see ourselves exactly as we are.

For me, the great attraction of the desert is that it challenges our perspective, disturbs our comfort zone, takes us beyond our normal boundaries, and invites us to ask ourselves some hard and important questions. And that is why, in 2008, accompanied by two first-rate colleagues, an award-winning writer and explorer, and an engaging assortment of Bedouin tribesmen, I found myself co-leading parties of senior managers and leaders from a high profile global organisation to and fro across Abu Muharriq and the vast expanses of desert on either side.

***

There is a well known anecdote about the great hypnotherapist Milton Erickson that also has a desert resonance, for deserts come in many shapes and forms, especially in the guise of metaphor. An alcoholic journalist approached Erikson and asked for help. Having established that the journalist had failed to complete any previous programme of treatment or therapy, Erickson dismissed him with a curt, 'If you can't help yourself, there's nothing I can do for you.' The journalist gave him one last pleading shot, 'Please.' 'Then I can offer you a *suggestion*,' Erickson said wryly. 'Go sit in the public gardens—there are a couple of cacti there. Take a long, close look at them, consider how they survive in the desert, and do a lot of thinking.'

I did a lot of thinking in the desert. The desert is a great place to contemplate. The stillness and silence are perfect. Two thousand years ago, the Coptic Christians, having had enough of the excesses of the Roman Empire in local Alexandria, fled to the desert founding small hermitages in the caves not far from Abu Muharriq. The caves are still there. Having passed several days in Cairo I could see the attraction of some quiet time.

Sunrise was my favourite time to contemplate. I'd slough off my sleeping bag, and leaving my companions gently susurrating in the makeshift camp, I'd head up the sandy slopes to the rocky outcrops high above, some ten minute's climb away. From here, the camp and the 4×4s, the tents and the tiny figures in their sleeping bags were like children's toys in a doll's house. In the soft light before sun-up I could see over forty kilometres in every direction across dunes, hills, outcrops, wadis, and on into the huge infinity of the dawn sky. And then the sun would rise, surprising each time with its huge languid gracefulness as it eased itself from the ridged horizon like a solitary red soap bubble blown from a child's mouth. The day was still cool.

There were two strands to my contemplation. The first was just to empty my mind, to quieten the inner chatter, to sit in a Zen-like state of non-striving, non-doing mind. Sense the breath, sense the body, feel the growing heat of the sun. Nothing more than a letting go and a connecting with the great and limitless spirit of the place.

The second strand was to give thought, with as much clarity and attention as I could muster, to what had been on my mind for many weeks: the writing of a book, this book, this collection of stories, anecdotes, and metaphors. What *exactly* did I want to say? What did I want to explore? How would I hold it together? What would be the key themes? I had no preconceived ideas, except to be as authentic as possible about what had become important to me on my own journey in recent years.

I have a very good mate, an Australian, who has the gift of saying extraordinarily wise and perspicacious things just when the moment calls for them. Well, half of what he says is extraordinarily wise, the rest goes over my head, but that's entirely due to my limits not his. I say to him, 'Pete, where do you find these things to say?' He replies, 'Jeez, I dunno, Nick. I just let my mind go blank, stay very quiet inside, and then all of a sudden, a bloody great PowerPoint slide appears before my eyes ... and I just read it!'

And that's it. That's exactly what can happen when I do manage to quieten all the inner chatter. The answer just emerges. It was there all the time waiting to be noticed. And in the desert, on that rocky outcrop, over a period of several sunrises, the desert itself became my guide. There were four key themes that emerged as each sunrise climbed slowly towards breakfast time.

1. Work and Busy-ness

The desert divides people into two camps. You love it or you hate it. It's like Marmite. You can't afford to be indifferent to the desert. You either enter into its spirit or you don't. People who enter into its spirit tend to be the ones who find it easier to leave their Blackberry or mobile phone back in the hotel mini-safe. They are the ones who can sit comfortably in that vast silent space, let go of the need to be constantly busy with minutiae and self-talk, and just *be* with themselves and with the desert.

The ability to be inwardly quiet, to focus with great attention on one issue at a time, to sort the wheat from the chaff, is a prerequisite for making better quality, more sustainable choices in life and work. All of us need to be busy sometimes. The problem is when the busy-ness becomes an addiction, a way of deliberately avoiding analysis and exploration of an issue or of ourselves at a deeper level.

From time to time we need to step back from busying ourselves in overwhelming detail and courageously face the bigger picture. The fact is that sometimes we can become so busy that we lose sight of ourselves and the point of our busy-ness. We need to ask ourselves: Who is being busy and for what purpose? This is the time for courageous conversations: firstly with ourselves, then perhaps with others.

When we find ourselves mired in detail, or out of touch with our vision, when we find ourselves working long hours simply to stand still, it is not uncommon to feel anxious. Anxiety is a product of feeling out of control: of self, of others, of the world in general, and of the future. Anxiety is rife in the world, especially the business world.

It's a fascinating fact but the etymological root of the modern word 'business' is the Old English *bisignis*, meaning—unsurprisingly —*anxiety, worry, concern*. The roots of modern English often have much to teach us if we probe into their original meanings and referents. Somehow it's rather disturbing to realise that anxiety and the addiction to busy-ness in the world of work have been around for more than a thousand years. It seems we're slow learners.

One antidote to being caught in the trap of busy-ness is reflection or contemplation. Get up in the helicopter, get out on the balcony, look down and see what is going on from a more dispassionate, distant perspective. From here you are much more likely to notice interconnections and the systemic relationships between things and people. From here you can engage in some real strategy, rather than the day-to-day tactics and operations that go on at ground level. From here you can ask yourself: Where am I going and what is it that I really want? You can begin to get some sense of direction once more and take charge of your life and your work again. But don't get stuck here, just spend more time here.

Whether we are sitting on a rocky outcrop in the desert, or just taking ten minutes of quiet time in our office or living room, the ability to shift to this more dispassionate, reflective perspective is essential to our health and well-being. It can shift us out of just doing and teach us how to both *do* and *be*. It can shift us away from a narrow focus on getting tasks done, to the realisation that tasks are more easily accomplished through the building of strong relationships and shared visions.

The stories and anecdotes in this book on the themes of work and busy-ness explore—among other things—ways to think more systemically, build better relationships, create a more integral vision, and avoid getting stuck in old patterns and behaviours when the world has moved on. Other stories invite the reader to consider ways to avoid the traps of narrow or conventional thinking.

2. Life and Desire

One of the great desert experiences is to take a mat and sleeping bag and observe the sky at night. A full moon is extraordinary. The desert becomes a lunar landscape—the dunes, rocks, and hills are bathed in soft, warm moonlight; light and shade create contrast and drama. No torches are needed. If you're quiet and lucky you might see a lizard or fennec fox. But best of all is when there is no moon and therefore no light pollution.

Then the great vault of heaven reveals its awesome beauty: billions of jewelled points of light—galaxies, planets, stars, meteorites, shooting stars—pulsing and shimmering against the vast dark backdrop of infinite blue-blackness. In the quiet of a moonless night, you can watch stars rise, as the world spins, and if you have time and patience, follow them to their zenith and on across the great expanse of darkness till they drop below the opposite horizon.

Now is a good time to contemplate important matters, like the purpose and direction of your life. It's a fascinating paradox. Here you are, wrapped in a warm sleeping bag to keep out the night chill, with the greatest light show on earth giving you a command performance. And yet, you are so insignificant lying here on the desert floor, surrounded by the fossilised bones of long dead animals. And above you, many of the stars are long dead too. All that's left of these dead suns is their brilliance that has travelled millions of light years to greet you tonight.

Waking up to one's cosmic insignificance and mortality can be a great liberation. How do I make the most of this short life? Am I doing work that fully allows me to express myself? What is it I really desire and how do I make it happen? Do I actually have the power to make anything happen or am I just deluding myself? Is it all just mirage?

The great attraction of *desire* is that it brings our mind into narrow focus on something we have not yet attained; we may not even be sure exactly what it is that we desire, but we sense deeply that it is worth having. It is desire that motivates us to get out of our beds or sleeping bags in the morning and make things happen, even if we're still groping blindly towards what it might be.

Providing we're not operating out of survival mode, in which case we probably wouldn't be out here in the desert, we can lie back and use this time under the stars to consider some more etymology. Desire: the root is Latin, *de + sider*, meaning *of or concerning the stars*. Having a desire means keeping your star in sight. You must pursue it, even when it shimmers, disappears from time to time, or gets obscured by fog or cloud. Sometimes, for a really great desire, you'll have to follow your star as it dips over the metaphorical horizon. If you really wish to reach your destiny you may have to venture into territories that at present you can scarcely imagine, and let go of the safety of your known world for what is as yet barely glimpsed.

The stories in this book on the theme of life and desire are—like the Pole Star—pointers towards a direction that may be useful or of value. Whatever we want to do with our life is a very personal thing. The stories are simply an invitation to reflect, consider, and take a glimpse into the possible.

Happiness

A man won the lottery and had more money than he ever dreamed; another became chief of a huge global organisation and had more power than he ever imagined; a third married into a wealthy and well-connected family and had as much status as any royalty. Yet none were happy.

They each went to see a psychologist to whom they expressed their frustration. She said, 'You each sound as if you think wealth, luxury, comfort, power, status, and absence from poverty are ingredients of happiness. They are not. All you need to be truly happy in life is to find something you can commit to with total passion, enthusiasm, and wholeheartedness.'

3. Darkness and Shadow

In the late afternoon, darkness comes quickly to the desert and with it respite from the day's heat and bright illumination. But darkness has always been associated in the human psyche with fear and foreboding; and not without reason. To enter willingly into the darkness, into a world that is obscure and hidden from us, takes courage. Darkness can be the blackness of night when creatures of another world emerge from their dens and hiding places, or a more insidious, metaphorical darkness when those parts of ourselves that we would rather not acknowledge remake their acquaintance with us. The energy we have expended during daylight hours suppressing these unacknowledged parts—our shadow—is exhausted and the long night's darkness subtly invades our defences.

It takes courage to step into the dark and face up to whatever it is that we most fear. It takes huge courage to own what we most dislike or deny or fear in ourselves. But if we do cross that threshold the rewards are enormous. For when we take this step, and begin to accept ourselves as we are, in both our strengths (which we also deny) and our frailties, we find we have crossed a significant boundary. The first thing we're likely to discover when we cross that edge of self-acceptance is that we become much more compassionate of ourselves. The second thing we may discover is that we can become more accepting and compassionate of others.

When we deny our power, or our ability, or our mortality, or our narcissism, or our envy, or our anger, or our fear (the list is endless) we distort our reality. We become disconnected from ourselves and from others, and then it is almost impossible to remain connected to our life's journey. Denial saps our energy: it takes huge amounts of attention to stay on guard all our waking hours. As soon as we learn to own our shadow we can let it go and redivert the energy into more productive channels, empowering ourselves and others.

The desert challenges our comfort zone, our desire to be safe and secure, at all levels. Only by sleeping out under the vast vault of the night sky—small, human, and vulnerable—can we ever see the brilliant illumination that awaits us amid and beyond the darkness. Only by enquiring into our own shadow can we connect with who we truly are and let go of what is keeping us small.

Courage comes from the heart, from the French word *coeur*. The stories on the theme of darkness and shadow explore what it might mean to face up to our inner dragons, accept the call to action and self-honesty, and cross the threshold into a larger, more mature, awakened, and *enlightened* future.

4. Connection and Separation: Exploring OneSelf

Is a fish aware that it swims in water? What keeps us in shadow is our inability to see ourselves as we are. The secret of all transformation is to see ourselves in a more objective way. Float up from the desert floor, attach yourself to any star and from that distant perspective take a long hard look at yourself. From here we may be able to see that life is not all about me, after all! We need to recognise our qualities and strengths, of course. But notice too how we are stuck, set in our ways, oblivious to the wider patterns and interconnections that sustain our existence. Only at a distance, from where we can observe with detachment, can we begin to see and appreciate our current limitations and stuckness. But now, from a more remote perspective, perhaps we can begin to see a way out of our self-imposed maze.

From a cosmic perspective, a person lying on the desert floor is not much different to a grain of sand; although the grain of sand will probably keep its chemical and physical structure rather longer! Nevertheless, the self has a fierce will and resolve, and a firm belief that it *is* all about me! So there! And that's good. It gives us purpose and direction in our lives. But if the small self is not prepared to explore its shadow, it's likely to feel judgemental, disconnected, and very, very separate: I stop at my skin and then there's the rest of the world. That can be quite a lonely place; a place where we need lots of distractions to keep us sane. And our modern world certainly serves up an almost unlimited number of ways in which we can distract ourselves to our heart's content.

On the other hand, in the desert under the great vault of the night sky I am in my element. Here there are no distractions, only my breath and my thoughts, and the feel of the sand against my back. Here there is quietness and clarity. Here I can sense the spirit of the place and feel completely at one with it. And again the old roots of language emerge in the silence. *Spirit, spiritus, aspirare.* At root, spirit simply means breath. To be spiritual is to be in our breath, inspired, connected to self, and to the world around us. What we generally call air is also breath, inhaled and exhaled over thousands of millennia, by animals and plants beyond count. It is breath that connects us—it is breath that connects everything. Pure *spiritus.*

Imagine standing on a cliff edge, looking far out over the sea, or better still lying on your back in the desert gazing up at the stars. Now breathe that whole limitless space. And notice how the breath roots down to your very centre and fills you with energy, fills you with the very spirit of the place.

***

Back on the rocky ledge as the sun rises I am aware of many thoughts emerging. I am aware that the quality of my life depends upon the quality of my attention. And I make a note to keep these thoughts in mind for the book I have *in mind*. And here on this ledge, looking down on the camp far below, and the vast Sahara stretching away on all sides, I can't escape the realisation that I am ultimately alone. And it feels intensely right and very comfortable.

I am alone but not lonely. There is all the difference in the world between the loneliness and separation of the small self and the connection and integration of the OneSelf. Like one small wave I have my own unique and shifting identity, yet I am always and inseparably nothing less than an indivisible part of the whole great ocean.

This deep awareness is fully embodied in the ancient wisdom of my language, for all language is ultimately based on human experience handed down from one generation to another. What does *aloneness* really mean we might ask? Separate the word into its component parts and a forgotten mystery is illuminated: *all + one + ness*. To taste the indivisibility of *oneness*, the etymology reveals, we first have to enquire within ourselves. We need to take time alone to reflect, contemplate, and meditate. We need to have some courageous conversations with ourselves. We need to confront our inner dragons, and that we can only do for ourselves and within ourselves, although we may engage a friend, or a skilful coach or mentor, or even an insightful story or two to hold a space for us as we do it. For, as the saying goes, if you want to know the Buddha, first you must study yourself.

The stories in this book on the themes of connection, separation, and OneSelf invite us to study ourselves, to look inside, ride our wave, follow our star, and above all find our own way of doing so.

Appendix A

Big Mind, Big Heart

The Big Mind website (www.genpo.org) describes the Big Mind process in the following way:

> Big Mind Big Heart is the name given, by American Zen Master Dennis Genpo Merzel Roshi to a special new way to discover, experience and appreciate your life. It's also a good way of working out the kinks, the stuck places, and the unhealthy patterns that keep us down. Life is complex, and the inner self is an exquisite network of the psychological and the spiritual. Understanding it well naturally leads one to a better life.
>
> The Big Mind Big Heart approach to life is a method of self-investigation and analysis that is straightforward and effective, and working with it will open your heart and mind to a new appreciation of the fullness and richness of life. It's a new combination of tools, a blend of Western psychology and science, and the Eastern traditions passed on to us, and it's been developed for the express purpose of helping us to better understand the mind and the nature of human life.

I personally have found the Big Mind process an extraordinarily engaging and fast-track way to connect to deep states of conscious awareness; it readily offers, even to beginners, powerful glimpses of the transcendent, the non-dual. Most Westerners don't have time to sit in meditation for months or years on end. The Big Mind process enables easy access to deep states of awareness even at a first sitting. Yet it's not only a serious process of deep and valuable self-reflection; I tend to find I spend a lot of time just laughing at my own ridiculousness. A well-run Big Mind session tends to have a lot of laughs and a high level of energy, as well as moments of profound self-revelation.

The process combines the Voice Dialogue process developed by Western psychologists Hal and Sidra Stone with Zen meditation, or *zazen*. But Big Mind does not need to be seen as a Zen practice. It is totally compatible with the contemplative practices of all wisdom and spiritual pathways such as meditation and prayer. I am not a Buddhist and Big Mind works just fine for me. The aim of Big Mind is to connect each one of us with our true self or true nature. Whether we call this God, Jahweh, Allah, Buddha, Tao, or Ein Sof is neither here nor there. For Big Mind connects us with emptiness itself which embraces and integrates everything that arises.

One way to describe the Big Mind process is to use the analogy of a large corporation. A well-organised, smoothly functioning company will have a CEO, a board, directors, senior managers, and so on. There will be clearly identified lines of business, and well-defined channels of communication and reporting. Information flows in all directions, there is a clear sense of identity and vision, and relationships are harmonious, respectful, and open.

Now when we think of ourselves, we can also recognise that we are an organisation. Within us exist innumerable voices or aspects of ourselves: these are our employees. But how many are there? We don't know. How odd! We've hired all these folks for our company but we've never got round to telling them exactly what their jobs or functions are. They don't even have job titles or job descriptions! They don't even know who reports to whom or who their boss is. And we expect them to work well together.

What would we call a business organisation that was organised like this? A mess! Dysfunctional! To make matters worse, there are certain employees who didn't fit in with the others and they've been made redundant. They're locked outside the factory gates demonstrating and protesting and attempting to overthrow the organisation. These are our shadow aspects, the ones we've disowned, the ones that don't fit in with our vague idea of our company's brand.

In the Big Mind process, we interview each employee one at a time. Not everyone, but certainly the key ones, and especially some of the key players we've locked out. We ask them questions and get their perspective on what they do and who they think they serve, and we help them clarify their role and how they fit in with the other employees. We let them know what it is we want them to do and what we expect of them. Together we create a clear and meaningful job description. Eventually, we'll introduce them to the CEO of the company. In a surprisingly short amount of time the corporation can begin to function much more effectively and much more maturely.

This is just a snapshot of the process. It's both serious and fun; simple and profound. And because it works hand in hand with the egoic, relative mind, and does not attempt to judge or deny it, there is little resistance. And so, as the relative mind, the marketplace mind begins to relax into the game, it becomes easy and natural for the transcendental mind, Big Mind, to emerge and for us to engage deeply with it.

Appendix B

Developmental Psychology

The basic notion of developmental psychology is that human beings have the potential to develop complexity throughout their life. We are not all at the same level of development nor would we wish to be so.

Jean Piaget was one of the first to introduce this concept with his work on children's development, yet clearly we do not stop developing and growing at the age of 16 or so. While some of us may not change at all after adolescence, many of us do keep moving on as we become more engaged in an increasingly complex world that demands ever more complex coping strategies to keep abreast of more and more challenging situations, relationships, and contexts.

Developmental psychology offers us many practical tools for developing both awareness of ourselves and of others, and understanding how we may need to be flexible and deeply conscious when connecting to and communicating with others who see the world differently from ourselves. It also reminds us that our own, and often provisional, ways of seeing the world are not right or better. They are just the current navigating system we are using to make sense of the world as we experience it.

Developmental psychology explores how we make meaning, how we construct our reality, and how we interpret events and relationships. Earlier stages tend to think they are 'there', that they have arrived. It's only at the later post-conventional stages that an ability to recognise and accept incompleteness emerges. Earlier stages tend to be blind to their stuckness and the particular limitations that attend each mindset, whereas later stages are significantly more aware of their entrapments. The later the stage of our development, the more complex our thinking tends to be, the more systemically aware we are, and the more uncertain we become of whether we can truly ever know anything,

When a person is centred fully in their particular stage of development it can feel exactly the right place for them to be. Their coping strategies fit the requirements of the environment and culture that they inhabit. Other times, when their coping strategies no longer fit the external environment, they can feel confused, disturbed, and lost. This may indicate that they are moving towards a transition to another stage. They may shift to another stage or they may not. Shifts can be to earlier or later stages depending on the contexts in which they are living.

Developmental psychology assumes a hierarchy, but not an oppressive *dominator* hierarchy as may be found in certain exploitative political or economic systems. Rather it is a natural and interdependent *actualisation* hierarchy (see Riane Eisler, *The Chalice and the Blade*) in which every element is essential to all the others. A good example might be a naturally occurring growth hierarchy in which atoms can transform to molecules, molecules to cells, cells to organisms, organisms to ecosystems, and on into biosphere, and so on. As Ken Wilber has pointed out, 'growth hierarchies convert heaps into wholes, fragments into integration, alienation into co-operation' (*A Theory of Everything*: p. 26).

No stage is better or more desirable than others; each is fit for particular purposes, and each contains the codes that have to be mastered to a significant extent in order to proceed to the next stage. In theory, it is not possible to jump stages. If a stage is not fully integrated before shifting to a subsequent stage, certain elements may become a shadow aspect. For example, the stage described as RED in Spiral Dynamics is concerned with power. If this is not fully integrated so that a person knows how to deal with aggression, bullying, and even assertiveness in others, the chances are that this person will seek to avoid conflict at all costs and back down in situations where they most need to stand as the warrior-self. This serves neither themselves, nor others, nor their communities.

I explored the Spiral Dynamics model in some depth in a previous book, *More Magic of Metaphor*. Here I just wish to give a brief overview and description of this model and also of the Harthill Leadership Development Framework, which are the two models I am most familiar with. Readers may also wish to explore the work of Susanne Cook-Greuter, Clare Graves, Robert Kegan, Lawrence Kohlberg, and Jane Loevinger, among others.

Spiral Dynamics

Basic Characteristics of the Eight Systems

> We do not see the world the way it is,
> we see the world the way we think it is.
>
> Dudley Lynch and Paul Kordis, *The Way of the Dolphin*

As the complexity of the conditions in which we live increases, we have to develop the complexity of our thinking and behavioural strategies to cope. The thinking and valuing system each of us adopts to deal with the conditions absolutely influences the way we perceive reality. Each of the eight systems experiences reality differently, is motivated differently, and responds to stimuli differently.

It is not possible, however, to recognise the operating system in a person or group simply by observing their behaviour—*what* they do. You need to discover the underlying valuing patterns by asking *why* a person is doing or saying certain things *and* pay attention to what they are doing. Patterns of behaviour observed over time are one of the most reliable forms of feedback. Observe what the feet do just as much as what the mouth says.

BEIGE:
Emerges mainly when survival is threatened. For example, deep grief, serious illness, intensive-care units.
Leadership role: Caretaker

PURPLE:
Repetition, routines and rituals help people centred here feel safe and secure in a mysterious, unknowable world.
Leadership role: Caring Parent

RED:
People centred here see the world as a jungle. They play the role of warrior or aggressor to survive.
Leadership role: Big Boss who can give tough love and police the boundaries

BLUE:
People centred here believe there is only 'one right way' and with this belief seek order, meaning and purpose in life.
Leadership role: Rightful Authority

ORANGE:
People centred here seek influence, possibilities, status and hi-tech tools and toys to play and work with. They like to be winners and will negotiate win–win situations.
Leadership role: Snappy, well-briefed colleague who demands the best

GREEN:
People centred here seek mutually agreed ways of working together with management and colleagues. Their concerns are to build a better world for all and share common resources with those who have less.
Leadership role: Sensitive Facilitator

YELLOW:
People centred here seek ways to understand the complexity of integrated living systems of which they are a part. Their key drivers are knowledge and competence. They often prefer working alone. Leaders need to get out of their way and be available as a resource.
Leadership role: Competent Partner/Consultant

TURQUOISE:
Few people are centred here. The system is only just beginning to emerge.
Leadership role: Spiritual Counsellor

For further information, see Nick Owen, *More Magic of Metaphor: Stories for Leaders, Influencers and Motivators* (Appendix A: A Short Introduction to Spiral Dynamics: pp. 307–324).

Useful websites:
www.claregraves.com
www.integralinstitute.org
www.integralnaked.org
www.nordicintegral.com
www.spiraldynamics.net
www.spiraldynamics.org

The Transformational Leadership Development Framework

The Seven Main Stages of the Leadership Development Framework

Stage	Spiral Coding	Focus of Attention	Leadership Characteristics
Opportunist	RED	Me, my world, my own interests first	Exploit and manipulate as might makes right; act with little regard to consequences; my way or the highway
Diplomat	Red/BLUE	Belong, fit in, don't rock the boat, avoid overt conflict	Create safe relationships, conform, avoid or appease whenever conflict arises
Expert	BLUE/orange	Efficient problem-solving, seek the one right way, technical mastery	Deep knowledge of craft expertise; follow rules and procedures; can be stubborn and rigid; may lack people skills
Achiever	ORANGE/green	Effective strategic performance, deliver the results, seek success	Focus on tasks, results, planning, and strategy; has enough people skills to work with and within teams; pace setting, entrepreneurial style
Individualist	GREEN/yellow	Seek work–life balance and independence, Who am I?, self-development	Enquiring and reflective; becoming less decisive and certain than previous stages; inclusive and facilitative; sees multiple viewpoints; less driven
Strategist	YELLOW/turquoise	Seeks to generate organisational and personal transformation in self and others	Seeks to empower self *and* others through mutual enquiry; expresses vulnerability; questions assumptions; seeks transformation; less concerned with ego and power; wide systemic awareness
Alchemist	TURQUOISE	Continually enquiring and listening in the midst of action	Able to integrate present/longer term; material/ spiritual; personal/societal transformations; clown/sage

Pre-conventional: Opportunist   5% of leaders and managers
profile here

Conventional: Diplomat   15% of leaders and managers
profile here

Expert   35% of leaders and managers
profile here

Achiever   30% of leaders and managers
profile here

Post-conventional: Individualist 10% of leaders and managers
profile here

Strategist   4% of leaders and managers
profile here

Alchemist   1% of leaders and managers
profile here

In the post-conventional stages, uncertainty increases (there are more possible viewpoints), systemic awareness widens, ego becomes less dominant, gender and ethnicity issues diminish as competency and contribution are emphasised, 'reality' is increasingly recognised as socially constructed, and awareness of own filters is acknowledged.

For further information, see Nick Owen, *More Magic of Metaphor: Stories for Leaders, Influencers and Motivators* (Appendix B: The Leadership Development Framework: pp. 325–328); David Rooke and William Torbert, 'Seven Transformations of Leadership'; William Torbert, *Action Inquiry*.

Useful website:
www.harthill.co.uk

Sources

The stories collected within the covers of this book have wide and varied provenance. Some are my own, some I have heard informally and at storytelling events over the years, some have been sent to me by friends and readers via e-mail, and there are vast collections of stories to be found on the internet.

There are also a great many excellent collections of stories to be found in books. Where I have found a story in only one book I have included the name of the book and the book's author below. Where I have found stories that appear in more than one book, these sources are listed in the Bibliography.

With the exception of Rumi's short poem 'Beyond Words' (7.18), which is my own adaptation from various translations, every other story in the book has been reworked and reframed in my own way. This is very much in the spirit of the storytelling tradition, handed down through the ages, in which every storyteller inherits a story from its previous guardians—often going back through many generations—and makes his or her own variations on the theme and on the language in which the story is expressed.

Chautauqua 1

1.1   Zen tradition.
1.2   Zen tradition.
1.3   Zen tradition.
1.4   Zen tradition.
1.5   Taoist tradition.
1.6   Persian tradition. Retold from Nossrat Peseschkian, *Oriental Stories as Tools in Psychotherapy*.
1.7   Originally from the Native American tradition. David Wagoner's poem 'Lost' is a similar reworking.
1.8   Sufi/Persian tradition.
1.9   Sufi/Persian tradition.
1.10 Buddhist tradition.
1.11 I heard this story many years ago in Tanzania but the idea that reality is socially constructed is common to many traditions.

1.12 Adapted from Anthony de Mello, *Awareness.*
1.13 Adapted from Clarissa Pinkola Estés, *Women Who Run with the Wolves.*
1.14 Rick Cooper and Henri Corduroy du Tiers. Retold from an e-mail sent to me by Rick.
1.15 Retold from a case history in W. Chan Kim and Rene Mauborgogne, *Blue Ocean Strategy.*
1.16 Retold from an e-mail sent to me by Pete Lawry.
1.17 First heard from Curly Martin. There are plenty of references to Cliff Young's adventure on the internet.

Chautauqua 2

2.1 Zen tradition.
2.2 Zen tradition.
2.3 Zen tradition.
2.4 Zen tradition.
2.5 Chinese tradition.
2.6 Taoist tradition. Adapted from Mark Forstater, *The Spiritual Teachings of the Tao.*
2.7 Sufi tradition. I first heard this from Sandra Maitri at an Enneagram seminar.
2.8 Sufi tradition.
2.9 Sufi tradition.
2.10 Sufi/Mullah Nasruddin tradition.
2.11 Jewish/Kabbalah tradition. Adapted from Rabbi Nilton Bonder, *Yiddishe Kop: Creative Problem Solving in Jewish Learning, Lore and Humor.*
2.12 Jewish tradition.
2.13 There are several websites on the internet recording Anthony de Mello's collections of stories. A Jesuit priest, de Mello's work embraced all the great spiritual traditions and his many writings illustrate his enormous wisdom, compassion, and humanity.
2.14 The Brothers Grimm.
2.15 There are versions of this story in all the great spiritual and wisdom traditions.
2.16 I've been telling this story so long I have no idea where I first came across it.
2.17 Same as 2.16.
2.18 Anecdotal.

2.19 Adapted from Anthony de Mello's collections of stories.
2.20 Adapted from the Sufi/Mullah Nasruddin tradition via Peter Hawkins, *The Wise Fool's Guide to Leadership*.
2.21 Anecdotal.
2.22 Sikh tradition. There is a very similar story from the Sufi tradition in Nick Owen, *The Magic of Metaphor* (Story 2.2).

Chautauqua 3

3.1 Zen tradition.
3.2 Zen tradition.
3.3 Various sources.
3.4 Various traditions.
3.5 Sufi tradition/Mullah Nasruddin.
3.6 Sufi/Persian tradition. Adapted from Nossrat Peseschkian, *Oriental Stories as Tools in Psychotherapy*.
3.7 Sufi tradition. Adapted from Idries Shah, *The Way of the Sufi*.
3.8 Sufi tradition. I first heard this from a participant at a retreat in mid-Wales.
3.9 Anthony Gibson told this story about himself at a Big Mind seminar in Salt Lake City, November 2007.
3.10 Anecdotal.
3.11 Sufi tradition. Retold from Nossrat Peseschkian, *Oriental Stories as Tools in Psychotherapy*.
3.12 Adapted from Rabbi Nilton Bonder, *Yiddishe Kop: Creative Problem Solving in Jewish Learning, Lore and Humor*.
3.13 This is my own amalgamation of a number of different stories and proverbs.
3.14 I came across this case history on the internet. This is my adaptation of the story.
3.15 Adapted from a case history in Anne Deering, Robert Dilts, and Julian Russell, *Alpha Leadership*.
3.16 I first heard this story from Genpo Roshi in January 2007.
3.17 Adapted from Mihaly Csikszentmihalyi, *Flow*.

Chautauqua 4

4.1 Zen tradition.
4.2 The internet.

4.3   Sufi tradition. Adapted from Idries Shah, *The Way of the Sufi.*
4.4   Sufi/Mullah Nasruddin tradition. Heard from David Whyte at a seminar, September 2008.
4.5   Christian tradition. Heard from David Whyte at a seminar, September 2008.
4.6   Sufi/Persian tradition. Adapted from Nossrat Peseschkian, *Oriental Stories as Tools in Psychotherapy.*
4.7   Adapted from Louis de Bernieres, *Birds without Wings.* The incident is copiously covered in history books and on the internet.
4.8   Adapted very freely from Louis de Bernieres, *Birds without Wings.* The story is meant not as a historical account but as a loosely designed description of the life and work of a single man to make some points about the pursuit of quality.
4.9   Kabbalah tradition.
4.10 Various traditions. I first heard this story while working in Tanzania and Kenya in 1982.
4.11 Anecdotal.
4.12 Anecdotal. There is a version of this in David Whyte, *Crossing the Unknown Sea.*
4.13 Pete Lawry. The original version of this story is on Pete's website: www.plconsulting.com.au
4.14 A version of this story first appeared on Standard Chartered Bank's intranet as an element in their Great Manager Programme.
4.15 I first heard this story from Martin Woods.
4.16 Jonathan Geard-Beney sent me this as an attachment to an e-mail.

Chautauqua 5

5.1   Zen tradition.
5.2   Zen tradition.
5.3   Zen tradition.
5.4   Sufi tradition.
5.5   Sufi tradition/Mullah Nasruddin. I first heard this from Martin Woods. There is a version of this story in Peter Hawkins, *The Wise Fool's Guide to Leadership.*
5.6   Sufi/Persian tradition. Adapted from Nossrat Peseschkian, *Oriental Stories as Tools in Psychotherapy.*
5.7   Sufi tradition.

5.8   Sufi tradition. Another version of this story can be found in Nick Owen, *The Magic of Metaphor* (Story 4.14).

5.9   Various traditions.

5.10   Various traditions.

5.11   Sufi tradition. I first heard this from Sandra Maitri at a seminar in 2002.

5.12   I heard this from Diane Musho Hamilton at a Big Mind retreat in Salt Lake City in 2007.

5.13   Tibetan Buddhist tradition.

5.14   I heard this from Robert Twigger at a camp in the Sahara Desert in April 2008. Robert is an intrepid British explorer and award-winning writer.

5.15   David Callaghan told this story as part of his presentation at a leadership development seminar in Evian in March 2008—after arriving an hour late!

5.16   Based on Robert Dilts's modelling of Disney's creativity strategy. I have heard Robert talking about this himself at various neuro-linguistic programming events. You can find more in Robert Dilts, *Strategies of Genius*, Vol. 1.

5.17   Anecdotal.

5.18   Adapted from an internet site.

Chautauqua 6

6.1   Zen tradition.

6.2   Zen tradition. I first heard this story from Genpo Roshi at a Big Mind seminar in London, January 2007.

6.3   Various traditions. I heard it as a humorous story in my childhood. I've also heard it from Genpo Roshi at a retreat.

6.4   Various traditions.

6.5   Adapted from Anthony de Mello, *Awareness*.

6.6   Sufi tradition. Adapted from Idries Shah, *The Way of the Sufi*.

6.7   According to Allan B. Chinen, in *Once Upon a Midlife*, this story originates from a collection of Italian stories gathered together by the great Italian author Italo Calvino. Versions of it appear in Chinen (ibid.) and also in David Whyte, *The Heart Aroused*.

6.8   Sufi tradition. I first heard this story at a Diamond Heart retreat in mid-Wales.

6.9   Tibetan Buddhist tradition.

6.10   Buddhist tradition.

6.11 Chinese tradition. There is a version of this story in Allan B. Chinen, *Once Upon a Midlife*.

6.12 Russ Hudson told this story of his own experience at an Enneagram seminar in London in 2005.

6.13 Various traditions.

6.14 Pete Lawry sent me this story. This is my version of it.

6.15 Heard from many sources. There is a version of it in Rosamund and Ben Zander, *The Art of Possibility*.

Chautauqua 7

7.1 Various traditions.

7.2 Zen tradition.

7.3 Zen tradition.

7.4 Zen tradition.

7.5 Zen tradition.

7.6 Taoist tradition.

7.7 Found on the internet.

7.8 Adapted from Margaret Wheatley and Myron Kellner-Rogers, 'The Irresistible Future of Organising'.

7.9 I heard this story from Steve Carter at a seminar in Cairo.

7.10 Zen tradition. Genpo Roshi told this story at a Big Mind seminar in London, January 2009.

7.11 Various traditions. There is a version in David Whyte, *The Heart Aroused*.

7.12 Prakash Dulip told me this story at a seminar in Budapest.

7.13 Adapted from a story attributed to Osho on an internet story site.

7.14 My take on Wei Wu Wei's much quoted epigram. Wei Wu Wei is a pen name of the Irish writer and thinker Terence Gray.

7.15 Various traditions.

7.16 Various traditions.

7.17 Sufi tradition. A version exists in Idries Shah, *Tales of the Dervishes*.

7.18 Jalal ad-Din Rumi.

Notes

Prologue

1. The story originates from the Fenian Cycle, recounting the legends of the great Irish heroes of the third century AD. The principal characters in the stories of *Tir na n'Og* and *The Salmon of Knowledge* are Oisin [ɒʃiːn], Niamh [njiːəv], Fionn Mac Cumhail [fjɒnn mək kuːəl], Fionngas [fjɒnngæs], Uail Mac Baiscne [uːəl mək bæʃknə].

2. Allen B. Chinen's books on stories, myths, and life stages offer deep insights into this rich area of literature.

3. I have found Carole S. Pearson's work on archetypes and shadow very informative and useful, and also the work of James Hillman, and the Ridhwan School's 'Diamond Heart Approach'. However, the most accessible and practical framework I have come across yet for the exploration of Shadow is within Genpo Roshi's Big Mind process. For more on Big Mind see notes 6, 8 and 9 below, the introduction to Chautauqua 5, the notes on story 7.15, and Appendix A.

4. I am rather attracted to Zen, however, which appeals to the nonconformist in me, and through the simplicity and directness of its ritual.

5. The 'I' disappears. Much contemporary psychology and psychotherapy refers to I-positions or sub-personalities to explain the contradictory nature of the self. In this view the 'I' does not actually exist; it is simply a useful generalisation. While most people are perfectly content with this illusion, it can get in the way of a deeper understanding of ourselves and our potential. It is useful to consider that many different voices exist within us, each seeking to express different aspects of our nature. The more organised and aligned they are, the more aware and serene we are likely to be.

6. Big Mind is a synthesis of Zen meditation and enquiry with the Western psychological tool of Voice Dialogue. Its no-nonsense directness enables Western minds that find it impractical to

spend months in retreat to experience deep states of self-awareness quickly and easily. It facilitates access to awakened states
of non-duality usually at the first sitting.

7.   Kabbalah is the mystic branch of Judaism; Sufism is the mystic
      branch of Islam. The Tao literally means 'the Way'. Zen is a
      school of Buddhism emphasising experiential wisdom, medita-
      tive sitting, and conscious action in the marketplace.

8.   This elegant gloss on the concept of what it means to be a
      'fully mature, free functioning human being'—*human* in our
      marketplace manifestation; *being* in our spiritual manifestation;
      that we are spiritual beings in human form—is an observation
      frequently used by Genpo Roshi when teaching the Big Mind
      process.

9.   The apex and triangle are core elements of the Big Mind process.
      A deeper exploration of the triangles can be found in Genpo
      Roshi's book: *Big Mind, Big Heart*. The book is very accessible
      and sets out the key teachings of the Big Mind process very
      clearly. I must also acknowledge my personal debt and grati-
      tude to Genpo Roshi. His teachings and guidance over the last
      few years have given me key insights into my own development
      and have helped me clarify many of the key ideas expressed in
      the Prologue and throughout the book.

10.   In *More Magic of Metaphor*, I explored stories in relation to stages
      of psychological development. In it I referred particularly to the
      model known as Spiral Dynamics and there is also a descrip-
      tion of the Harthill Leadership Development Framework in
      that book's appendices. Other models include Professor Robert
      Kegan's Six Stages of the Evolving Self.

11.   I have not been able to find the actual source for this quotation.
      However, it is so frequently attributed to Einstein, and resonates
      with so much else that he has said and written, that I have little
      doubt of its authenticity in spirit if nothing else.

12.   Quoted in Max Planck and James Murphy: *Where is Science
      Going?*, p. 10.

13   For a marvellously accessible introduction to quantum
      mechanics watch this interview with David Bohm on YouTube:
      http://uk.youtube.com/watch?v=SvyD2o7w24g

14. The yin–yang principle of classical Chinese thought recognises the crucial interdependency of seeming opposites: light/shade, mountain/valley, hard/soft, sun/moon, ebb/flow, order/chaos, masculine/feminine. The relationship between yin and yang is frequently depicted through metaphor, for example, as sunlight shining on mountainsides and into valleys. At one stage in the day, yang—the sunlit slopes of the mountains—are bathed in sunlight, while yin—the shady valleys—are deep in shadow, hidden from the sun's rays by the huge mass of mountain. But as the sun moves across the sky, yin and yang gradually change places. What was revealed is now obscured and what was obscured is now revealed.

Yin–yang is central to Chinese thought and medicine: health and healing are not possible without the proper balance between natural bipolar opposites. It is this deep sense of interconnection, and the dynamic equilibrium between forces that arise naturally within and between ourselves and the material world, that allows us to experience wholeness and harmony in our lives.

15. The myth of Apollo and Cassandra—with its central themes of separation, distrust, spurned love, and enmity—darkly underscores the events depicted in Homer's epic narrative *The Iliad* and in Aeschylus' tragedy, *Agamemnon*.

Cassandra agreed to have sex with Apollo, God of Reason and Wise Discernment, in return for the gift of intuition or second sight. But having received the gift, Cassandra reneged on her promise. Betrayed, Apollo decreed that although her prophecies would always be accurate, none would ever be believed.

And that's exactly how it is in *The Iliad* where no one pays the slightest attention to the accuracy of Cassandra's dire warnings; she is simply dismissed as a hysterical woman. But she has brought this on herself by breaking the pact she had agreed with Apollo. The poet's message is clear. Intuition without the tempering of reason and wise discernment—the realm of Apollo—is of no value whatsoever. It will simply present as emotional self-indulgence lacking all frame or structure. When the contradictory powers of reason and intuition lack a healthy and mutually informing relationship there will be disorder in the psyche, distrust in the land, and discord between nations.

The story is taken up in *Agamemnon*. Troy has fallen and is sacked by the Greeks. Cassandra, the most beautiful of Priam's daughters, has been taken as a prize by Agamemnon, King of Mycenae. On the journey to Greece, Cassandra repeatedly warns of impending tragedy but Agamemnon refuses to listen to her emotional ranting.

If Cassandra represents untempered feminine emotionality without boundaries, Agamemnon represents untempered masculine reason without imagination or sensitivity. Ten years earlier, Agamemnon had sacrificed his daughter, Iphigenia, to propitiate the gods before his fleet sailed to Troy. His wife, Clytemnestra, has not forgiven him. On Agamemnon's return to Mycenae, Clytemnestra ensnares him in a fishing net as he takes his bath and murders him. Outside on the palace steps, the palace guards assassinate Cassandra.

Agamemnon and Cassandra symbolise the total split of the human psyche; she connected only to intuition and he only to reason. The masculine and feminine principles, whose inner admixture is essential for each person's interior well-being and integrity, are sundered and each is implicit in the other's curse and downfall.

16. From Genpo Roshi's Big Mind process. See note 9 above.

Chautauqua 3

17. Quoted in Margaret Wheatley and Myron Kellner-Rogers, 'The Irresistible Future of Organising'.

Chautauqua 4

18. In his book *The Hero with a Thousand Faces*, Joseph Campbell introduced the idea of the monomyth, a structure common to stories across the planet. The monomyth is often referred to as the Hero's Journey. The monomyth has seventeen stages but is frequently simplified to the following seven:

• The ordinary world

- The call to adventure
- Refusal of the call
- Crossing the threshold
- The road of trials
- Seizing the Grail
- The return.

Many Hollywood movies have been based on this outline, *Star Wars* being a particularly notable example. A well-known example in literature would be Tolkien's *The Lord of the Rings*, and the pattern can be also noted in sacred texts, for example the stories of Moses, the Buddha, Jesus, and Mohammed.

Chautauqua 6

19.   The trainer was Tad James during a Time Line Therapy Master Practitioner programme.

Notes on the Chautauquas

Chautauqua 1

1.6   This story is a good antidote for any risk-averse culture. In a crisis conventional methods usually won't help. Often it was conventional thinking that caused the crisis in the first place. External circumstances changed, but the coping strategies weren't upgraded. Creative thinking, based on a wider systemic understanding, is required along with a willingness to take risks.

Human beings and organisations operate between the polarities of structure and chaos. Too much structure and we ossify; too much chaos and we have nothing tangible to hold on to. We need to find a tension between them: tension not balance. Structure is important to provide a foundation; chaos provides a creative edge. We need both but the relationship between them constantly changes depending on factors such as context, situation, relationship, and environment.

Music provides a good analogy. Sometimes our mood might require something quite structured like sacred music or a lyrical song; at other times we might prefer the more chaotic and discordant harmonies of jazz or rock. Either way, improvisation cannot work without some core element of structure; and structure—to maintain interest—requires some level of creativity.

1.7   My inspiration for this piece was David Wagoner's well known poem 'Lost'. My understanding is that his original poem was adapted from the words of a Native American elder which he had heard at a conference or similar gathering. The power of the message is in the simplicity of its form and language and in the metaphors and images of the natural world. To be present requires access to the non-efforting mind; the mind of the one who is not hard at it. The story is a great antidote to personal and organisational busy-ness.

1.8   This story is shocking. And yet it is in many ways a parable of our times. The villagers demonstrate a shallow morality. Underneath their righteous judgement is a desire to enrich themselves with as little effort as possible. They are prepared to listen to and accept the most outrageous ideas uncritically and take actions which go against all notions of common sense. They collude to allow the tricksters to get away with their scams entirely unpunished. It does not take a great deal of metaphorical awareness to translate this ancient story into many social and economic contexts of the modern day.

1.10   This is a great double bind story. The thief simply can't understand how he is trapped by Nagarjuna until it is too late for him to do anything about it. Nagarjuna simply asks 'Would you prefer to become awakened now or later?' Just as a parent might say to a child, 'Would you prefer to clean your room before or after you've had your dinner?' Either way the assumption is that it will happen. The story elegantly illustrates the old proverb: Whatever you resist, persists.

1.13   The title of this story *Uhuru* literally means 'emancipation from slavery' in Kiswahili and, by extension, freedom and independence. It is a story that works on several levels. At one level it's a story about culture and cultural difference, about shame and innocence, ignorance and knowing, and about polarity assumptions based on these factors. At another level it deals with the politics of conquerors and the conquered, and ways in which the disempowered can regain their sense of freedom and spirit through artful naivety and scarcely suppressed mirth. At yet another level it celebrates the strength and centredness of feminine sexuality even as it mocks the disowned sexuality of the British male establishment.

In *Women Who Run with the Wolves*, Clarissa Pinkola Estés interprets this story as medicine: 'the sexual and the irreverent as sacred'. It makes us laugh and it therefore heals: 'When the laughter helps without doing harm, when the laughter lightens, realigns, reorders, reasserts power and strength, this is the laughter that causes health.' It is, as she says, 'Good, clean fun.'

It's also worth noting in passing that this story only makes sense within certain cultural frames of reference. While the British, German, and United States establishments might be shocked at the behaviour of the women in the story, it's hard to imagine the same of the French and Italians. Bravo!

Sexuality casts a huge shadow over much of the globe, especially where religion is concerned. Most monotheistic religions appear to assume that the human body only exists from the waist up.

1.15 It doesn't matter what business you are in—banking, education, real estate, entertainment—you have to continuously improve the quality of your offer or product. If you don't, your competitors will leave you for dead; if you don't, your customers will leave you for a better deal; if you don't, you'll be looking for alternative employment.

One of the best ways to create continuous improvement is to listen to what your customers—internal and external—are saying and find ways to deliver what they want. It's not rocket science. You just need to listen, think, and take action. And be prepared to challenge conventional wisdom by being ready to think differently!

The same is true for personal relationships, including the relationship you have with yourself ... which of course is the most important one of all.

1.16 This is a parable about how we are sleepwalking towards destruction: too many assumptions; trusting others rather than relying on our own instincts and resources; unwillingness to take personal responsibility; a loss of connection to the mysteries and wisdoms of older generations; over-reliance on reason and modern technology; naive belief in the powers of native wisdom. The message is: Wake up!

Chautauqua 2

2.6 The world is full of opportunities for the discerning person to seize and apply advantage. The advantage may be to the individual; but many others too may benefit from the development of an effective technology made widely available.

So do not take for granted the many wonderful secrets and deep knowledge you possess. Because they have been with you long, and because you consider them ordinary, does not mean they lack value. Nor does it mean they have only the application that is obvious. Be true to yourself and be creative in your thinking.

Success in life is not accidental although we often attribute it to luck. It comes through looking at things in new ways, being awake to what is happening around us, and investing in possibility. The stranger created the future he wanted by being alert to what he was noticing at a particular moment. He made it happen through the power of presence, mindfulness, and application.

The story also reminds us that true awakening and enlightenment is not about withdrawing from the world but actively engaging in it with increasing levels of consciousness.

2.8 Anger is one of the most disowned of all our inner voices. It therefore casts a long and dark shadow. This story explores the range of emotional energy and consequences that exists between immature and self-indulgent anger and its mature, sublimated form.

Our immature anger, rage, rushes upon us like a tidal wave, rendering our rational faculties nigh on useless. Overwhelmed with emotion, we make poor choices and may do things to ourselves and others that we come to regret.

Owning our anger, and the underlying fear that usually drives it, articulating it, and where necessary verbally sharing it with others, can go a long way to taking back our control over it. Owning our anger and honestly expressing it liberates us from huge amounts of stress and bitterness. In the introduction to Chautauqua 6, I describe my own experience of the negative effects that disowning my anger caused within my own mind–body system.

At its most mature expression, the anger that passes through us may feel like an energy force for which we are merely the conduit. It is an intuitive expression of righteous, cleansing energy that serves the deepest values and expectations of society. It is a warrior energy in service of what is right and true. It is the human expression of the wrath of god; it is the wielding of Manjushri's sword, representing the noblest execution of discriminating wisdom.

That is the powerful message of this story, symbolised by the blossoming of the stunted tree. In the service of the community, the man transcends his shadow by owning his anger, and serves society by intuitively discerning and dealing with the malice of the assassin.

2.10 My computer is much too sophisticated for me. My guess is that I use only about ten per cent of the software wizardry available to me. That's my interpretation of this story. I spend so much time and energy being clever, sophisticated, and intellectually busy that I fail to see the simple and effective answers right under my nose. And I then end up astounded when the world reminds me it has rhythms and wisdom of its own.

2.11 A version of this adaptation of a Kabbalah story first appeared on the intranet of Standard Chartered Bank's Great Manager Programme in 2007. I had been invited to write a number of stories on key management themes over a twelve-month period. This story was one of the stories on the theme of sustainability. The introductory framework of the story went as follows:

A senior management team was struggling with another serious crisis. They brought in a consultant to give them guidance. 'Today's world is so complex,' they said, 'How do we know what are the right choices to get out of this mess?' The consultant looked at the group and replied, 'Forget success just for yourselves. The world is too complex for that. Success is only truly available when the whole community benefits. Seek the Third Win. Don't seek just a win for yourselves, but seek also a win for others, and a win for the wider context too. And if you want to achieve truly sustainable growth and wealth, then focus on building excellent relationships, sharing resources, and working together to achieve your key ambitions.'

'But how do we do that?'

'Observe more, listen more, and don't believe that you have all the answers. The answers we seek often lie with our clients, with junior members of our staff, and with all the resources with which are constantly surrounded.'

They still looked puzzled, so she told them a story ...

2.17 In February 2002 an article appeared in the *Harvard Business Review* by Heike Bruch and Sumantra Ghoshal entitled 'Beware the Busy Manager'. One of the biggest problems in large organisations is getting people to stop acting busy and to start using some quality thinking time before making important decisions; particularly when the decisions that are made are likely to have long-term consequences and ramifications. This story offers an antidote.

2.21 It is always useful to remind ourselves that the etymology of *enthusiasm* comes from the Greek, meaning 'possessed by God'. It is also useful to remind ourselves that our healing and our happiness can very much depend on the presence of this state within us too.

Chautauqua 3

3.3 I may be reading too much into this simple yet amusing anec-dote, but it brings the question of deep sustainability to my mind. Sustainability requires serious investment. Not only of money, but resources, intellect, values, attitude, perspective, and above all contextual awareness—as this Chinese story illu-strates.

One of the greatest obstacles to achieving successful and sustai-nable change is the wish of certain people to explore no further than simple cause and effect relationships when things go wrong or get difficult. These people tend to look for someone or something to blame for a problem. Reality is usually much more complex. To create sustainable change, the whole context needs to be considered, and the complex web of relationships between people, processes, and their environment needs to be explored as a systemic and dynamic whole.

3.7 Hundreds of years before integral, systems, and quantum theo-ries became fashionable in the West, the Sufis had their own ideas about systemic interconnectedness, as this unlikely tale illustrates. Buddhists have talked about Karma—the notion that all actions have consequences—for over two thousand years. So it can be useful to remind ourselves of the nature of systems and to enquire more frequently and more deeply about the possible future consequences of whatever actions we take.

3.14 This story reminds me very much of the power of Harrison Owen's *Open Space Technology*. OST is a fabulous format for engaging everyone in reaching collective problem space solu-tions in which the full resources of the whole community are brought to bear on the issues at hand. This story illustrates the inevitable messiness of full-on engagement with many different sections of a community, and also the great benefits that can be derived from doing so.

3.15 Micro-management can be the scourge of modern organisations. It is a failure to recognise that human beings, and the organisa-tions they create, are self-organising systems. Human beings are also naturally engineered to be creative, find solutions to challenges, and to have a built-in sense of order and structure.

Micro-management simply brings out the rebel in people as well as deep frustration.

Experts who have been promoted to managerial positions need to let go of their expertise and use their skills to coach their teams where necessary and to sponsor a space in which their people can learn and thrive.

Lars Kolind at Oticon took this idea to the edge and succeeded brilliantly. When individuals are encouraged to exercise their intelligence, creativity, and responsibility they tend to respond well. When leaders learn to sponsor and support arenas of activity in service of a shared vision things happen. When all the people in an organisation treat each other as adults we can move towards the realisation of what a twenty-first century business organisation could look like.

3.16   I really appreciate the simplicity of this story. It offers such a powerful insight, which is so often ignored in all relationships, whether personal or professional. People are not mind readers, so whenever you communicate do so with honesty and clarity.

3.17   The ability to work with and through paradox and contradiction are key qualities of post-conventional thinking and leadership. The importance of embracing contradictions is embodied in the idea of the apex of the triangle (discussed in the Prologue), in classical Chinese thought as yin–yang, and in many wisdom traditions.

The ability to embrace paradox is also a consequence of accepting and owning our shadow elements. Then we can truly recognise that apparent opposites are simply aspects of who we truly are: smart *and* stupid, wise *and* ignorant, magnificent *and* insignificant, good *and* evil, loving *and* fearful, masculine *and* feminine. The list is endless (*and* finite!).

Chautauqua 4

4.1   There is a Swahili proverb that says much the same: *Haraka haraka haina baraka* (More haste, less blessing).

4.5   Three themes that strongly stand out for me in the story are patience, perseverance, and stewardship. They are core elements of excellent leadership across many contexts, including business, teaching, and parenting. A project is not ready until it has developed wings of its own: it needs time to establish itself, it requires nurturing, and it requires protection. Projects, of course, come in many shapes and forms.

4.8   As described in the Sources section (above) this story is filleted from the many chapters about Atatürk in Louis de Berniere's excellent novel *Birds without Wings*. It is not meant to be an accurate historical portrayal but a sketch about qualities that enable success. Key among these are the importance of having honest conversations with self and others, taking into account that people are different and differently gifted, giving quality behavioural feedback to self and others, taking personal responsibility for whatever happens, sharing information freely, and recognising and owning one's personal limitations. Atatürk also recognises three clearly defined yet interrelated arenas of engagement: operations, tactics, and strategy. He also highly values taking the simplest possible route to achieve whatever is necessary.

4.12   This tragedy highlights the fundamental importance of recognising and valuing our own personal integrity and of trusting our own judgement and authority when those who are in positions of leadership let us down. David Whyte calls this quality of unconditional personal responsibility our 'Inner Captain' and it is a remarkably apposite description. Who else can steer our course but ourselves? How else can we maintain our true bearing without reference to our own moral compass? It is not unusual for people in positions of authority to let us down, and when this happens we must look to ourselves and be prepared to take full responsibility for whatever we do or fail to do.

At its best, the Inner Captain is the voice that says—whatever happens, and whoever caused it—I did it. Economic recession: I did it! Someone crashes into the back of my car while I wait at a red light: I did it!

Why? Because I chose to be there. I chose to put myself in harm's way. I know it's a difficult, dangerous world where things can go wrong. Some people are dishonest; car crashes happen. Once I stop being naive and start to take responsibility for whatever happens, I am liberated. I can let go of anger and unforgiveness, and move on with my life.

Or to put it another way: the only part of this world I have any direct influence over is myself. I do not have the power to change in any direct way what is outside of me. Therefore every time I blame or judge others for problems and difficulties, I make myself a victim. That's not smart; it imprisons me and makes me small. The antidote is simple: I did it!

Chautauqua 5

5.2   One of the easiest ways in which people, teams, and organisations get stuck is in failing to adapt to changing conditions. Rules and regulations, rituals and practices get set in stone as *the* way to do things. Very often there was—once upon a time—a very good reason for doing a certain thing in a certain way. But time moved on, circumstances changed. This simple story lightly mocks this stuckness syndrome. There is a similar story, 'The Tale of the Rogue Monkeys', in Nick Owen, *More Magic of Metaphor* (Story 21).

5.5   A version of this story appeared in the Great Manager Programme for Standard Chartered Bank. I used the following framing device to offer an interpretation of the story in an appropriate business context:

> Many businesses make the mistake of seeking out the perfect product, or the perfect client, or the perfect market. No such things exist. Sustainable success, that serves the long-term needs of the community as a whole, is the result not so much of doing the right things as of building the right relationships. It is open, respectful relationships that create truly productive and sustainable partnerships.
>
> The best, it is often said, is the enemy of the good enough. A business leader was becoming increasingly frustrated by the tendency of some of his senior managers to waste huge amounts of time and energy refining the perfect project or writing the perfect report. He argued that most people

didn't want perfection, just something that worked well enough for their needs. 'What percentage of the software on your computer do you actually use?' he would demand. But it can be hard to get experts to let go of old habits. Eventually he told an old story to make the point that perfection is ultimately unattainable and usually rebounds against those who seek it.

And the story of the Mullah's quest for the perfect bride followed.

5.9 It is usually a good idea to face up to and confront whatever pressing issues need to be addressed. Even if the choices are not easy or comfortable. Seeking to avoid tough choices and uncomfortable situations frequently results in them catching up with us anyway, leaving us without either integrity or self-possession.

5.11 This story offers a brief but chilling description of what occurs in societies when the rule of law has broken down, trust has evaporated, and malice runs amok. Sadly, this situation occurs in both developed and less developed societies and nations.

A Chinese saying goes like this:

If there is light in the soul,
There will be beauty in the person.
If there is beauty in the person,
There will be harmony in the house.
If there is harmony in the house,
There will be order in the nation.
If there is order in the nation,
There will be peace in the world.

When there is no light in the soul, whether of the wolf or his enemies, the manifestation of fear and maliciousness described in the story will be widespread. There will be discord in the house and in the nation. Everybody will spend their energies protecting themselves or denouncing others.

In the workplace or in a classroom, where there is a sense that security and safety are lacking, where social cohesion and any forms of trust are absent, where there is fear of exploitation, such attitudes will arise and make productive endeavour hard or impossible. Such situations also occur where political leadership in a nation has been destabilised, overthrown, or is abused.

The Chinese proverb points to a way forward. The antidotes are harmony, order, and peace. The need for a stable society in which a shared sense of justice prevails, and where individuals can fully contribute to the collective community, and the collective community can support each individual in their right to self-expression are foundational prerequisites for progress, peace, and prosperity.

5.16 Our busy monkey minds are forever overloading themselves by trying to do too many things at once. The beauty of the Disney Creativity Strategy, like Edward de Bono's Six Thinking Hats, is that it separates out our thinking into discrete elements.

Many successful people tend to use variations of this model. The key elements are that ideas are welcomed and validated no matter how off the wall they may at first appear to be. No initial editing or critiquing is permitted! This encourages openness and creativity and a respectful innovative culture. Secondly, all dreams ultimately have to be tested to see if they are doable, and *finally* subjected to rigorous but respectful critiquing. Then the original Dreams can be revisited so that they can be refined and actualised. Note: this takes discipline and time but the rewards are huge.

In any team, you can run 'experts' who are specialist Dreamers, Realists, or Critics. But it is perhaps useful to get everyone to play all three roles in turn. 'Let's now put on our Dreamer hats. OK, time for Realist hats,' and so on. The key thing is to separate the thinking so the different hats aren't all fighting for attention at the same time, a phenomenon not unknown in many family gatherings and business meetings!

Continuous improvement doesn't usually come from Eureka! or Aha! moments, but from the steady and incremental building up of better and better ideas and ways of working together.

Some suggestions for Dreamer questions:

- What's our vision?
- What could we do in an ideal world?
- What's my dream?
- If I could have it all, what would that look, sound, and feel like?

Every idea is permissible; the sky is the limit; resources are limitless.

Some suggestions for Realist questions:

- What are the steps and stages?
- What skills will be needed?
- How long will it take?
- Who are the right people?
- What budget do we have?

The Realists take the Dream and make it practical. The Dream is intact but it is now a scaled down Dream, yet still vivid and exciting. Above all, a plan now exists for the Dream's realisation.

Some suggestions for Critic questions:

- How do you propose to achieve this result with that much budget?
- Do you really believe that two-minute sequence will keep the audience entertained?
- What might be the public's response to that piece of political incorrectness?
- How do you propose to convince the Finance Director of the validity of these ideas?

The Critics ask the tough questions and respectfully challenge the validity of the proposals. The key is that they ask questions to the Dreamers and Realists; they do not make demotivating and judgemental statements. And they only critique the Dream and the Plan, never the Dreamers or the Realists.

Chautauqua 6

6.1 This story is the perfect antidote to both suffering and hubris: ideal for weathering an economic recession and many other setbacks and successes. The theme is found in many other traditions than Zen Buddhism; in the Old Testament the prophet speaks of seven years of feast followed by seven of famine. Everything is temporary and impermanent; there is nothing else but change.

The Greek Sophist Heraclitus famously observed that you can't step into the same river twice. In Anglo Saxon literature there is a short poem about a small bird that flies into a baronial hall: out of the dark into the bright intensity and energy of warriors feasting, singing, and drinking, and on out again into the darkness. Tolkien summed up the essence of this bleak view of life as:

> *Lif is læne;*
> *Eal scæced; leoht and lif somod.*
>
> Life is short;
> Everything hastens away; light and life together.
>
> J. R. R. Tolkien, *The Monsters and the Critics*

6.7 This is a tale of extraordinary richness. Both Allan B. Chinen and David Whyte have offered masterful interpretations in their books, which are not only complementary but also intriguingly different in terms of the different nuances they elicit. Both agree that it is a story that charts the journey from late youth to mature mid-life, and both agree that the central theme is the exploration of how the journey is beset by suffering, self-sacrifice, and absence from ourselves and those we love, until finally we come to realise that there are more mature ways of dealing with the existence of evil than through avoidance or confrontation.

I have no desire to go into the depth of interpretation offered by these two writers, but strongly urge those who may be interested to do so. But I would like to make some observations of my own.

The body on the threshold of the shop represents a realisation of passing from one stage of our life, youth, to the beginnings of the middle years. In our youth we find it nigh on impossible to recognise evil in ourselves—instead we project it onto others. And we are idealistic; we believe in our moral certitudes that we can change the world through battling against the ranged forces of evil—which are all *out there*.

The body on the threshold cannot be ignored, however, and rather than fight to defend his innocence, the shopkeeper takes to his heels. He begins a twenty-year absence from his home, symbolising the traditional male breadwinner's role in dedicating the main portion of his middle years to working to pay for the mortgage, school fees, pension, and whatever else may be required. Many men, and women too these days, sacrifice what their hearts desire to the practical requirements of financial survival.

Then too, the shopkeeper entering into Solomon's service reflects how so many of us enter a willing slavery to an employer, an organisation, an institution which we believe we can learn from, offer service to, and who in turn we believe will protect us, develop us, and we fervently hope fairly reward us.

But there comes a time when we long to reconnect to the dreams and passions of our former existence. And when this time comes, Solomon is keen to keep the shopkeeper on the straight and narrow. His advice is merely commonplace but above all it is intensely practical and guides the shopkeeper to come to terms with his own shadows, especially those of aging and evil.

The first piece of advice counsels the shopkeeper to put aside youthful dreams of dangerous exploration, or the lures perhaps of inappropriate romantic attachments, that many in mid-life may be tempted to pursue in order to deny their advancing years. Solomon's first piece of advice is to deepen experience not to widen it.

His second piece of advice is to counsel that we cannot change the world, only ourselves. The shopkeeper's experience in the cottage in the forest brings him face to face with two shadow aspects of himself. First he must recognise that evil exists in the world and his judgementalism will never eradicate it. He must learn to accept what is and to recognise that his first duty is to himself; his own self-preservation. Secondly, he needs to recognise his own feminine side, locked in the basement, the victim of his own masculine envy and jealousy. He must own and accept his own fear of the feminine.

Notice how this part of the narrative foreshadows the next. When he sees his wife embracing another man all his suppressed fear, anger, and jealousy is activated. The final advice of Solomon gives him time to come to terms with the evil that exists within himself, the judgements, the hot-headed unwillingness to find out the complexities that have come together to create this present situation.

As the shopkeeper enters a new phase of mature mid-life, fully embodying the three pieces of Solomon's wisdom he can fully own and take responsibility for his behaviours and actions. And in so doing he begins to liberate himself. The journey and the experiences he has had on the journey enable him to take control of his emotions through *reason*, and to fully engage with his *intuitive* side through the full acceptance of his shadow. Now he is free to accept himself *just as he is*.

There is also another way to interpret this story: not in terms of age but in terms of developmental psychology. Developmental psychology suggests that people may go through stages of increasing complexity as they grapple with changes in an increasingly complex exterior environment. As our old coping strategies no longer work in the new and changing conditions, we must seek more complex strategies from within to overcome these challenges. For more on this see Nick Owen, *More Magic of Metaphor*, and refer to the appropriate section in the bibliography for other works on this topic. Also, refer to Appendix B later in this book.

6.9 The metaphor of impermanence embedded in this story is extraordinarily powerful. I find it so easy to take everything in my life, including myself, for granted. Every day is a gift, every breath is a gift, every experience is a gift. In fact, even painful and unpleasant experiences are gifts; they are signs we are still alive, that things can always change for the better, and that life is the greatest gift of all. See also Story 6.12.

6.11 I couldn't have written this book four or five years ago. Then I would have been amazed if someone had told me that death could ever seem attractive and even desirable.

6.14 There are two things I particularly enjoy about this story. One is the symbolic arrangement of the doorways, each one embedded within the other, representing our journey through life as a constant invitation to deepen our experience. And as we do that we can begin to perceive ever more richness within our inner and outer lives—providing of course that we are willing to be open to this journey. The hidden doors of course are always there; we are just blind to them. We erect curtains of our own.

The second thing is the answer the man gives the monks on his return to the monastery after his years of questing. It is one of the simplest yet most perceptive insights I have come across as a description of our human condition.

Finally, the hidden doorways remind me of the notion of the gateless gate in Buddhism. Our busy mind constructs a gate between the rational, relative, marketplace mind and the awakened, absolute mind of the non-dual universe. No such gate exists.

In the Koran and the Bible this is expressed in the idea that it is easier for a camel to pass through the eye of a needle than a rich man to enter the Kingdom of Heaven. Busy mind, rational mind, human mind always gets in the way.

Chautauqua 7

7.5 All pathways lead to the same destination.

7.7 This story offers a real insight into how we construct the reality we perceive in our lives. It's all in our heads. We don't see the world the way it is; we see the world the way we think it is. This story laughs at our ridiculousness.

7.8 I found this information about termites in Margaret Wheatley's excellent article, 'The Irresistible Future of Organising' (available on her website). In it she explores the amazing shifts that can occur in our leadership and management strategies when we start to accept that each human being and every organisation is a self-organising system.

She puts forward a well-argued case that crisis management becomes self-perpetuating when leaders focus mainly on the micro-organising traditional practices of structure, process, and behaviour. This approach to leadership and management assumes that organisations and people are machines whose behaviours can be predicted and programmed. In the twenty-first century? Dream on.

A self-organising system, Wheatley suggests, requires a different three-pronged approach: (1) the development of corporate and personal *identity* which leads to shared vision and direction; (2) the sharing of *information* throughout the organisation which promotes flow and multidirectional communication; and (3) the building of excellent *relationships* throughout the organisation so that a culture of openness is engendered and each person feels sufficiently engaged to take personal responsibility for themselves and their actions.

Termites score on all three counts, and perhaps if more financial organisations had had this kind of transparency and openness the current financial crisis could have been avoided. Still *now* is always a great time to learn from our mistakes.

7.10   Many people profess to wishing they had more presence or charisma. The key to these qualities, it seems to me, is the ability to live in the present moment and the awareness to notice what is happening both within ourselves and in the outside environment. When we develop these abilities energy naturally seems to flow through us. We can feel more awake, more alert, and more imbued with direction and purpose, and seem so to others too.

The ability to live in the present moment, to be connected to our breath and body, to empty our mind of preconceptions so that we can truly notice what is, offers us one of the most direct passageways through the gateless gate.

7.11   This story reminds me of the power available to each of us when we take our passion and enthusiasm into whatever work it is that we do. I meet too many people working in organisations that have lost connection with their passion, who don't bring into their work that part of themselves that doesn't belong to the organisation, that part of themselves which has never been shackled or imprisoned, that part of us that knows how to say: Yes! Yes! Yes!

It is most noticeable when people approach mid-life. They are no longer driven by the desires to achieve and succeed they had when climbing the ladder and were desperately earning to pay the mortgage, the school fees, the pension. They no longer desire to serve the company from dawn to dusk, to take work home in the evenings and at weekends. They want to know: Who am I really? What am I here for?

Doubt and uncertainty assail them. They feel disconnected and fragmented; out of touch with the dreams and ideals they left behind so far back in their past. Like the Master Potter in the story, they need to let go of the old software that no longer serves them, and die to their past so they can be reborn to the authentic self that still faithfully awaits them in their future. Only then can they commit fully and freely to whatever it is they really want in the world.

And if you recognise an element of this in you, let me add one thing to Solomon's wisdom. Just as the Potter didn't consult his family, friends, or colleagues before making his choice it also makes sense for you not to rely too much on the consent of others. They will only resist you, for whatever movement you make will most likely disturb their comfortable sense of identity and they may not want to wake up from their sleep.

7.13 This story illuminates how it is so easy for us to imprison ourselves in comfort, assumptions, and illusions about ourselves and the world. Above all, our sense of identity is an illusion that ensnares us and keeps us pinioned. Maximus's example is a powerful wake-up call.

7.14 This essential concept of No-Self occurs in almost all spiritual pathways. In psychological terms we could say that the notion of *self* is simply a generalisation of all the different inner voices, sub-personalities, or I-positions. Wei Wu Wei has described this concept very elegantly in his book, *Ask The Awakened*.

7.15 This story is found in many traditions. It calls attention to the consequences that may occur when we lose touch with our non-dual or spiritual self. Some parts of our small self, particularly the ego and all its different voices, have a great desire and ambition to talk up their identity in order to make the small self feel big and important. They want to take over the running of the establishment. Other parts of the self sense there is something important behind the 'door' but fail to take ownership or responsibility for doing anything about it.

This story has a great deal of resonance with the Big Mind process which seeks the deep integration of our dual and non-dual selves. If the Master, our deeply wise and aware spiritual self, is absent then the many other marketplace selves will squabble with each other for precedence, serving their own particular purposes rather than the needs of the whole system. For a concise explanation and description of the Big Mind process see Appendix A.

7.17   This beautiful Sufi story speaks for itself. And I was intrigued to notice that when I sorted the stories in this book by theme, this story fitted more themes than any other story—by far.

7.18   Rumi. One of the few voices who consistently and brilliantly succeeds in conveying the non-dual in words and images. I'll meet you in that meadow!

Bibliography

Ansari, Shaykh Taner. *What About My Wood!* Ansari Publications, 2006.

Baldwin, Jill and Williams, Hank. *Active Learning: A Trainer's Guide.* Oxford: Blackwell, 1988.

Beck, Don E. and Cowan, Christopher. *Spiral Dynamics: Mastering Values, Leadership, and Change.* Oxford and Cambridge, MA: Blackwell, 1996.

Bodian, Stephan. *Meditation for Dummies.* Hoboken, NJ: Wiley, 2006.

Bohm, David. *Wholeness and the Implicate Order.* London and New York: Art Paperbacks, 1980.

Bonder, Rabbi Nilton. *Yiddishe Kop: Creative Problem Solving in Jewish Learning, Lore and Humor.* Boston, MA: Shambhala, 1999.

Bruch, Heike and Ghoshal, Sumantra. 'Beware the Busy Manager,' *Harvard Business Review* 80 (2), Feb. 2002: 62–69.

Campbell, Joseph. *The Hero with a Thousand Faces.* Fontana, 1993.

Carter, Stephen. *The Road to Audacity: Being Adventurous in Life and Work.* Basingstoke: Macmillan, 2003.

Casteneda, Carlos. *Journey to Ixtlan.* London: Penguin, 1974.

——— *Tales of Power.* London: Penguin, 1976.

Charvet, Shelle Rose. *Words That Change Minds: Mastering the Language of Influence.* Dubuque, IA: Kendall/Hunt, 1997.

Chatterjee, Debjani. *The Elephant Headed God and Other Hindu Tales.* Cambridge: Lutterworth, 1989.

——— *Sufi Stories from around the World.* London: Soma, 1999.

Chinen, Allan B. *Once Upon a Midlife.* New York: Putnam, 1992.

Coelho, Paulo. *The Alchemist.* London: HarperCollins, 1993.

——— *The Pilgrimage.* London: HarperCollins 1997.

Collins, Jim. *Good to Great.* London: Random House, 2001.

Csikszentmihalyi, Mihaly. *Flow: The Psychology of Optimal Experience.* New York: HarperCollins, 1990.

de Bernieres, Louis. *Birds without Wings.* New York: Vintage, 2005.

de Bono, Edward. *Six Thinking Hats.* Harmondsworth: Penguin, 2000.

de Mello, Anthony S. J. *Awareness.* London and New York: HarperCollins, 1990.

Deering, Anne, Dilts, Robert, and Russell, Julian. *Alpha Leadership: Tools for Business Leaders Who Want More from Life.* Chichester: Wiley, 2002.

Denning, Stephen. *The Leader's Guide to Storytelling.* San Francisco, CA: Jossey-Bass, 2005.

Dilts, Robert. *Strategies of Genius,* Vol. 1. Capitola, CA: Meta Publications, 1995.

Ehrenberg, Victor. *From Solon to Socrates.* London: Methuen, 1968.

Eisler, Riane. *The Chalice and the Blade.* New York: HarperCollins, 1998.

Erickson, Milton H. *My Voice Will Go With You.* New York: Norton, 1991.

Forest, Heather. *Wisdom Tales from Around the World.* Little Rock, AR: August House, 2008.

Forstater, Mark. *The Spiritual Teachings of the Tao.* London: Hodder & Stoughton, 2001.

Gardner, Howard. *Frames of Mind: The Theory of Multiple Intelligences.* New York: Basic Books, 1993.

Gladwell, Malcolm. *Blink: The Power of Thinking without Thinking.* Harmondsworth: Allen Lane, 2005.

Goffee, Rob and Jones, Gareth. *Why Should Anyone Want to be Led by YOU?* Boston, MA: Harvard Business School, 2006.

Goleman, Daniel. *Emotional Intelligence: Why it Can Matter More than IQ.* London: Bloomsbury, 1996.

Gray, John. *Straw Dogs.* London: Granta, 2002.

Harvey, Andrew and Hanut, Eryk. *Perfume of the Desert: Inspirations from Sufi Wisdom.* Portland, OR: Metamorphous, 1999.

Hawkins, Peter. *The Wise Fool's Guide to Leadership.* Ropley: John Hunt, 2005.

Heaney, Seamus (tr.). *Beowulf.* London: Faber & Faber, 1999.

Jensen, Eric. *The Learning Brain.* San Diego, CA: Turning Point, 1994.

Johnstone, Keith. *Impro: Improvisation and the Theatre*. London: Methuen, 2007.

Kauffman, Stuart A. *At Home in the Universe: The Search for the Laws of Self-Organisation*. Oxford: Oxford University Press, 1995.

—— *Re-inventing the Sacred: A New View of Science, Reason and Religion*. New York: Basic Books, 2008.

Kegan, Robert. *The Evolving Self: Problem and Process in Human Development*. Cambridge, MA: Harvard University Press, 1982.

—— *In Over Our Heads*. Cambridge, MA: Harvard University Press, 1994.

—— and Lahey, Lisa. *How the Way We Talk Can Change the Way We Work*. San Francisco, CA: Jossey-Bass, 2003.

Kim, W. Chan and Mauborgne, Renee. *Blue Ocean Strategy*. Boston, MA: Harvard Business School, 2005.

Laborde, Genie Z. *Influencing with Integrity*. Carmarthen: Crown House, 1998.

Lakoff, George and Johnson, Mark. *Metaphors We Live By*. Chicago, IL: University of Chicago Press, 1980.

Lawley, James and Tompkins, Penny. *Metaphors in Mind*. London: Developing Company, 2000.

Lynch, Dudley and Kordis, Paul K. *Strategy of the Dolphin*. London: Random House, 1988.

Maguire, Jack. *The Power of Personal Storytelling*. New York: Putnam, 1998.

Merzel, Dennis Genpo. *The Path of the Human Being*. Boston, MA: Shambhala, 2005.

—— *Big Mind, Big Heart: Finding Your Way*. Salt Lake City, UT: Big Mind Publishing, 2007.

O'Connor, Joseph. *NLP Workbook*. London: HarperCollins, 2001.

Owen, Harrison. *Open Space Technology: A User's Guide*. San Francisco, CA: Berrett-Koehler, 1997.

Owen, Nick. *The Magic of Metaphor: 77 Stories for Teachers, Trainers and Thinkers*. Carmarthen: Crown House, 2001.

Owen, Nick. *More Magic of Metaphor: Stories for Leaders, Influencers and Motivators.* Carmarthen: Crown House, 2004.

Pearson, Carol S. *Awakening the Heroes Within.* New York: HarperCollins, 1991.

Peseschkian, Nossrat. *Oriental Stories as Tools in Psychotherapy.* New Delhi: Sterling, 1982.

Pinkola Estés, Clarissa. *Women Who Run with the Wolves.* London: Rider, 1993.

Pirsig, Robert M. *Zen and the Art of Motorcycle Maintenance.* London: Bodley Head, 1974.

———— *Lila: An Inquiry into Morals.* London: Bantam, 1991.

Planck, Max and Murphy, James. *Where is Science Going?* New York: Norton, 1932.

Rehman, Rachel Naomi. *Kitchen Table Wisdom.* London: Macmillan, 1996.

Riso, Don Richard and Hudson, Russ. *The Wisdom of the Enneagram.* New York: Bantam, 1999.

Roach, Michael Geshe. *The Diamond Cutter: The Buddha on Managing Your Business and Your Life.* New York: Doubleday, 2000.

Rooke, David and Torbert, William R. 'Seven Transformations of Leadership', *Harvard Business Review* 83 (4), April 2005: 66–76.

Rose, Colin and Nichol, Malcolm J. *Accelerated Learning for the 21st Century.* London: Piatkus, 1997.

Rumi, Jalal ad-Din. *The Essential Rumi.* New York: HarperCollins, 1994.

———— *Whispers of the Beloved.* London: Thorsons, 1999.

———— *Selected Poems.* London: Penguin, 2004.

Sarno, John E. *Healing Back Pain.* New York: Warner, 1991.

Scott Peck, M. *The Road Less Travelled.* New York: Simon & Schuster, 1978.

Senge, Peter, Scharmer, C. Otto, Jaworski, Joseph, and Flowers, Betty Sue. *Presence: Exploring Profound Change in People, Organizations, and Society.* London: Nicholas Brealey, 2005.

Senge, Peter M. *The Fifth Discipline.* London: Random House, 1990.

Shah, Idries. *Tales of the Dervishes.* New York: Dutton, 1967.

———*Thinkers of the East.* London: Octagon, 1971.

——— *The Way of the Sufi.* London: Penguin, 1974.

——— *The Pleasantries of the Incredible Mulla Nasrudin.* London: Penguin, 1993.

Shlain, Leonard. *The Alphabet versus the Goddess: The Conflict between Word and Image.* London: Penguin, 1998.

Simmons, Annette. *The Story Factor.* Cambridge, MA: Perseus, 2001.

Spencer, Sabina. *The Heart of Leadership.* London: Rider, 2004.

——— and Adams, John D. *Life Changes: A Guide to the Seven Stages of Personal Growth.* New York: Paraview, 2002.

Stone, Hal and Stone, Sidra. *Embracing Our Selves: Voice Dialogue Manual.* Novato, CA: Nataraj, 1989.

Sullivan, Wendy and Rees, Judy. *Clean Language: Revealing Metaphors and Opening Minds.* Carmarthen: Crown House, 2008.

Sun Tzu. *The Art of War,* tr. Samuel B. Griffith. Oxford: Oxford University Press, 1963.

Tolkien, J. R. R. *The Lord of the Rings.* London: Allen & Unwin, 1954.

——— *The Monsters and the Critics and Other Essays.* London: George Allen & Unwin, 1983.

Tolle, Eckhart. *The Power of Now.* London: Hodder & Stoughton, 2001.

Torbert, William. *Action Inquiry: The Secret of Timely and Transforming Leadership.* San Francisco, CA: Berrett-Koehler, 2004.

Trompenaars, Fons and Hampden-Turner, Charles. *Riding the Waves of Culture.* London: Nicholas Brealey, 1997.

Twigger, Robert. *Angry White Pyjamas.* London: Orion, 1997.

——— *Big Snake.* London: Victor Gollancz, 1999.

Wagoner, David. *Traveling Light: Collected and New Poems.* Champaign, IL: University of Illinois Press, 1999.

Wei Wu Wei. *Ask the Enlightened: The Negative Way.* Boulder, CO: Sentient Publications, 2002.

Wheatley, Margaret. *Leadership and the New Science: Discovering Order in a Chaotic World.* San Francisco, CA: Berrett-Koehler, 1999.

Wheatley, Margaret and Kellner-Rogers, Myron. 'The Irresistible Future of Organising', available at www.margaretwheatley.com

Whyte, David. *The Heart Aroused.* New York: Doubleday, 1994.

———— *The House of Belonging.* Langley, WA: Many Rivers, 1996.

———— *Crossing the Unknown Sea.* London and New York: Penguin, 2001.

Wilber, Ken. *Integral Psychology: Consciousness, Spirit, Psychology, Therapy.* Boston, MA: Shambhala, 2000.

———— *A Theory of Everything.* Boston, MA: Shambhala, 2001.

Wineman, Aryeh. *Ethical Tales from the Kabbalah.* Philadelphia, PA: Jewish Publication Society, 1999.

Zander, Rosamund and Zander, Ben. *The Art of Possibility.* London: Penguin, 2000.

Useful websites:
www.101zenstories/com
www.haqq.com.au/~salam
www.katinkahesselink.net
www.margaretwheatley.com
www.rider.edu/suler/zenstory
www.soulwise.net/99adm00.htm
www.spiritualinquiry.com
www.sufism.org/society/stories
www.tzfat-kabbalah.org
www.zensufi.com

About the Author

Nick Owen is an experienced trainer, consultant, and coach. He has also enjoyed successful careers as a professional actor and theatre director, radio and print journalist, writer and storyteller. He combines work in the corporate and professional sectors with work in the arts and education, bringing a broad range of creative and innovative perspectives to the work at hand.

As well as working in the UK with many top FTSE organisations, he has worked internationally across a wide variety of contexts. His work ranges from organisational and professional development across Europe in large corporations and SMEs to change work with some of the poorest and most disadvantaged communities in Africa and South-East Asia.

He is the author of two bestselling books on creativity, personal development, and leadership, an associate at the de Baak Management Centrum in the Netherlands, and has been a Visiting Professor at Insead/Cedep Business School in France. He is an NLP Trainer and Master Practitioner, holds qualifications in Reversal Theory, Time Line Therapy, and Spiral Dynamics, and is a certified practitioner of the Harthill Leadership Development Framework. He is Director of Nick Owen Associates Ltd, London.

About Nick Owen Associates Ltd

Nick Owen Associates Ltd focuses on discovering and developing leadership potential at every level of an organisation and enhancing the necessary communication, awareness, and relationship skills which support that. To this end they offer hands-on programmes that combine their knowledge of what the workplace demands with a sensitivity to what each individual may need for the next stage of his or her development.

They aim to deliver life-enhancing as well as skills-enhancing programmes. What makes them different from most other providers is that they combine hard-edged research and analysis from the worlds of applied and developmental psychology with the very best models from the performing and creative arts. The resulting blend is engagingly experiential, communicative, and hands-on while underpinned by disciplined rigour and structure. Their programmes are relevant, authoritative, engaging, and great fun. Above all, they build a framework for sustainable change, deeper awareness of self and other, and immediate benefits for the workplace.

Typical programmes include:

- Mindful leadership
- Professional and personal development for leaders and high flyers
- Influencing beyond boundaries
- Working with archetypes: exploring the natural patterns of personal and professional leadership
- Business storytelling and organisational narrative: the art of effective corporate and professional persuasion
- Credibility, mastery, and professional communication skills
- Building sustainable and compelling professional relationships
- Coaching skills for managers
- One-to-one executive coaching.

Every programme they run is individually tailored for their clients.

For more information contact:

nick@nickowen.net
info@nickowen.net

Acknowledgements

This book is the product of my interaction with many people, many ideas, many books, and many stories over many years. It reflects where I am placing attention in my life as I come to the completion of this manuscript. I wasn't ready to write this book a year or two ago; I was in a different space. Tomorrow I'll probably be framing my thoughts and intuitions in different ways again. Yet there is a flow, a continuity that holds all together and that is the pathway along which I've been travelling in the company of so much inspiration from so many others, alive and dead.

I'd like to thank those who have read and offered their insightful comments on my manuscript: Elaine Barker, Kamie Buddemeier, Mark Esterman, Cilian Fennel, Eleonora Gilbert, Simon Heale, Bruce Lambson, and Pete Lawry.

I owe a particular debt of gratitude to those whose personal contributions, stories, and assistance with other matters have found their way onto these pages. I hope they will feel that I have done sufficient justice to their generosity: Rick Cooper, Henri Corduroy du Tiers, Rory Deane, Cilian Fennel, Jonathan Geard-Beney, Anthony Gibson, Kilian Gilbert, Pete Lawry, Robert Twigger, and Martin Woods.

I don't often get a chance to state publicly my wholehearted appreciation of those whose creativity and genius, or support and love, has brought joy, insight, and clarity to my own awareness and personal development over many years. So my deep gratitude to: Chinua Achebe, J. S. Bach, Amilcar Cabral, Miles Davis, Franz Fanon, Claudia Ferradas, Paolo Freire, Jan Garbarek, Eleonora Gilbert, Hermann Hesse, Keith Johnstone, Pete Lawry, Gabriel García Márquez, Anthony de Mello, Sofija Mitreva, Mullah Nasruddin, Dave Pammenter, Robert Pirsig, Jalal ad-Din Rumi, Franz Schubert, William Shakespeare, Sun Tzu, Firma Caccam Viray, and David Whyte. There are of course countless others; my thanks to them too.

Many teachers have supported my learning over the years. I cannot mention all of them, but to these a special thanks: Chris

Cowan, Sheelagh Deller, Robert Dilts, Pete Lawry, Judith de Lozier, Sandra Maitri, Joseph O'Connor, Mario Rinvolucri, Genpo Roshi, Ted Stead, and Colin Turner.

Certain places have particular significance and energy for me. One meaning of *genius* is 'the spirit of the place'. So my thanks to the spirits of the following places at which this book emerged: Cairo, Corney Reach, Lane End, the Sahara Desert, and Supetar on the island of Brac.

My deep thanks too to all the team at Crown House Publishing. They may not be the biggest publisher in the world but they do have a passion and enthusiasm that makes it an absolute delight to work with them.

Finally I'd like to thank my mother, Noreen Jones, who was the first to introduce me to the power and imaginative invention of story and narrative. As I lay tucked up in my childhood bed anticipating the unknown journey into darkest night, hers was the voice that smoothed the transition.

Praise for *The Salmon of Knowledge*

This book elegantly typifies a theme in Nick Owen's work of not attempting to enforce change on others. Instead it mainly teaches through metaphor and story so that each reader can find deep meaning and significance for themselves. The use of metaphor enables people to access those hard-to-describe aspects of all human experience such as paradox, multiple perspectives and polarities, and to recognise how these influence decisions, choices, fears and desires. This kind of 'inside' knowing can create the conditions for our next developmental step and is self-learning at its finest. We heartily recommend this book.

Penny Tompkins and James Lawley, authors of *Metaphors in Mind: Transformation through Symbolic Modelling*

This is a superb book from Nick Owen; it's like no other book I have ever read. If the reader is ready, the stories and the insights from Nick will take them on a journey that holds a mirror to the genius, naivety and potential of the human spirit. For the mind that is open a gift of true knowledge and learning awaits within these pages.

Alex Maw, Assistant Director of Public Health, North East Lincolnshire Care Trust Plus

Nick Owen, in his wonderful book *The Salmon of Knowledge*, uses the power of 'story' to share the wisdom of ages in a language that has meaning and relevance in today's reality. It is full of rich metaphors that allow the reader to challenge deeply held assumptions, and learn how to live more comfortably in a world of polarity and paradox. Nick provides us with recipes of simplicity for dealing with ever increasing levels of complexity!

Sabina Spencer PhD, author of *The Heart of Leadership: Unlock your Inner Wisdom and Inspire Others*

Another tour de force by life explorer Nick Owen, one of the most wide ranging and eclectic of cutting edge theorists and a man with a real eye for brilliant stories of more than one dimension.

Robert Twigger, British explorer, and award-winning author of *Angry White Pyjamas* and *Real Men Eat Puffer Fish*

A bubbling stream of stories to refresh any traveller on a personal development journey.
Nick Owen cleverly combines the variety of diverse spiritual and storytelling traditions—ancient and modern—with universal human themes such as stuckness, fear, life direction, relationships and self-knowledge. A book to dip into, again and again.

Judy Rees, co-author of *Clean Language: Revealing Metaphors and Opening Minds*

The Salmon of Knowledge is the perfect book for these uncertain times. Whether you need a practical guide, creative inspiration or a philosophical companion, it's all here. We're going to have to define a new map of the world of business and Nick's stories give clues and inspiration of how we might find our way. Are you sitting comfortably? Then begin the journey of *The Salmon of Knowledge*.

Alex McKie, The Next Step

Nick Owen is a master of storytelling and metaphor. He inspires us to reflection and fresh discovery, particularly about ourselves. He invites us to wrestle with paradox—or transcend it. For example, in an opening story about a man digging a well to find water, the lessons he offers includes a series of do's and don'ts, including, 'Advice is cheap and often unreliable.' I have to believe he also appreciates such irony. By drawing on the many rich wisdom traditions in the world, he even subtly offers a path to the discovery of our connections with each other—and with our often separated and disjointed ways of knowing and meaning making. Through his narratives he joins science and spirit, the individual with her community, the perspectives of self and society. He links us to our enduring cultures and the brevity of our own existence. And he challenges us to use his work to help us reshape our perspectives to engage the many aspects of life revealed to us. This is a book to which I can return again and again for both solace in the face of life's challenges and stimulus to embrace the richness of life and living.

Russ Volckmann, PhD; publisher and editor, *Integral Leadership Review*

Are we much more than the stories we tell of ourselves? And do not the stories we hear make, shape, or break us? In which case we should choose our stories well. Nick Owen's subtle and subversive retellings open a world of possibility for personal change and adventurous exploration.

Steve Carter, psychologist, consultant and author of *The Road To Audacity*

It took quite a while to read *The Salmon of Knowledge*: each story begged to be reflected on and learnt from—and there are a lot of stories!

This book of bite-sized stories, anecdotes and metaphors provides a wealth of material for self-reflection, leading to deep insights. You are sure to know yourself better long before you finish the book. The stories explore such universals as the shadow side, letting go, presence, mastery, and leadership, and entice you to step back from day-to-day life, take stock and return with more clarity about who you are, what is important and how to proceed.

Wendy Sullivan, co-author of *Clean Language: Revealing Metaphors and Opening Minds*

This little book is full of treasure; the kind of treasure that the folds of the earth and the folds of man's mind have protected and yet searched for, for countless centuries. This book seeks to unpick the lock of fable, story and folklore. It saviours the beauty, magic, and depth of the human discourse with itself, through the happening of life. It is a remarkable book that whispers of infinity and eternal life. Take for example, the few simple words on *separate self* and *extended self*. Nick manages to treat the most esoteric and mystical aspects of human life with a wonderful depth and reality; he helps us name 'it', name that which eludes us. He makes the coin of man with its persistent two-sidedness finally stop hankering with the pursuit of what is not obtainable and settle, finally knowing itself as rare, rare metal. I loved this book, it is full of wisdom. It brought me joy, and quiet illumination; may it lighten your way.

Adrian Machon, Director, Executive and Leadership Development, Corporate Leadership and Organisation Development, GSK Pharmaceutical Company

From my point of view, being a professional storyteller for almost thirty years, I thought that I had seen it all, read it all, and heard it all. But with great happiness

I found that Nick's stories and examples could both move and surprise me. And in his bouquet of flowers there are samples that I will ask if I may 'gently steal'. Both for my personal purpose and eventually to share with a future audience. May I Nick?

Anders Granström, actor and storyteller, member of the Swedish Actors Association

This is a book full of wonderful stories and deep insights which can be used by anyone who wants to inspire themselves and others. It gently, yet profoundly, challenges us to explore more deeply our relationship with ourselves and with the world: enabling us to become more insightful, resourceful, and creative. It is easy and compelling to read. I read it from cover to cover in a few hours. At the same time you can dip in and out of it to find what you are looking for since it is clearly and simply set out. The stories in themselves are wonderful and would be powerful enough on their own. The way Nick has grouped them and framed them with personal and honest commentaries deepens and enriches them enormously. This is a wonderful and generous book that, like the many stories it contains, is powerful and engaging.

Honest, generous and thought-provoking.

Barbara Houseman, voice, acting, and communication coach

Nick Owen has done us a favour. This generous book is essential for anyone who wonders why great stories survive, why we tell them, and how we can use them to create greater understanding of the world we live in.

Cilian Fennell, media consultant and TV producer

In this information-overloaded, mass mediated world, we resonate not with data but stories.

A collector of the world's stories in the Joseph Campbell tradition, Nick Owen has assembled a treasury of the world's great wisdom tales that delight, inspire, provoke, and awaken the reader.

Retold without a trace of folksiness, these tales engage us directly across the centuries, illuminating the dilemmas and paradoxes we often feel are new and unique to us; they leave us feeling 'how did the storyteller know this about me or my organisation?'

Like a thoughtful curator Nick has shaped the collection into powerfully relevant themes which help direct our attention to the most illuminating tales. And make real use of them. Nick's easy-going style makes it easy to browse or immerse yourself.

Highly recommended whether you want to apply this wisdom to yourself or offer it to clients.

David Pearl, creative coach to senior business leaders, CEO, David Pearl Group

Nick Owen's latest book of stories brings together an eclectic international collection of tales ancient and modern, secular and non-secular. Some are familiar, others not so, yet, as with all good stories, they speak to themes we can recognise. Of course, that is the point. The stories here will challenge, amuse, entertain, and stretch, enabling the reader to explore him or herself and potentially gain a new perspective. Certainly reading these stories left me feeling refreshed and ready to look at the world differently. They provoked a few 'ah-ha' moments and initiated possibilities. Equally interesting is Nick's own story, partly about the genesis of the book and partly about things/situations/ideas which have influenced him and hence the book, which is interwoven into the sections and towards the end of the book.

Nick has organised the stories according to seven sections or Chautauquas and four key themes. These classifications have provided a framework for Nick's commentary—which sometimes seems a little didactic. You might choose to overlook the commentary and dive straight into the stories themselves taking out whatever they provoke in you or for you. However, for many, the commentary will prove useful at some point as it provides a guide to stories for certain situations and aids interpretation.

The book works well on a number of levels—for the individual looking for inspiration and stimulation as well as for professionals looking for stories to illustrate/aid their own work. For me, as an executive coach and trainer, the book will be a valuable source of stories to dip into. Taken as a whole the book also provides an informed look into the way stories are constructed and have, throughout history, helped us examine, and make sense of, ourselves and the world around us.

Fiona Eldridge, director of The Coaching and Communication Centre, co-author of *The Seven Steps of Effective Executive Coaching*

Nick really has a unique talent for finding and putting in a wider context some fascinating and pertinent stores. In these times of growing confusion in where we are heading as individuals, and also collectively as the human race, this book can indeed provide us all with some valuable material for re-evaluation, reflection, and inspiration. Sometimes we all need to sit down and look deeply before heading off again.

Iain McNay, conscious.tv

This work is amazing. It embodies the capacity to mirror wholeness. The reader can choose to see and interpret each reflection. As a physician, my focus in medical practice is on wholeness and its relationship to healing. Nick Owen provides the reader with multifaceted reflections of wholeness. This is a tool that can facilitate awareness as healing in our often fragmented lives.

Kamilla Buddemeier MD

All it takes are six little words to catch and hold an individual's attention: 'Let me tell you a story.'

No matter our age, from infant to nonagenarian, the thought of hearing or telling a story acts at the deepest level of our neural structures and prepares us for a shift in consciousness—sometimes slight, sometimes profound. Telling and listening to stories are acts that define and distinguish us from most of the animal kingdom. Our stories reflect our humanity and our sense of being. Without stories, we would not be sitting at the current pinnacle of our development.

Nobody understands this better than Nick Owen. A master storyteller in his own right, he seeks out stories and records them in his own inimitable style, sometimes remaining true to the original text, other times tweaking them to ensure that they resonate with a modern listener or reader. More importantly, his finely tuned radar is ever watchful for the stories that evolve out of everyday happenings in his life and in the lives of those that he interacts with. Like the Maggid, the travelling storyteller of Jewish Chassidic times, he captures these stories without any purpose or intent other than knowing that they are gifts that he will be able to use at some future point in time.

Nick understands better than most that stories are the most powerful of the tools available to him in his life's work of helping individuals and organisations transform themselves. In *The Salmon of Knowledge*, he has brought together another fabulous collection of short stories that anybody who is serious about transforming their lives, workplaces, families, communities, or even the world should not be without. Some are old friends that we welcome back warmly, others are new or twists on a theme that take us, even momentarily, to some new place of thinking; a place where things will be different because that story is now part of our story.

Yet, if we are to make real change and real transformation we need to overcome a malaise that is upon us. In a world dominated by rational thinking, our stories strive to be factual with a mechanistic purpose and intent from the teller to the listener/reader. Important as rational thinking is, it pales into insignificance compared to the potential that can be unlocked by moving individuals into a post-rational consciousness. To achieve this through stories requires that we learn how to unpack the stories, to read between the lines to understand the intentions and wisdom that exist at multiple levels of consciousness.

The second gift that the *Salmon* delivers to us is a framework to help individuals to unpack the stories presented not only in the book but also in their everyday life. Enjoy the stories in this book by all means, but more importantly take the framework offered and start using it to view life differently. Adapt it, modify it, extend it, throw away parts that don't work for you, in short make it your own. If you follow this path, you will notice that your stories grow richer, at the same time you will start to see greater depth in all the stories of those around you.

As Heraclitus said, 'A man can never step into the same river twice—for it is never the same river, and he is not the same man.' Similarly, with Nick Owen's assistance and the Salmon's Knowledge, you will never step into the same story twice. And that, my friends, can only be for the better.

Keith Bellamy, independent futurist

This splendid book is an invaluable tool with powerful insights and stories that enlighten and entertain the reader—written with great wisdom, humour, and love.

Leah Conway, managing director, 4humanKIND

In 2001 Nick Owen brought out *The Magic of Metaphor* with Crown House Publishing and three years later *More Magic of Metaphor*. This year, 2009, sees Nick offering us *The Salmon of Knowledge* and to quote his own words 'one hundred stories on the themes of wholeness, integration, connection, awareness, oneness, wakefulness ...'

Nick is a teacher, educator, and business trainer and uses metaphor and stories in his day-to-day work. My feeling is that his voice has changed over the nine years that these three books have taken to produce. The nimble-footed, brilliant and, yes, partly narcissistic younger man has given way to the Nick of today whose voice in *The Salmon of Knowledge* is deeper, more vibrant and I feel that in this last book, much older in the best sense of the word.

Somehow Nick seems to have found the right voice for retelling these wisdom tales from deep within them and I think I fully understand what he means when he writes: 'wisdom stories offer us a remote vantage point from which to observe, evaluate, and engage with the world of human interaction'.

Enjoy his deep, whole, and vibrant voice.

Mario Rinvolucri, colleague and fellow storyteller

I've found I can always trust that the stories that Nick shares with me—interweaves and situates for me—will reach into those hidden and transformative places that my rational mind tries in vain to attain. He's repaid that faith again with this latest treasure trove.

Matthew Kalman, MA, FRSA, founder of London Integral Circle and founder member of the Integral Institute

With *The Salmon of Knowledge*, Nick Owen gently compels us to explore our life and self with a series of fascinating and intriguing stories. He skilfully guides us to realise grander and grander perspectives on ever deepening satisfaction and by doing so we release a cacophony of as yet unknown potentials.

Mick Quinn and Debora Prieto, husband–wife team teaching conscious evolution and awakening potential

A wake-up call, an opportunity to stop, to consider and evaluate how we truly 'be' delivered through a series of insightful, timeless, and often humorous stories, anecdotes, and observations with hints of Nick's own journey makes *The Salmon of Knowledge* a compelling reading both in its entirety or as a coaching, leadership development, and personal development aide.

Richard Coulthwaite, finance director, Underwriting, Brit Insurance

Through story, Nick engagingly sets out different angles on how we choose to live; whether we abide to a set of learned rules or whether we select to acknowledge, embrace, and reach beyond our confines and so experience more of *ourselves*. I enjoyed his fables and legends as they feel eternal—their wisdom reaches far back into our history and continues to make sense today. *The Salmon of Knowledge* is an enticing read; it reminds us that even if we are dealing with issues like cosmic consciousness we can remain childlike in our delight in learning from mystery and lore.

Elaine Herdman-Barker, Harthill associate and independent coach for leaders in organisation and consulting

The old and new truth—*if you wish to know God, the Buddha, True Nature or Truth—first you must study yourself*—speaks to us all, especially those of us in the 'helping' professions who seek to understand others' emotional tribulations.

Through his stories, Work, Life, the Dark Shadow, and Oneself are all explored with a linking text that is like a conversation and a narrative that helps us make meaning from and link with profound, powerful and affecting themes.

The stories serve to remind us of our vulnerability—our all + one + ness that is the core of our links to both earth and heaven. We learn again of our spiritual quest through the many masters who teach us what we (somehow) feel we already know, but lose touch with in the 'bisignis' of life.

There is real richness in the excellent and illuminating stories from a huge variety of sources and different belief systems, past, present, mythic, psychological, literary, and personal to the author—slaying internal dragons. Story 5.13 is truly helpful and thought-provoking—how profoundly we must own our own demons, and Story 7.7 is a particular favourite of mine.

Angy Man, Dip. Counselling (Roehampton), Master of Psychodynamic Practice, Oxon, MBACP

Other Books by Nick Owen

The Magic of Metaphor: 77 Stories for Teachers, Trainers and Thinkers
(Carmarthen: Crown House, 2001)

The Magic of Metaphor presents a collection of stories designed to engage, inspire, and transform the listener and the reader. Some of the stories motivate, some are spiritual, and some provide strategies for excellence. All promote positive feelings, encouraging confidence, direction, and vision.

Containing sixteen suggestions for effective storytelling, advice on organisation, style, and storytelling skills, and a selection of seventy-seven stories that can be adapted and developed, *The Magic of Metaphor* is an inspirational sourcebook for counsellors, health workers, psychologists, professional speakers, managers, leaders, and NLP practitioners, as well as for teachers, trainers, and therapists.

The Magic of Metaphor is recommended reading in many institutions and organisations around the world and has been translated into seven languages including Russian, Chinese, Spanish, and Italian.

More Magic of Metaphor: Stories for Leaders, Influencers and Motivators
(Carmarthen: Crown House, 2004)

More Magic of Metaphor explores the notion of leadership in its widest sense. Whether you lead in business, education, coaching, sports, health, parenting, or any other context this book offers insights into the many aspects of this complex, fascinating, and demanding role that we are all, from time to time, called upon to fulfil.

Containing over sixty stories from a wide range of traditions and eras, the book explores them in the context of two great contemporary models for understanding ourselves and others with deeper awareness and compassion. Ken Wilber's Integral 4-Quadrant 'Theory of Everything' model maps out the four great territories in which human beings operate and demonstrates the importance of bringing them together in holistic and integral ways. The Spiral Dynamics model offers a profound and elegant way to make sense of how people think, how they are motivated, what kind of leaders they prefer, how they learn, how they change, and how development and transformation occur in individuals, groups, organisations, nation states, and the world generally.

Yet the book not only offers profound insights into the human condition, it also manages to be fun, light, and amusing. It is a book for bedtime reading as much as for serious study. For anyone fascinated by the complex demands of leadership, and its attend-ant skills of relationship building, influencing, motivating, and contextual analysis, this book makes a very valuable addition to the library.